STRUCTURAL

PROBLEMS IN

SHAKESPEARE:

LECTURES AND ESSAYS BY

HAROLD JENKINS

STRUCTURAL PROBLEMS IN SHAKESPEARE:

LECTURES AND ESSAYS BY HAROLD JENKINS

Edited by
Ernst Honigmann

The Arden website is at
http://www.ardenshakespeare.com

The general editors of the Arden Shakespeare have been W.J. Craig and
R.H. Case (first series 1899–1944) Una Ellis-Fermor, Harold F. Brooks,
Harold Jenkins and Brian Morris (second series 1946–82)

Present general editors (third series)
Richard Proudfoot, Ann Thompson and David Scott Kastan

This edition of *Structural Problems in Shakespeare: Lectures and Essays by
Harold Jenkins*, first published 2001 by The Arden Shakespeare

Editorial matter © 2001 Ernst Honigmann

Arden Shakespeare is an imprint of Thomson Learning

Thomson Learning
Berkshire House
168–173 High Holborn
London WC1V 7AA

Typeset by LaserScript, Mitcham, Surrey

Printed and bound by Antony Rowe Ltd, Eastbourne

British Library Cataloguing in Publication Data
A catalogue record for this book is available from the British Library

Library of Congress Cataloguing in Publication Data
A catalogue record has been requested

ISBN 1-903436-72-9 (pbk)

NPN 9 8 7 6 5 4 3 2 1

CONTENTS

INTRODUCTION

by Ernst Honigmann

What have Vaughan Williams, Graham Greene, Paul Scofield, Peter Brook, Graham Sutherland, Philip Larkin, Tom Stoppard, David Hockney, Doris Lessing, Alec Guinness and Harold Jenkins in common? Answer: they were all awarded the annual Shakespeare Prize of the FVS Foundation, Hamburg, for outstanding contributions to European culture. Harold (as I shall call him) was the first Shakespeare scholar in fifty years to win the prize, in 1986, in recognition of his work as general editor of the Arden Shakespeare and as editor of the magnificent Arden edition of *Hamlet* (1982). If they had been collected in one or more volumes, the citation might also have mentioned Harold's lectures and essays, which together make another very important contribution. Published on their own, as most of them were, these essays could not have the impact of a major book, yet those who first read them no doubt recognized a very unusual literary sensitivity. They heard a quite distinctive voice, and will have admired an equally distinctive command of all the resources of scholarship and criticism. A mere thirteen, issued in a single volume as they are now, will be found to have, collectively, no less originality and wit and powers of analysis and argument than the edition of *Hamlet* itself.

When Harold asked me to be his literary executor I told him that I would particularly like to issue a volume such as this, a collection of published and unpublished essays. He wrote to me (21 March 1988) that 'there is hardly anything, unless the odd unpublished lecture, worthy of publication that hasn't been published already ... But I should see that you were given absolute and unfettered discretion.' And again (23 August 1997): 'Of course you are right (in what you said to me privately) that I ought to have collected my fugitive pieces myself and not have left others to do it ... but, though the thought had occasionally passed fleetingly through my mind, I was chary of approaching publishers or indeed pursuing such an enterprise.' My wish to issue such a volume was known to Harold and sanctioned by him. Aware that he was his own most severe critic I assumed that his disclaimer – that little remained that was worthy of publication – could hardly be right. In this, as in most of our rare disagreements over a period of almost fifty years, I later saw that his judgement was sounder than mine.

Why did he speak so dismissively of his unpublished lectures when all his work, his shortest articles no less than his books, appears to aim at the same very high standards? I was not aware of one crucial fact – that his published work was always revised many times, whereas lectures that he had not prepared for the press did not benefit from afterthoughts to the same extent. It did not occur to me that this might be the case because in his letters his command of language seemed as faultless as in his published work – to adapt the words of Heminges and Condell, 'His mind and hand went together: and what he thought he uttered, with that easiness that I have scarce received from him a blot in his papers.' The 'Letter to a Sixthformer' (pages 193–5) gives some idea of Harold's facility as a writer. Or does it? I discovered after his death, sorting through boxes of his papers, that he also prepared drafts of many of his letters. The easiness and indeed perfection of his style was partly natural to him, as also in his conversation, and partly the result of labour. The lecture on *Much Ado* survives in at least three versions in typescript, each one preceded by others in manuscript; and in what I take to be the final typescript of the lecture on *King Lear* there are forty-nine afterthoughts, all improvements, usually a neater turn of phrase.

When so many lectures and essays are available, how should one put together a posthumous collection? While it would have been possible to select splendid lectures from many fields – Metaphysical poetry, Elizabethan or Restoration drama, Bunyan,

Smollett, Graham Greene, to name just a few – it seemed to me, from a publishing point of view, desirable to focus on a single writer or theme. The obvious single writer was Shakespeare, and, I soon discovered, much of Harold's criticism of Shakespeare returned to the same central preoccupation – the structure or design of the plays. In his edition of *Hamlet* he opposed T.S. Eliot's view of the play as 'an artistic failure', insisting instead on its 'coherent dramatic design';[1] Shakespeare, he claimed, 'holds in assured grasp the many threads of his complicated plot'.[2] Several of the longer essays in this volume deal with structure and related matters – how one episode points forward to another, the 'shaping' of the action, expectancy, the necessary or appropriate conclusion. Hence the volume's title (for which I am responsible: we discussed the collection a number of times, though not its contents or title). It seemed to me fitting that the title should allude to this central motif and to Harold's first inaugural lecture, 'The structural problem in Shakespeare's *Henry IV*', since he, better than almost anyone else, excelled in explaining the many different problems of construction in the plays.

Of course, others have examined Shakespeare's art of construction, some in essays that will live as long as Shakespeare is read. Dryden on Caliban, Morgann on the dramatic character of Sir John Falstaff, De Quincey on the knocking at the gate in *Macbeth* – these are classics in their own right. Harold's lectures and essays, free from jargon and fashion, dealing with problems that every Shakespeare critic must ponder, have the same timeless appeal. They are 'not of an age, but for all time'.

Although ten of the essays included in this volume have been printed before and four were reprinted or partly reprinted in anthologies, most of the ten can only be seen in specialist libraries and some not even there. It would have been possible to exclude all previously printed pieces: after consulting with colleagues I decided not to, for two reasons. Chiefly, because I wanted Harold to be represented by his best work; secondly, because few 'general readers' have access to learned journals and specialist libraries, and these lectures and essays ought to be much more widely known.

The arrangement of the volume in two parts also calls for a brief word. Harold's edition of *Hamlet* is his best-known book (it outsold all other plays in the Arden Shakespeare for many years); in the edition he refers to his preliminary studies, published in British and American and German journals, or summarizes their conclusions. I assume that many readers will want to see for themselves how he reached those conclusions, and indeed that any of his thoughts about *Hamlet*, be it only 'Hamlet and the fishmonger' or 'How many gravediggers?', will be of interest to those who have learned to value his expert judgement. This, therefore, should be seen as a memorial volume and also as a companion volume for the edition of *Hamlet*.

～

Harold Jenkins (1909–2000) was educated at University College, London (BA 1930; MA 1933). After five years of graduate study as Quain Student at UCL, supervised by W.W. Greg, he moved to the University of Liverpool as William Noble Fellow (1935–6), and then to the University of the Witwatersrand, Johannesburg, as Lecturer and Senior Lecturer (1936–45). He returned to UCL as Lecturer and Reader (1945–54), served as Professor of English at Westfield College, University of London (1954–67), and later as Regius Professor of Rhetoric and English Literature at the University of Edinburgh (1967–71). He lectured on a very wide range of writers, from the sixteenth to the twentieth century, but in his published work concentrated on sixteenth- and seventeenth-century literature, especially Shakespeare. His contribution as joint general editor of the Arden Shakespeare (1958–82) and as editor of the Arden *Hamlet* (1982) won international recognition (see page vii) and many honours, including a Festschrift, *'Fanned and Winnowed Opinions': Shakespearean Essays presented to Harold Jenkins* (1987).[3] He was elected a Senior Fellow of the British Academy in 1989. A longer *Memoir* appeared in the *Proceedings* of the British Academy (2001).

The books and papers of Harold Jenkins, including different versions of the lectures and other material printed in this volume, have been deposited in the Library of Queen Mary and Westfield College, University of London.

PUBLICATION HISTORY

This list gives the publication history of each item. The bibliographical details are reprinted, with the permission of the editors, from 'Harold Jenkins: List of publications', in John W. Mahon and Thomas A. Pendleton (eds), *'Fanned and Winnowed Opinions': Shakespearean Essays presented to Harold Jenkins* (London: Methuen, 1987). '*King Lear*', '*Macbeth*' and 'Letter to a Sixthformer' have not been printed before. For '*Much Ado About Nothing*', see below.

'The structural problem in Shakespeare's *Henry IV*': inaugural lecture, Westfield College, London, 19 May 1955 (London: Methuen, 1956), iv + 28 pp. Reprinted in R.J. Dorius (ed.), *Discussions of Shakespeare's Histories* (Boston: D.C. Heath, 1964), 41–55; Norman N. Holland (ed.), *Henry IV, Part Two*, Signet Classic Shakespeare (New York: Signet, 1965), 212–33; G.K. Hunter (ed.), *Shakespeare: Henry IV Parts I and II*, Macmillan Casebook (London: Macmillan, 1970), 155–73; William A. Armstrong (ed.), *Shakespeare's Histories: An Anthology of Modern Criticism* (Harmondsworth: Penguin, 1972), 202–21.

'The catastrophe in Shakespearean tragedy': inaugural lecture, University of Edinburgh, 3 November 1967 (Edinburgh: Edinburgh University Press, 1969), 22 pp.

'*Much Ado About Nothing*': *The Shakespeare Newsletter*, extra issue (1997), 5–16. Published after '*Fanned and Winnowed Opinions*' (London: Methuen, 1987).

'*As You Like It*': *Shakespeare Survey*, 8 (1955), 40–51. Reprinted in Leonard F. Dean (ed.), *Shakespeare: Modern Essays in Criticism* (New York: Oxford University Press, 1957), 108–27; rev. edn (1967), 114–33; Eleanor Terry Lincoln (ed.), *Pastoral and Romance: Modern Essays in Criticism* (Englewood Cliffs, NJ: Prentice-Hall, 1969), 102–18.

'*Twelfth Night*': 'Shakespeare's *Twelfth Night*', *Rice Institute Pamphlet*, 45 (1959), 19–42. Reprinted in Kenneth Muir (ed.), *Shakespeare: The Comedies* (Englewood Cliffs, NJ: Prentice-Hall, 1965), 72–87.

'Hamlet and Ophelia': British Academy Shakespeare Lecture, 3 April 1963, *Proceedings of the British Academy*, 49 (1963), 135–51. Reprinted in *Interpretations of Shakespeare: British Academy Shakespeare Lectures*, selected by Kenneth Muir (Oxford: Oxford University Press, 1985), 142–60.

'Fortinbras and Laertes and the composition of *Hamlet*': *Rice University Studies*, 60 (1974), 95–108.

'Hamlet and the fishmonger': *Jahrbuch* of the Deutsche Shakespeare-Gesellschaft West (1975), 109–20.

'How many grave-diggers has *Hamlet*?': *Modern Language Review*, 51 (1956), 562–5.

'Thus diest thou': from 'Two readings in *Hamlet*', *Modern Language Review*, 54 (1959), 391–5.

As far as possible, the text of each of the above reproduces the text as originally printed. It should be noted that every journal has its own 'house style', some very different from others: in this edition the 'style' has sometimes been silently altered, for the sake of greater uniformity. Act, scene and line references remain as Harold cited them (and, quite often, did not cite them), even if, as in the case of *Hamlet*, they do not tally with Harold's own edition, which was published later.

'*King Lear*' and '*Macbeth*' were both originally written, I believe, as two of a series of intercollegiate lectures on Shakespeare's tragedies, delivered in the University of London; 'The catastrophe in Shakespearean tragedy' may have started life as part of the same series. Harold at one time considered publishing these lectures under the title *Hyperion and the Satyr*.

'Letter to a Sixthformer': I heard of the existence of this letter from Dr Elizabeth Brennan (Mrs Eric Lowden), who heard of it from her stepson, Mr Stephen Lowden, an English master at St Paul's School. Mr Jotischky tells me that he and his sixth form set at St Paul's 'were drawn into increasingly detailed debates about the text of *Hamlet*, impressed by Professor Jenkins's 'obvious fervour for the subject'. Very daringly the sixthformer wrote to the Arden editor with a suggestion, and received a charming and characteristic reply. I am grateful to Mr Jotischky for permission to publish it.

Harold provided footnotes for some but not all of the above. Where it seemed necessary I have added more footnotes (signed 'E.H.').

Ernst Honigmann
Newcastle upon Tyne
March 2001

PART 1

SHAKESPEARE ESSAYS

1

THE STRUCTURAL PROBLEM IN SHAKESPEARE'S *HENRY IV*

In having the honour to inaugurate a chair of English in this college, I have thought it appropriate to devote my inaugural lecture to the pre-eminent writer in English.[1] A professor of English who gives to Shakespeare such priority of his attention needs, I hope, no defence. But, if defence were necessary, I could of course plead the authority of that distinguished body which has honoured me this afternoon by the attendance of so many of its members, the Board of Studies in English, whose collective wisdom has ensured that the syllabus studied in our London school of English gives to Shakespeare a greater prominence than to any other author, not even excepting the author of *Beowulf*. To confine myself to two – or is it indeed only one? – of Shakespeare's masterpieces may be less obviously justifiable. But it cannot be the task of an hour to survey Shakespeare whole, much less Shakespearean criticism. By accepting a restricted scope I must, I am aware, forgo what Dr Johnson called 'the grandeur of generality'. But, whatever may be the poet's business, the scholar and the critic, in their humbler field, before they can come at the grandeur of generality, must be willing to 'number the streaks of the tulip'. Though they may properly avoid the esoteric, they cannot ignore the particular. The qualm that I am left with is lest the particular two-headed bloom I have picked for this occasion should not seem the most suitable to present to a women's college. For I am told by one of the most remarkable women in the history of the British theatre that *Henry IV* 'is a play which ... most women dislike'. According to Mrs Inchbald, 'many revolting expressions in the comic parts, much boisterous courage in the graver scenes, together with Falstaff's unwieldy person, offend every female auditor; and whilst a facetious Prince of Wales is employed taking purses on the highway, a lady would rather see him stealing hearts at a ball.'[2] That, however, was before the emancipation. It would be small compliment to Westfield College if I failed to recognize the great change that has come about since Mrs Inchbald's day. I take this opportunity of paying my respect to the part that Westfield College has taken in the education of women and in the consequent enlargement of women's freedom, which has been so conspicuous a feature of recent social history. A subsidiary aspect of this social change, though one that Constance Maynard can hardly at first have envisaged, is that battlefields and even taverns are now less closed to women than they were. So it is without apology that I cheerfully commend to my students the 'infinite entertainment and instruction' that Mrs Inchbald herself admitted might 'be obtained from this drama even by the most delicate readers'.

The first problem that confronts one in approaching *Henry IV*, and the one about which I propose to be particular, has inevitably introduced itself already. Is it one play or two? Some of you will dismiss this as an academic question, the sort of thing that only people like professors bother their heads about. Some of you will look askance at it as a metaphysical question, which in a sense it is. But it is also, surely, a practical question: how satisfactorily can either the first part or the second be shown in the theatre without the other? What is gained, or indeed lost, by presenting the two parts, as the Old Vic are doing at the moment, on successive evenings? And thus of course the question becomes a problem of literary criticism. Until it has been answered, how can the dramatic quality of *Henry IV* be fully appreciated, or even defined? Yet the numerous literary critics who have attempted an answer to the question have reached surprisingly opposite conclusions.[3]

Answers began more than two hundred years ago in the *Critical Observations on Shakespeare* by John Upton, a man who deserves our regard for trying to scotch the notion so strangely current in the eighteenth century that 'Shakespeare had no learning'. Far from accepting that Shakespeare's plays were the happy, or the not so happy, products of untutored nature, Upton maintained that they were constructed according to some principles of art; and his examination of *Henry IV* suggested to him that each of its two parts had, what Aristotle of course demanded, its own beginning, middle and end. Upton held it to be an injury to Shakespeare even to speak of a first and second *part* and thus conceal the fact that there were here two quite independent plays.[4] To this Dr Johnson retorted that these two plays, so far from being independent, are 'two only because they are too long to be one'. They could appear as separate plays, he thought, only to those who looked at them with the 'ambition of critical discoveries'. In these tart words Johnson shrewdly defined what, if not one of the deadly sins, is still a vice and one to which universities are prone. The 'ambition of critical discoveries', a natural human vanity unnaturally nourished in our day by the requirements of the PhD thesis and the demand for 'publications', has been responsible for many interpretations of Shakespeare whose merit is in their being new rather than their being true. Yet one must not always accept the accepted. Dr Johnson's contemporaries did not all find it as plain as he did that *Henry IV* was just one continuous composition. It seemed probable to Malone that Part 2 was not even 'conceived' until Part 1 had been a roaring success. Capell, on the other hand, thought that both parts were 'planned at the same time, and with great judgment'.[5]

Among present-day scholars Professor Dover Wilson is on Johnson's side. He insists that the two parts of *Henry IV* are 'a single structure' with the 'normal dramatic curve' stretched over ten acts instead of five. Professor R.A. Law, however, declares that *Henry IV* is 'not a single ten-act play', but two organic units 'written with different purposes in view'. On the contrary, says Dr Tillyard, 'The two parts of the play are a single organism.' Part 1 by itself is 'patently incomplete'. 'Each part is a drama complete in itself,' says Kittredge flatly.[6] In short, some two centuries after Upton and Johnson, scholars are still about equally divided as to whether *Henry IV* was 'planned' as 'one long drama' or whether the second part was, as they put it, an 'unpremeditated sequel'. A new professor, his ambition already dwindling at Johnson's warning, might well lapse into melancholy, or even modesty. Modest or not, he can hardly escape the conclusion, reached by another eighteenth-century dignitary in a somewhat different situation, that 'much might be said on both sides'. Like Sir Roger de Coverley, he 'would not give his judgment rashly', yet like the late R.W. Chambers, whose pupil I am proud to have been, he may think that the modesty which forbears to make a judgement is disastrous.[7]

Words like 'planned' and 'unpremeditated' figure largely in this controversy; and of course they imply intention or the lack of it, and will therefore be suspect in those circles which denounce what is called 'the intentional fallacy'.[8] I am far from belonging to that school of criticism which holds that an author's own intention is irrelevant to our reading of his work; yet, as Lascelles Abercrombie says, aesthetic criticism must ultimately judge by results: a man's work is evidence of what he did, but you can never be sure what he intended.[9] This position, with the coming of the Freudian psychology, is finally inescapable, but in its extreme form it seems to me unnecessarily defeatist. When I find *Much Ado About Nothing* beginning with talk of a battle in which those killed are 'few of any sort, and none of name', I may infer that Shakespeare intended to write a comedy and not a realistic one at that. But if I wish to play for safety I may use a phrase of Lascelles Abercrombie's own and speak not of what Shakespeare intended but of what he 'warned his audience to expect'.[10] If we leave aside for the present all question of Shakespeare's intention, what does *Henry IV* itself, as it begins and proceeds along its course, warn us to expect?

The short first scene, filled with reports of wars – wars this time in which multitudes are 'butchered' – makes an apt beginning for a history play. But its dialogue announces no main action. Yet certain topics, brought in with apparent casualness, naturally engage our interest. There is talk of two young men who do not yet appear, both called 'young Harry', yet apparently unlike. The first of them, Hotspur, is introduced as 'gallant', an epithet which is very soon repeated when he is said to have won 'a gallant prize'. The prisoners he has taken are, we are told, 'a conquest for a prince to boast of '. Already, before Prince Hal is even named, a contrast is being begun between a man who behaves like a prince though he is not one and another who is in fact a prince but does not act the part. The King makes this explicit. Hotspur, who has gained 'an honourable spoil', is 'a son who is the theme of honour's tongue', while the King's own son is stained with 'riot and dishonour'. In the second and third scenes the two Harrys in turn appear. First, the Prince, already associated with dishonour, instead of, like Hotspur, taking prisoners in battle, plans to engage in highway robbery. Then, when he has arranged to sup next night in a tavern, he is followed on the stage by Hotspur telling how, when he took his prisoners, he was 'dry with rage and extreme toil'. This practice of juxtaposing characters who exhibit opposite codes of conduct is a common one in Shakespeare's drama. After the 'unsavoury similes' that Hal swaps with Falstaff, in which a squalling cat and a stinking ditch are prominent, there is Hotspur's hyperbole about plucking 'bright honour from the pale-faced moon'. It may not be a classical construction, but there is enough suggestion here of arrangement to justify Upton's claim for Shakespeare's art. We expect that central to the play will be the antithesis between these two young men and the lives they lead. And we shall find that this antithesis precipitates a moral contest which is an important aspect of the historical action of the drama.

The historical action presents Hotspur's rebellion. It is an action that develops with a fine structural proportion throughout Part 1. The act divisions, although they are not Shakespeare's of course, being first found in the Folio, may serve nevertheless as a convenient register of the way the action is disposed. In the first act the rebel plot is hatched, in the second Hotspur prepares to leave home, in the third he joins forces with the other rebel leaders, in the fourth the rebel army is encamped ready to give battle, in the fifth it is defeated and Hotspur is killed. Meantime, along with the military contest between Hotspur and the King, the moral contest between the Prince and Hotspur proceeds with an equally perfect balance. The opposition of honour and riot established in the first act is intensified in the second, where a scene of Hotspur at home preparing for war is set against one of Hal revelling in the tavern. The revelry even includes a little skit by Hal on Hotspur's conversation with his wife, which serves not only to adjust our view of Hotspur's honour by subjecting it to ridicule, but also to emphasize that the Prince is – with gleeful understatement – 'not yet of Percy's mind'. That he is not of Percy's mind leads the King in the third act to resume his opening plaint: it is not the Prince but Percy, with his 'never-dying honour', who is fit to be a king's son. At this point the Prince vows to outshine his rival. He will meet 'this gallant Hotspur' – the words echo the opening scene – this 'child of honour', and overcome him. And so, when the rebels see the Prince in Act 4, he is 'gallantly arm'd' – Hotspur's word is now applied to him – and he vaults upon his horse 'as if an angel dropp'd down from the clouds' – with a glory, that is, already beyond Hotspur. All that then remains is that the Prince shall demonstrate his new chivalry in action, which of course he does in the fifth act, first saving his father's life and finally slaying Hotspur in single combat. Opposed to one another throughout the play, constantly spoken of together, these two are nevertheless kept apart till the fifth act, when their first and last encounter completes in the expected manner the pattern of their rivalry that began in the opening words. The two have exchanged places. Supremacy in honour has passed from Hotspur to the Prince, and the wayward hero of the opening ends by exhibiting his true princely nature.

What then is one to make of the view of Professor Dover Wilson that the Battle of Shrewsbury, in which the Prince kills Hotspur, is not an adequate conclusion but merely the 'nodal point we expect in a third act'? If we do expect a 'nodal point' in a third act, then *Henry IV* Part 1 will not disappoint us. For there *is* a nodal point, and – I am tempted to say this categorically – it is in the third act of Part 1 that it occurs. In this third act, when the King rebukes his son, the Prince replies, 'I will redeem all this'; in the fifth act he fulfils this vow at Shrewsbury, as is signalized by the King's admission that the Prince has 'redeem'd' his 'lost opinion'. Again, in the third act, the Prince swears that he will take from Hotspur 'every honour sitting on his helm'; in the fifth act Hotspur is brought to confess that the Prince has won 'proud titles' from him.[11] More significantly still, the third act ends with the Prince saying,

> Percy stands on high;
> And either we or they must lower lie;

and then the fifth act shows us the spectacle of the hero looking down upon his rival's prostrate form. The curve of the plot could hardly be more firmly or more symmetrically drawn. It does not seem easy to agree with Dr Johnson and Professor Dover Wilson that *Henry IV* Part 1 is only the first half of a play.

If this were all there were to *Henry IV* Part 1, the matter would be simple. But the Prince's conquest of honour is only one aspect of his progress; the other is his break with the companions of his riots. Interwoven with the story of the Prince and Hotspur are the Prince's relations with Falstaff, and these, from Falstaff's first appearance in the second scene of the play, are presented in a way which leads us to expect a similar reversal. The essential thing about Hal is that, scapegrace that he is, he is the future king – the 'true prince', the 'sweet young prince', the 'king's son', the 'heir apparent', as Falstaff variously calls him, with whatever degree of mockery, in their first dialogue together. More than that, this dialogue is constantly pointing forward to the moment when he will come to the throne. 'When thou art king' – Falstaff uses these words four times in the first seventy lines and yet again before the scene is over. 'Shall there be gallows standing in England when thou art king?' 'Do not thou, when thou art king, hang a thief.' And so on. With these words ringing in our ears, then, we are continually being reminded of what is to come. The words seem, however, to refer to some vague time in the distant future. The Prince's reign will inescapably become reality, but it is at present apprehended as a dream. Falstaff's irrepressible fancy blows up a vast gaily-coloured bubble, and, as Bradley recognized,[12] it is because this bubble encloses the dreams of all of us that we feel for Falstaff so much affection. In our dreams we all do exactly as we like, and the date of their realization is to be when Hal is king. Then, everything will be changed – except of course ourselves.

We shall go on as before, our friend Falstaff will continue his nocturnal depredations, but highwaymen will not be regarded as thieves and punishments will be abolished. Unfortunately, in the real world outside the bubble, it is not the law but we ourselves that should change, as Falstaff recognizes when he says, 'I must give over this life, and I will give it over ... I'll be damned for never a king's son in Christendom.' The joke of this is that we know that Falstaff will never give over, nor means to; but the joke does not quite conceal the seriousness of the alternatives – give over or be damned; and the idea of damnation continues to dance before us, now and later, in further jests about Falstaff's selling his soul to the devil, wishing to repent, and having to 'give the devil his due'. What Falstaff's eventual doom is to be could be discerned more than dimly by a mind that came to this play unfurnished by literature or folklore. And none of us is quite as innocent as that. We cannot help being aware of an archetypal situation in which a man dallies with a diabolical tempter whom he either renounces or is destroyed by; and to the first audience of *Henry IV* this situation was already familiar in a long line of Christian plays, in some of which man's succumbing to temptation was symbolized in his selling his soul to the devil and being carried off to hell. It is because it is so familiar that it is readily accepted as matter for jesting, while the jests give a hint of Falstaff's role in the play. I merely pick out one or two threads in the very complex fabric of the dialogue: you will be good enough, I trust, to believe that, in spite of some dubious precedents in the recent criticism of other plays, I am not seeking to interpret *Henry IV* as an allegory of sin and damnation. Falstaff is not a type-figure, though within his vast person several types are contained. And one of them is a sinner and provokes many piquant allusions to the typical fate of sinners, whether on the earthly gallows or in the infernal fire. There is also an ambiguity, to use the modern jargon, which permits Falstaff to be not only the sinner but the tempter as well. The jokes of a later scene will call him indeed a devil who haunts the Prince, a 'reverend vice', an 'old white-bearded Satan'. What I think the play makes clear from the beginning is that neither as sinner nor as tempter will

Falstaff come to triumph. Even as we share his dream of what will happen when Hal is king, we confidently await the bursting of his bubble.

To strengthen our expectation even further is what we know of history, or at least of that traditional world where the territories of history and legend have no clear boundaries. The peculiarity of the history play is that, while pursuing its dramatic ends, it must also obey history and steer a course reasonably close to an already known pattern of events. The story of Prince Hal was perfectly familiar to the Elizabethan audience before the play began, and it was the story of a prince who had a madcap youth, including at least one escapade of highway robbery, and then, on succeeding to the throne, banished his riotous companions from court and became the most valorous king England had ever had. Not only was this story vouched for in the chronicles, but it had already found its way on to the stage, as an extant play, *The Famous Victories of Henry the Fifth*, bears witness, in however garbled a text. It is hardly open to *our* play, then, to depart from the accepted pattern, in which the banishment of the tavern friends is an essential feature. Moreover, that they are to be banished the Prince himself assures us at the end of his first scene with Poins and Falstaff in that soliloquy which generations of critics have made notorious.

> I know you all, and will awhile uphold
> The unyoked humour of your idleness.

The word 'awhile' plants its threat of a different time to come when a 'humour' now 'unyoked' will be brought under restraint. The soliloquy tells us as plain as any prologue what the end of the play is to be.

Yet, although *Henry IV* Part 1 thus from its first act directs our interest to the time when Hal will be king, it is not of course until the last act of Part 2 that Pistol comes to announce, 'Sir John, thy tender lambkin now is king.' It is not until the last act of Part 2 that the Prince is able to institute the new regime which makes mock of Falstaff's dream-world. And it is not of course till the final scene of all that the newly crowned king makes his ceremonial entrance and pronounces the words that have threatened since he and Falstaff first were shown together: 'I banish thee.' To all that has been said about the rejection of Falstaff I propose to add very little. The chief of those who objected to it, Bradley himself, recognized the necessity of it while complaining of how it was done. Granted that the new king had to drop his former friend, might he not have spared him the sermon and parted from him in private?[13] Yet Professor Dover Wilson is surely right to maintain that the public utterance is the essential thing.[14] From the first, as I have shown, interest is concentrated on the Prince as the future sovereign, and Falstaff builds hopes on the nature of his rule. Their separation, when it comes, is not then a reluctant parting between friends, but a royal decree promulgated with due solemnity. This is also the perfect moment for it, when the crown that has hovered over the hero from the beginning is seen, a striking symbol in the theatre, fixed firmly on his head. The first words of the rejection speech elevate him still further – 'I know thee not' – for the scriptural overtones here make the speaker more than a king.[15] The situation presents many aspects, but one of them shows the tempter vanquished and another the sinner cast into outer darkness. In either case the devil, we may say, gets his due.

The last act of Part 2 thus works out a design which is begun in the first act of Part 1. How then can we agree with Kittredge that each part is a complete play? Such a pronouncement fits the text no better than the opposite view of Johnson and Dover Wilson that Part 1, though it ends in Hotspur's death and the Prince's glory, is yet only the first half of a play. If it were a question of what Shakespeare intended in the matter, the evidence provided by what he wrote would not suggest either that the two parts were planned as a single drama or that Part 2 was an 'unpremeditated sequel'.

An escape from this dilemma has sometimes been sought in a theory, expounded especially by Professor Dover Wilson and Dr Tillyard, that what *Henry IV* shows is one action with two phases. While the whole drama shows the transformation of the madcap youth into the virtuous ruler, the first part, we are told, deals with the chivalric virtues, the second with the civil. In the first part the hero acquires honour, in the second he establishes justice. But I see no solution of the structural problem here. For, though it is left to Part 2 to embody the idea of justice in the upright judge, the interest in justice and law is present from the start. On Falstaff's first appearance in Part 1 he gibes at the law as 'old father antic'. And he goes further. Included within his bubble is a vision of his future self not simply as a man freed from 'the rusty curb' of the law but as a man who actually administers the law himself. 'By the Lord, I'll be a brave judge,' he says, making a mistake about his destined office which provokes Hal's retort, 'Thou judgest false already.' It is in the last act of Part 2 that we have the completion of this motif. Its climax comes when on Hal's accession Falstaff brags, 'The laws of England are at my commandment', and its resolution when the true judge sends the false judge off to prison. But it begins, we see, in the first act of Part 1. The Prince's achievement in justice cannot, then, be regarded simply as the second phase of his progress. Certainly he has two contests: in one he outstrips Hotspur, in the other he puts down Falstaff. But these contests are not distributed at the rate of one per part. The plain fact is that in *Henry IV* two actions, each with the Prince as hero, begin together in the first act of Part 1, though one of them ends with the death of Hotspur at the end of Part 1, the other with the banishment of Falstaff at the end of Part 2.

Now, since the Falstaff plot is to take twice as long to complete its course, it might well be expected to develop from the beginning more slowly than the other. Certainly, if it is to keep symmetry, it must come later to its turning point. But is this in fact what we find? Frankly it is not. On the contrary, through the first half of Part 1 the Hotspur plot and the Falstaff plot show every sign of moving towards their crisis together.

Both plots, for example, are presented, though I think both are not usually observed, in the Prince's soliloquy in the first act which I have already quoted as foretelling the banishment of his tavern companions. It is unfortunate that this speech has usually been studied for its bearing on Falstaff's rejection; its emphasis is really elsewhere. It is only the first two lines, with the reference to the 'unyoked humour' of the Prince's companions, that allude specifically to them, and what is primarily in question is not what is to happen to the companions but what is to happen to the Prince. In the splendid image which follows of the sun breaking through the clouds we recognize a royal emblem and behold the promise of a radiant king who is to come forth from the 'ugly mists' which at present obscure the Prince's real self. Since Falstaff has just been rejoicing at the thought that they 'go by the moon ... and not by Phoebus', it is apparent that his fortunes will decline when the Prince emerges like Phoebus himself. It is equally apparent, or should be, that the brilliant Hotspur will be outshone.[16] There is certainly no clue at this stage that the catastrophes of Hotspur and Falstaff will not be simultaneous.

Our expectation that they will be is indeed encouraged as the two actions now move forward. While Hotspur in pursuit of honour is preparing war, Falstaff displays his cowardice (I use the word advisedly) at Gadshill. While Hotspur rides forth from home on the journey that will take him to his downfall, the exposure of Falstaff's make-believe in the matter of the men in buckram is the foreshadowing of his. The news of Hotspur's rebellion brings the Falstaffian revels to a climax at the same time as it summons the Prince to that interview with his father which will prove, as we have seen, the crisis of his career and the 'nodal point' of the drama. That this interview is to be dramatically momentous is clear enough in advance: before we come to it, it is twice prefigured by the Prince and Falstaff in burlesque. But not only do the two mock-interviews excite our interest in the real one to come; the mock-interviews are in the story of the Prince and Falstaff what the real interview is in the story of the Prince and Hotspur. First, Falstaff, whose dream it is that he may one day govern England, basks in the make-believe that he is king; and then Hal, who, as we have so often been reminded, is presently to be king, performs in masquerade his future part. The question they discuss is central to the play: 'Shall the son of England prove a thief and take purses?' Shall he in fact continue to associate with Falstaff? One should notice that, although the two actors exchange roles, they do not really change sides in this debate. Whether he acts the part of king or prince, Falstaff takes the opportunity of pleading for himself. When he is king he instructs the prince to 'keep with' Falstaff; as prince he begs, 'Banish not him thy Harry's company, banish not him thy Harry's company: banish plump Jack, and banish all the world.' Falstaff's relations to the future king, a theme of speculation since the opening of the play, now come to a focus in this repeated word 'banish'. And when the Prince replies, 'I do, I will', he anticipates in jest the sentence he is later to pronounce in earnest. If it were never to be pronounced in earnest, that would rob the masquerade of the dramatic irony from which comes its bouquet: those who accept Part 1 as a play complete in itself wrongly surrender their legitimate expectations. In this mock-interview the Prince declares his intentions towards Falstaff just as surely as in his real interview with his father he declares his intentions towards Hotspur. One declaration is a solemn vow, the other a glorious piece of fun, but they are equally prophetic and structurally their function is the same. We now approach the turning point not of one, but of both dramatic actions. Indeed, we miss the core of the play if we do not perceive that the two actions are really the same. The moment at the end of the third act when the Prince goes off to challenge Hotspur is also the moment when he leaves Falstaff's favourite tavern for what we well might think would be evermore. It is at the exit from the tavern that the road to Shrewsbury begins; and all the signposts I see indicate one-way traffic only. There should be no return.

The various dooms of Hotspur and Falstaff are now in sight; and we reasonably expect both dooms to be arrived at in Act 5. What we are not at all prepared for is that one of the two will be deferred till five acts later than the other. The symmetry so beautifully preserved in the story of Hotspur is in Falstaff's case abandoned. Statistics are known to be misleading, and nowhere more so than in literary criticism; but it is not without significance that in *Henry IV* Part 1 Falstaff's speeches in the first two acts number ninety-six and in the last two acts only twenty-five. As for Falstaff's satellites, with the exception of a single perfunctory appearance on the part of Bardolph, the whole galaxy vanishes altogether in the last two acts, only to reappear with some changes in personnel in Part 2. Falstaff, admittedly, goes on without a break, if broken in wind; and his diminished role does show some trace of the expected pattern of development. His going to war on foot while Hal is on horseback marks a separation of these erstwhile companions and a decline in Falstaff's status which was anticipated in jest when his horse was taken from him at Gadshill. When he nevertheless appears at one council of war his sole attempt at a characteristic joke is cut short by the Prince with 'Peace, chewet, peace!' A fine touch, this, which contributes to the picture of the Prince's transformation: the boon companion whose jests he has delighted in is now silenced in a word. There is even the shadow of a rejection of Falstaff; over his supposed corpse the Prince speaks words that, for all their affectionate regret, remind us that he has turned his back on 'vanity'. But these things, however significant, are details, no more than shorthand notes for the degradation of Falstaff that we have so confidently looked for. What it comes to is that after the middle of Part 1 *Henry IV* changes its shape. And that, it seems to me, is the root and cause of the structural problem.

Now that this change of shape has been, I hope I may say, demonstrated from within the play itself, it may at this stage be permissible to venture an opinion about the author's plan. I do not of course mean to imply that *Henry IV*, or indeed any other of Shakespeare's plays, ever had a plan precisely laid down for it in advance. But it has to be supposed that when Shakespeare began a play he had some idea of the general direction it would take, however ready he may have been to modify his idea as art or expediency might suggest. Though this is where I shall be told I pass the bounds of literary criticism into the province of biography or worse, I hold it reasonable to infer from the analysis I have given that in the course of writing *Henry IV* Shakespeare changed his mind. I am compelled to believe that the author himself foresaw, I will even say intended, that pattern which evolves through the early acts of Part 1 and which demands for its completion that the hero's rise to an eminence of valour shall be accompanied, or at least swiftly followed, by the banishment of the riotous friends who hope to profit from his reign. In other words, hard upon the Battle of Shrewsbury there was to come the coronation of the hero as king. This inference from the play is not without support from other evidence. The prince's penitence in the interview with his father in the middle of Part 1 corresponds to an episode which, both in Holinshed and in the play of *The Famous Victories of Henry the Fifth*, is placed only shortly before the old king's death. And still more remarkable is the sequence of events in a poem which has been shown to be one of Shakespeare's sources.[17] At the historical Battle of Shrewsbury the Prince was only sixteen years old, whereas Hotspur was thirty-nine. But in Samuel Daniel's poem, *The Civil Wars*, Hotspur is made 'young' and 'rash' and encounters a prince of equal age who emerges like a 'new-appearing glorious star'.[18] It is Daniel, that is to say, who sets in opposition these two splendid youths and so provides the germ from which grows the rivalry of the Prince and Hotspur which is structural to Shakespeare's play. And, in view of this resemblance between Daniel and Shakespeare, it is significant that Daniel ignores the ten years that in history elapsed between the death of Hotspur and the Prince's accession. Whereas in Holinshed the events of those ten years fill nearly twenty pages, Daniel goes straight from Shrewsbury to the old king's deathbed. This telescoping of events, which confronts the Prince with his kingly responsibilities directly after the slaying of Hotspur, adumbrates the pattern that Shakespeare, as I see it, must have had it in mind to follow out. The progress of a prince was to be presented not in two phases but in a single play of normal length which would show the hero wayward in its first half, pledging reform in the middle, and then in the second half climbing at Shrewsbury the ladder of honour by which, appropriately, he would ascend to the throne.

The exact point at which a new pattern supervenes I should not care to define. But I think the new pattern can be seen emerging during the fourth act. At a corresponding stage the history play of *Richard II* shows the deposition of its king, *Henry V* the victory at Agincourt, even *Henry IV* Part 2 the quelling of its rebellion in Gaultree Forest. By contrast *Henry IV* Part 1, postponing any such decisive action, is content with preparation. While the rebels gather, the Prince is arming and Falstaff recruiting to meet them. Until well into the fifth act ambassadors are going back and forth between the rival camps, and we may even hear a message twice over, once when it is dispatched and once when it is delivered. True, this is not undramatic: these scenes achieve a fine animation and suspense as well as the lowlier feat of verisimilitude. But the technique is obviously not one of compression. Any thought of crowding into the two-hour traffic of one play the death of the old king and the coronation of the new has by now been relinquished, and instead the Battle of Shrewsbury is being built up into a grand finale in its own right. In our eagerness to come to this battle and our gratification at the exciting climax it provides, we easily lose sight of our previous expectations. Most of us, I suspect, go from the theatre well satisfied with the improvised conclusion. It is not, of course, that we cease to care about the fate of individuals. On the contrary, the battle succeeds so well because amid the crowded tumult of the fighting it keeps the key figures in due prominence. Clearly showing who is killed, who is rescued and who shams dead, who slays a valiant foe and who only pretends to, it brings each man to a destiny that we perceive to be appropriate. We merely fail to notice that the destiny is not in every case exactly what was promised. There is no room now in Part 1 to banish Falstaff. A superb comic tact permits him instead the fate of reformation, in fact the alternative of giving over instead of being damned. It is a melancholy fate enough, for it means giving over being Falstaff: we leave him saying that, if he is rewarded, he will 'leave sack, and live cleanly as a nobleman should do'. But, since this resolution is conditional and need in any case be believed no more than Falstaff has already taught us to believe him, it has the advantage that it leaves the issue open, which, to judge from the outcry there has always been over the ending of Part 2, is how most people would prefer to have it left. Shakespeare's brilliant improvisation thus provides a denouement to Part 1 which has proved perfectly acceptable, while it still leaves opportunity for what I hope I may call the original ending, if the dramatist should choose to add a second part. I refrain, however, from assuming that a second part was necessarily planned before Part 1 was acted.

Part 2 itself does not require extended treatment. For, whenever it was 'planned', it is a consequence of Part 1. Its freedom is limited by the need to present what Part 1 so plainly prepared for and then left out. Falstaff cannot be allowed to escape a second time. His opposition to the law, being now the dominant interest, accordingly shapes the plot; and the law, now bodied forth in the half-legendary figure of the Lord Chief Justice, becomes a formidable person in the drama. The opening encounter between these two, in which Falstaff makes believe not to see or hear his reprover, is symbolic of Falstaff's whole attitude to law – he ignores its existence for as long as he can. But the voice which he at first refuses to hear is the voice which will pronounce his final sentence. The theme of the individual versus the law proves so fertile that it readily gives rise to subplots. Justice Shallow, of course, claims his place in the play by virtue of the life that is in him, exuberant in the capers of senility itself. He functions all the same as the Lord Chief Justice's antithesis: he is the foolish justice with whom Falstaff has his way and from whom he wrings the thousand pounds that the wise justice has denied him. Even Shallow's servant Davy has his relation to the law; and his view of law is that, though a man may be a knave, if he is my friend and I am the justice's servant, it is hard if the knave cannot win. In this humane sentiment Davy takes on full vitality as a person; but he simultaneously brings us back to confront at a different angle the main moral issue of the play. Is he to control the law or the law him? In fact, shall Falstaff flourish or shall a thief be hanged?

It has sometimes been objected that Falstaff runs away with Part 2. In truth he has to shoulder the burden of it because a dead man and a converted one can give him small assistance. Part 2 has less opportunity for the integrated double action of Part 1. To be sure, it attempts a double action, and has often been observed to be in some respects a close replica of Part 1 – 'almost a carbon

copy', Professor Shaaber says. At exactly the same point in each
part, for example, is a little domestic scene where a rebel leader
contemplates leaving home, and in each part this is directly
followed by the big tavern scene in which revelry rises to a climax.
And so on. An article in a recent number of *The Review of English
Studies* has even called *Henry IV* a diptych, finding the 'parallel
presentation of incidents' in the two parts the primary formal
feature. I do not wish to deny the aesthetic satisfaction to be got
from a recognition of this rhythmic repetition; yet it is only the
more superficial pattern that can be thus repeated. With history
and Holinshed obliging, rebellion can break out as before; yet the
rebellion of Part 2, though it occupies our attention, has no
significance, nor can have, for the principal characters of the play.
The story of the Prince and Hotspur is over, and the King has
only to die.

The one thing about history is that it does not repeat itself.
Hotspur, unlike Sherlock Holmes, cannot come back to life. But
there are degrees in all things; conversion has not quite the same
finality as death. And, besides, there is a type of hero whose
adventures always can recur. Robin Hood has no sooner
plundered one rich man than another comes along. It is the
nature of Brer Fox, and indeed of Dr Watson, to be incapable of
learning from experience. In folklore, that is to say, though not in
history, you can be at the same point twice. And it seems as if
Prince Hal may be sufficient of a folklore hero to be permitted to
go again through the cycle of riot and reform. In Part 2 as in Part
1 the King laments his son's unprincely life. Yet this folklore hero
is also a historical and, what is more to the point, a dramatic
personage, and it is not tolerable that the victor of Shrewsbury
should do as critics sometimes say he does, relapse into his
former wildness and then reform again. The Prince cannot come
into Part 2 unreclaimed without destroying the dramatic effect of
Part 1. Yet if Part 2 is not to forgo its own dramatic effect, and
especially its splendid last-act peripeteia, it requires a prince who
is unreclaimed. This is Part 2's dilemma, and the way that it takes
out of it is a bold one. When the King on his deathbed exclaims
against the Prince's 'headstrong riot', he has not forgotten that at

Shrewsbury he congratulated the Prince on his redemption. He has not forgotten it for the simple reason that it has never taken place. The only man at court who believes in the Prince's reformation, the Earl of Warwick, believes that it will happen, not that it has happened already. Even as we watch the hero repeating his folklore cycle, we are positively instructed that he has not been here before:

> The tide of blood in me
> Hath proudly flow'd in vanity till now.

In the two parts of *Henry IV* there are not two princely reformations but two versions of a single reformation. And they are mutually exclusive.[19] Though Part 2 frequently recalls and sometimes depends on what has happened in Part 1, it also denies that Part 1 exists. Accordingly the ideal spectator of either part must not cry with Shakespeare's Lucio, 'I know what I know.' He must sometimes remember what he knows and sometimes be content to forget it. This, however, is a requirement made in some degree by any work of fiction or, as they used to call it, feigning. And the feat is not a difficult one for those accustomed to grant the poet's demand for 'that willing suspension of disbelief ... which constitutes poetic faith'.

Henry IV, then, is both one play and two. Part 1 begins an action which it finds it has not scope for but which Part 2 rounds off. But, with one half of the action already concluded in Part 1, there is danger of a gap in Part 2. To stop the gap Part 2 expands the unfinished story of Falstaff and reduplicates what is already finished in the story of the Prince. The two parts are complementary; they are also independent and even incompatible. What they are, with their various formal anomalies, I suppose them to have become through what Johnson termed 'the necessity of exhibition'. Though it would be dangerous to dispute Coleridge's view that a work of art must 'contain in itself the reason why it is so', that its form must proceed from within,[20] yet even works of art, like other of man's productions, must submit to the bondage of the finite. Even the unwieldy novels of the Victorians, as recent criticism has been showing, obey the demands of their allotted three volumes of space; and the dramatic masterpieces of any age, no less than inaugural lectures, must acknowledge the dimensions of time. The inaugural lecture has, however, this unique advantage: as its occasion is single, the one thing that can never be required of it is to make good its own deficiencies in a second part.

2

KING LEAR

In my lecture on Shakespeare's tragedies I said that Shakespeare's tragedies are concerned with the mysteries of human existence. They dramatize in particular situations the workings of good and evil. The mystery of evil, as Shakespeare sees it, is that it is part of the process of nature. There is a natural instinct in beasts to feed their own lives by destroying other lives. Among the plants Hamlet sees weeds taking possession of the garden and the mildewed ear causing the healthy one to wither. It is interesting that one of the activities of the foul fiend referred to in *King Lear* is that he 'mildews the white wheat'. This propensity of the fiend which is in plants and beasts is also shared by humanity: the mildewed ear that Hamlet speaks of blasting his wholesome brother is Hamlet's uncle; Hamlet's mother in her union with Claudius surrenders to bestial appetite. Marriage which leads to procreation is sanctified by such holy vows as Hamlet gave to Ophelia, but it is also a means to the breeding of sinners, which is what repels him from her. Shakespeare is always fascinated by this dual quality of generation in nature, and in man as a part of nature. It is not the whole of his tragic vision, but his tragic vision always includes it, and it is the fact of life with which *King Lear* may be said to begin. This play is based upon the story of three sisters, two bad and one good, yet all daughters of the same father; and it is a story which embodies in its particular incidents what is recognizable as a type of universal experience.

The legend of King Lear and his three daughters was well known. It had appeared in Geoffrey of Monmouth's *Historia Regum Britanniae* in the twelfth century and had been many

times recounted since. It was to be found in most of the
sixteenth-century chroniclers, including Holinshed, as well as in
The Mirror for Magistrates and Spenser's *Faerie Queene*. Briefly,
it told how the old king sought from his daughters the profession
of their love and, mistaking their true characters, left his kingdom
to the two eldest and disinherited the youngest, who married a
King of France. The elder daughters then revealed, in Holinshed's
word, their 'unnaturalness', so that Lear went to France to join his
youngest daughter and her husband, who thereupon invaded
Britain and reinstated him on his throne. This story had already
been shown on the Elizabethan stage in a play which Shakespeare
evidently used as a source. Many of its elaborations of the story
he was content to disregard; yet from its rambling action he could
select some incidents that helped in the structure of his own. This
old play of *King Leir* has, for example, a scene in which Lear and
Cordelia, at the moment of their reunion, kneel to one another;
indeed they compete in alternately kneeling and rising, and, with
the King of France and his attendant joining in and kneeling too,
the scene, as Kenneth Muir says, 'topples over into absurdity'.[1] Yet
the ineptness of this original did not prevent it from striking
Shakespeare's imagination, and the act of kneeling, as we shall
see, becomes integral to his dramatic pattern. Shakespeare also
derived from the old play the role of the faithful Kent, to which,
however, he gives new point. For the banishment of Kent is
Shakespeare's innovation; and, by making Lear banish his loyal
subject as well as his loving daughter, Shakespeare duplicates
Lear's expulsion of the good. And, when Kent comes back to
serve Lear in disguise, Shakespeare shows the good which Lear
has rejected still ministering to him against his knowledge. In all
preceding versions of the story Lear goes to Cordelia in France.
Shakespeare, by keeping him in Britain, avoids unnecessary
diffuseness; but at the same time, by making the good Cordelia
come spontaneously to her father instead of sending Lear to seek
her out, he again enhances the story's moral force. Moreover, by
eliminating her husband's part in the invasion of Britain, he
concentrates the emphasis upon the relations of father and
children. In Shakespeare's play the story of King Lear and his

three daughters culminates in one grand catastrophe in which all four lie dead together on the stage. Shakespeare's tragic ending for Lear is revolutionary; for traditionally Lear regained his kingdom. In the old play he and Cordelia both end happily with the wicked sisters routed. In other versions, it is true, Cordelia, after inheriting from her father, is defeated in battle by her sisters' children and kills herself in prison. But Shakespeare rejects suicide for Cordelia no less than happiness; it seems significant that he found self-destruction more appropriate for Goneril. A more striking innovation still is that he has reversed the order of the deaths of Cordelia and Lear; so that Cordelia's death, instead of providing a melancholy epilogue to her father's story, becomes an ingredient in his now tragic fate. Shakespeare's Lear ends when that good and evil which he has both propagated and experienced have ended.

We may see, then, Shakespeare selecting, concentrating and modifying those features of the story from which it will derive its pattern. But if he concentrates and alters he also adds. He intensifies Lear's suffering with the creation of the storm; he makes Lear go mad, and thereby transfers the interest from his physical to his mental experience. And by giving him two companions who exhibit different kinds of madness, the Fool and the Tom o' Bedlam, he provides a complex commentary upon the world we take for sane. He also adds the subplot.

It is a feature of Shakespeare's dramatic art that he often combines his main action with others that show variations of it. In *Much Ado About Nothing* two lovers are forced apart through a trick when one is deceived by something he overhears; but another couple who are similarly tricked by what they overhear are through this brought together. In *Hamlet*, where a son avenges his father, he himself kills another man's father and has vengeance taken on him. In *King Lear*, as in *Hamlet*, there is also a second family to provide an image of the first. But, whereas Hamlet's revenge is both reflected and inverted in that of Laertes, in *King Lear* the story of Gloucester and his good and wicked sons simply repeats the story of Lear and his daughters. *King Lear* is unique in Shakespeare in exhibiting two actions which run parallel with and not counter to one another. Indeed, the fundamental correspondence is such that features belonging to one story can be transferred also to the other, as an instance will make clear. The story of Gloucester is based on that of the King of Paphlagonia in Sidney's *Arcadia*, which Shakespeare faithfully follows in his account of Gloucester's death. 'His flawed heart ... / 'Twixt two extremes of passion, joy and grief, / Burst smilingly.'[2] Yet the verbal echoes of *Arcadia* occur in the account not of Gloucester's death, but of Lear's. The old king in *Arcadia* has 'his *heart broken* with unkindness' and '*stretched* ... beyond his limits with this excess of comfort'; and at Lear's death Kent says, '*Break, heart*, I prithee break ... He hates him / That would upon the rack of this tough world / *Stretch* him out longer.' This transference to Lear of what in the source belongs to Gloucester shows how closely the two situations come together in Shakespeare's mind. The correspondence of the situations admits, of course, variations in detail. One father has three daughters, the other has two sons. Each has invited the harm his offspring do him, the one by giving them his kingdom, the other by bringing a bastard into the world. Each is turned out destitute, but the one is made mad and the other blind. And, while one cries out for vengeance, the other in despair seeks suicide. The parallel never becomes mechanical; too exact a repetition might provoke our disbelief. Yet the likeness is never obscured; and our perception of the common pattern underlying the variety not only affords aesthetic satisfaction but suggests to the imagination the operation of some universal law. As was said long ago by Schlegel, 'Were Lear alone to suffer from his daughters, the impression would be limited to the powerful compassion felt by us for his private misfortune. But two such unheard-of examples taking place at the same time have the appearance of a great commotion in the moral world. The picture becomes gigantic.'[3] It becomes still more gigantic when the commotion in the families is extended into the natural world which surrounds them. There is no storm in earlier versions of the King Lear story, though there is one in the *Arcadia*, where Gloucester's original takes shelter from the fury of wind and hail. This may be another instance of

Shakespeare's transferring to Lear what he found in his source for the other plot. The storm provides the terrible culmination of the afflictions that descend on Lear's defenceless head. But it is also more than that. It shows the reduplication throughout nature of the tumultuous disorder we are witnessing in the human society, as though one implies the other. It seems to be in one comprehensive process that fathers are set upon by their children and nature herself is riven by that violence of thunder and hurricane which she herself creates. The imagination beholds a universal order disintegrating into chaos.

So the tumult of Lear's experience, echoed in that of Gloucester and reverberating through the storm, detaches itself from the limits of particularity. This does not mean that it need lack the vividness of particular events. The quarrel at Goneril's arises plausibly out of household friction and leads on to the quarrel with Regan, to Lear's confrontation of the two of them together, the intervention of Gloucester on Lear's behalf and the putting out of Gloucester's eyes. Through a series of exciting scenes the plot is firmly blocked in. And these big crises in the action are given a solid enough setting, what with Lear calling for his dinner or his horse, the journeying back and forth from Goneril's house to Gloucester's castle, the messengers on their various errands, Kent put into the stocks and the crazed beggar Tom o' Bedlam roving the wild countryside. All this has something of the actuality of daily life in Shakespeare's England. Yet it blends with a world of romance in which a king is attended by a hundred knights and an unknown challenger comes forth to be victorious in single combat in the lists. And for all the apparent immediacy of incident there is, as Bradley and others have remarked, a vagueness as to time and place.[4] It is true the word 'Dover' echoes through the dialogue. To Dover Kent sends a messenger, Lear is to be conducted and Gloucester wants to go. But the importance of Dover is as much symbolic as geographical: Dover links England with France; it is the place from which Cordelia and help will come. The battle contributes something to the impression of a world in conflict, adding the strife of kingdoms to the division between families; but the political background is left quite shadowy: if we need an explanation for the disappearance of the King of France, it will do that he went back home to deal with 'something he left imperfect in the state, / Which since his coming forth is thought of '. The storm appropriately has no locality; for even the heath we talk about is an invention of Shakespeare's editors, who put it in the stage directions when Shakespeare never mentioned it in the text.

The action has that combination of precision at the centre with vagueness on the periphery which belongs to a fairy-tale. And that in a sense is what *King Lear* is. Once upon a time there was an old king who had three daughters, and the two eldest were wicked and the youngest was very good. This is the type of Cinderella, and Cordelia has of course her fairy prince. It is the very simplicity of the folk-tale situation, with its roots deep in the primitive mind, that holds us from the outset. We do not ask why the sisters are good or bad; it is enough that they are so. They inhabit an ideal world of the imagination where ordinary life is transcended. In all their speech and gestures they have of course the animation of real people; and the cruelty of Goneril and Regan has its verisimilitude when it is sparked off by Lear's irascibility. But the three sisters retain also an archetypal character. It is not singly but together that they represent human nature. The ingratitude which drives a man out of his mind and the loving-kindness which breaks his heart both belong to human nature, and Lear, who experiences both, has generated both. His daughters complement one another, like the brother kings in *Hamlet*, whom Shakespeare compares to Hyperion and the satyr.[5] But *King Lear*, in the symmetries of its plot, is further from naturalism than *Hamlet*. Goneril and Regan, unlike Claudius, have no moment of tenderness or conscience, no flicker of possible relenting. Yet, with Cordelia to balance them, the absolute of heartlessness is what the drama asks of them, just as it requires of Cordelia the perfection of truth and love.

If I here stress the obvious, it is because it seems not to be appreciated by those who object to the improbability of Shakespeare's opening scene in which the daughters are asked to declare their love. This is not to be excused, as it sometimes is, as a mere device for getting the plot started. On the contrary, it is essential in order to exhibit in all their stark simplicity the foundations on which the action rests. The simplified motivation here sometimes disquiets the modern reader, who has been brought up on novels and taught to psychologize the characters of fiction. But the love test belongs to folk-tale; and a dramatist who placated a demand for verisimilitude here would risk robbing the opening scene of its whole symbolic force. The critical uneasiness usually comes to a head in the discussion of Cordelia. She ought, it is sometimes suggested, to have humoured the old man. Granville-Barker, for example, agrees with her father in accusing her of pride, and says that youth owes to age a little more, and less, than the truth.[6] Others have regretted that her virtue should show so little tact. Still others have objected to her rectitude itself. But is it not to over-subtilize the play to observe with Professor Sewell that 'she is to blame ... for keeping herself blameless'?[7] Those who wish Cordelia had shown just a little of her sisters' cunning would blur the opposition between them. They are really asking that good should be content to look like evil. Cordelia's declaration that she loves her father according to her 'bond' descends from the folk-tale source, and it is one of those truthful equivocations in which folk-tale – and the seventeenth-century drama – takes delight. What the bond is the play in time will show. How the play means us to regard Cordelia seems perfectly apparent from the dialogue. She speaks of honour, love and duty, and these words receive an emphatic echo in those of Kent, who intervenes against her disinheriting to tell Lear plainly, 'Thy youngest daughter does not love thee least.' And when Kent in turn is banished all the drama of this episode throws great emphasis on his parting speech, in which he commends Cordelia to 'the gods' as one 'That *justly* think'st and hast most *rightly* said'. She is then rewarded with a royal husband, who loves her for precisely those virtues that her father has despised. When she called herself 'true', her father retorted, 'Thy truth then be thy dower'; but with this the King of France is satisfied. 'She is herself a dowry,' he says. Truth needs nothing but itself. And France's words to Burgundy afford yet one further comment:

> Love's not love
> When it is mingled with regards that stand
> Aloof from th'entire point.

Shakespeare has used every dramatic device to signal approval of Cordelia's conduct, and those who think she should have acted differently, like those who think Othello was easily jealous, would seem to go against the verdict given in the play.

As for Lear's own conduct, that is pronounced upon by Kent with equal clarity:

> Revoke thy gift;
> Or, whilst I can vent clamour from my throat,
> I'll tell thee thou dost evil.

Nor does the play leave doubt about what the evil is. It says nothing, though the commentators have said much, about the iniquity of dividing up a kingdom. Our little learning about Elizabethan political theory will be dangerous if it leads us to stress this. The evil that Lear does is not in giving up his kingdom, which is represented as an act of prudence in old age, but in whom he gives it to. He bestows everything on his wicked offspring and 'nothing' on the good, thus repudiating his own nobler part and yielding sovereignty to the baser. 'Hence and avoid my sight', he says to Cordelia; 'out of my sight', again to Kent. They manifest honour, love and duty; and he refuses to see them. Kent's retort, 'See better, Lear', emphasizes this.

The evil in this play, like that in *Hamlet* and *Macbeth*, springs from a violation of nature. Lear is to suffer from the crimes of unnatural children, but the pattern of wrong begins in him when he chooses to be an unnatural father. Casting off Cordelia, he says, 'Here I disclaim all my paternal care, / Propinquity and property of blood', and again, 'I give / Her father's heart from her.' These are terrible words, and most terrible of all is the vow that 'the barbarous Scythian, / Or he that makes his generation messes / To gorge his appetite' shall be as dear to him as his own daughter. When he refuses to distinguish between the child he has loved and barbarians who feed upon their offspring, Lear gives us our first glimpse in the play of that cannibalism, that devouring of one's own flesh, which Shakespeare repeatedly represents as the climax of the evil propensities in nature. We may remember how Rome, banishing Coriolanus, is compared to an unnatural parent eating up her own. We are presently to see in Goneril and Regan those passions which lead humanity to prey upon itself 'Like monsters of the deep'. But such passions are first associated with Lear and this first scene shows them to us. What the action of the play will reveal is how Lear suffers from what he here initiates and how, through his sufferings, he learns, as Kent exhorted him, to 'see better'.

The change that has taken place in Lear by the end of the play is very dramatically represented when the old king, whom we first saw on his throne in a fury of despotic power, on the stage before our eyes goes down humbly on his knees to the very daughter he then banished. Kneeling scenes in Shakespeare are always full of meaning; for kneeling is the visible act which proclaims a spiritual homage, as Shakespeare explicitly states in *Henry IV*. The story of the Prince who on his knees restores to his dying father the crown he was thought to have coveted was traditional. But in Shakespeare it acquires a new solemnity when the kneeling Prince declares that 'this prostrate and exterior bending' is a sign of his 'inward true and duteous spirit'. This, however, is the kneeling of the son to the father. For the parent to kneel to the child is a reversal of the natural order of things. As such it is monstrous when Volumnia kneels to Coriolanus (the mother kneeling to the son); and it is Coriolanus's recoil from 'this unnatural scene', at which 'the gods look down' in mockery, that brings him back to duty and affection and prevents the burning of Rome. But what Volumnia does with a sense of its outrageousness Lear does in a gesture of spontaneous humility which is immensely dramatic and moving. Cordelia, with the filial response of the natural child, asks her father for his blessing, 'Hold your hands in benediction o'er me', and then instead it is Lear who kneels to her. The authority and prerogatives of fatherhood, which Lear formerly insisted on and which Cordelia still acknowledges, Lear now tacitly relinquishes in favour of the sinner's need to ask forgiveness of one whom he has wronged. And all the emotions which this scene stirs in us will be presently revived when, in the last scene of all, just before they go off to prison together, Lear says to Cordelia,

> When thou dost ask me blessing, I'll kneel down
> And ask of thee forgiveness.

The scene of Lear kneeling to Cordelia shows, then, a reversal of what happened in the opening. It also gains additional force by its contrast with another scene in which Lear has knelt to another of his daughters. When Lear, after leaving Goneril, comes to his second daughter, Regan tells him to go back to Goneril and admit that he has wronged her. 'Ask her forgiveness?' he bursts out, and then in scorn goes through the motions of what seems to him ridiculous: 'Dear daughter ... on my knees I beg ...' That *this* reversal of the natural relationship of parent and child is monstrous even Regan agrees when she retorts, 'These are unsightly tricks.' But what at this stage Lear does only in bitter mockery he subsequently does sincerely. Having stormed at the idea of begging Goneril for forgiveness, he comes to the point when he can say to that other daughter, 'You must bear with me ... Forget and forgive.' In the earlier scene Regan has heartlessly reminded him, 'O, sir, you are old'; and, though he cannot deny this, his admission of it is again an act of mockery. 'Dear daughter, I confess that I am old.' But it is in a very different spirit that he later confesses to Cordelia, 'I am a very foolish, fond old man.' The later episode is enriched by our memory of the earlier one; it is by an art supremely dramatic that Shakespeare exhibits to us the revolution that takes place within Lear's mind and heart.

Yet not only is the fact of a change in Lear impressed upon us dramatically by such contrasting scenes; it is a feat of the play to link such scenes together in a continuously developing action. In all that Lear undergoes as he is taken through storm and madness, amid his rages, conflicts and bewilderments, we may witness a progressive transformation within him. Some of the crucial moments which show this transformation were well remarked by Bradley.[8] Any attempt to describe it, still more to summarize it, must result in simplification. But with this warning I must try briefly to suggest the course of Lear's inner drama and how the play conveys it to us.

The change begins early, even before the first act is over, with the dawning recognition of his initial error. At first, installed in Goneril's house, he is still the imperious monarch: 'Let me not stay a jot for dinner; go get it ready.' When servants do not jump to his bidding, he says, 'I think the world's asleep.' But, when his complaints to Goneril are met with counter-complaint and even reproof, he wonders whether it is the world that is asleep or himself. 'Ha! waking? 'Tis not so.' These are his first questionings about his own relations with the world around him. 'Are you our daughter?' he asks. 'This is not Lear ... where are his eyes?' Though he cannot yet do what Kent instructed him, 'see better', he takes the first step to this when he doubts the power of his own eyesight and admits that 'his discernings / Are lethargied'. Goneril and Regan, when they had received his kingdom, reflected on his 'poor judgement' and agreed that he had 'ever but slenderly known himself'. Now he is discovering this himself. 'Who is it that can tell me who I am?' In Goneril, later to be referred to as a disease of his own flesh, he now perceives the fiend, the predatory instinct of 'the sea-monster'; and with this comes the first acknowledgement of error. For the unnatural ingratitude of one daughter now reveals to him his own unnatural conduct towards another. What had seemed in Cordelia the utmost of offence now shrinks to a 'most small fault' and his vaunted 'judgement' turns out to have been 'folly'. The dialogues with the Fool now drive this home, and it is with these first doubts of himself that fears of madness begin. The world he has so confidently ruled is starting to reel about him.

Yet, when the man who has rejected his own daughter is himself rejected by his other daughters, the effect of this is to make him vent on them an even fiercer wrath than he had visited on her. Struggles to contain his grief mingle with threats to reassert his will; new admissions of his weakness alternate with dreadful curses. In the big scene where he confronts Goneril and Regan together a prayer for patience to endure his wrongs is followed by another that he may be given 'noble anger' to exact 'revenges' which 'shall be / The terrors of the earth'.

It is at this moment, with Lear torn between grief and rage, that the first sounds of the storm are heard, as though the human action sets up reverberations throughout nature. In Lear's mind the storm joins with his 'two pernicious daughters' against him. But if it seems, in all that it makes him suffer, an extension of their cruelty, it also unites with his own fury. As he stands bareheaded to the blast, epitome of frail humanity at the mercy of a world in turmoil, the warring elements which assail him appear also as the magnification of his own tumultuous passions. The man who has terribly cursed his own offspring is shown exhilarating in the self-destructive forces within nature, calling on the thunder to 'crack nature's moulds' and strike the round earth flat. He accepts the storm as an awful visitation of the gods to punish human crimes; but he sees himself as one 'more sinned against than sinning'.

Yet the storm continues the change which Goneril and Regan have begun when it forces him to recognize his weakness; he acknowledges himself 'a poor, infirm, weak and despised old man'. And presently the king who has insisted on a retinue of a hundred knights is glad to accept the barest shelter. 'Where is this straw?' he asks, 'Come, bring us to this hovel'. With this he begins to turn from his former way and to accept for the first time the necessities of his human condition. He does not submit in an instant. He lingers on the threshold of the hovel, held there by the tempest in his mind, as though reluctant to relinquish the storm; so that, when he at length goes in, this gesture, in contrast with all we have seen of him before, may strike as with great dramatic force. It is by the very simplest words and actions that the crises in the spiritual drama are conveyed. When Lear not only accepts for himself 'this hovel' and 'this straw' but says to his 'poor fool', 'How dost, my boy? Art cold?,' he shows for the first time thought and compassion for another human creature. He even says, 'In boy; go first'. Kingly pride is forgotten when, going into the hovel, the king gives precedence to his own attendant fool. Whereas he had besought the storm to destroy the humanity that offended him, he now feels pity for those whom the storm afflicts, 'poor naked wretches'. The 'pomp' of majesty to which he has clung he now exhorts to 'take physic'; 'Expose thyself to feel what wretches feel'; and this too is very dramatically rendered when at this moment a naked wretch appears suddenly on the stage. As Lear begins to take off his clothes to equate himself with the beggar, pomp taking physic is exhibited in action. Confronted with the naked wretch, Lear sees for the first time what man really is. Here is 'the thing itself, unaccommodated man ... a poor, bare, forked animal'. This is not the whole of what man is; but that man *is* this is one of the things Lear has to discover. The 'noble anger' with which he cursed and banished those who opposed his will is replaced by an eagerness to learn. The king humbles himself to the mad beggar whom he keeps calling his 'philosopher'. But in accepting the madman as a man of wisdom he has of course become mad himself. He enters a world of confusion, in which it is not too much perhaps to see a struggle between the new self and the old. For, if he equates himself with the beggar, he also identifies the beggar's situation with his own. 'Hast thou given all to thy two daughters, and art thou come to this?' And, when he installs the naked beggar as his 'robed man of justice', the justice he demands shows an obsession with his own wrongs. In the mock trial of his daughters, with a joint-stool to do duty for Goneril, the topsy-turvy world of madness parodies the sane. When the king bestowed his kingdom unjustly, Kent told him he was mad; but now in a different madness the king without a kingdom seeks justice from the witless and the outcast. The father who gave his heart from his loving daughter would now dissect his cruel daughters – 'Let them anatomize Regan' – to discover the cause which makes hard hearts.

It is when Lear ceases to look for justice in any human society that he will 'see better'. When this happens, his madness has reached a further stage. In the scene which brings him and Gloucester together, these two old fathers, both cast out by their children, the one without wits, the other without eyes, present a pitiful spectacle of humanity in the extremity of its suffering from the savagery it has bred. The drama of their meeting, with the blind man recognizing the madman by his voice and the madman claiming to remember the eyes of the man who has none, spares us nothing of their plight, while it gives the utmost poignancy to the situation of the mad teaching the blind to see. 'No eyes in your head', 'yet you see how this world goes ... A man may see how the world goes with no eyes.' For the man without wits may show him what the customs of society disguise from the sighted and the sane. The vision is still a confused one, since Lear has not yet shed all customary ways of thinking; the outcast still sees himself as a king. 'When I do stare, see how the subject quakes.' He acts again like the wrathful dragon of the opening when events have deprived the dragon of his power. Yet he has learnt that his sovereignty was not absolute; he could not command the thunder, and the dragon has changed his nature when he says, 'I pardon that man's life.' Not curses nor banishment, but pardon. 'Die for adultery? No!' For lechery is universal in that instinctive life which man shares with the animal world. 'The wren goes to't' and the 'gilded fly' and 'the soil'd horse', while the 'simpering dame' beneath her parade of virtue has the same 'riotous appetite' as the beasts. The animal, and the fiend, are in us all.

> But to the girdle do the gods inherit,
> Beneath is all the fiends';
> There's hell, there's darkness.

Lear has looked at unaccommodated man and seen him in his physical nakedness. Now at this further stage he sees him in his moral nakedness as well. This was something else the clothes concealed. For 'through tattered clothes small vices do appear', but 'robes and furred gowns hide all'. The man without eyes is not deterred by appearances from perceiving how all men are inwardly the same. The justice rails upon the thief, but 'change places and, handy-dandy, which is the justice, which is the thief?' All this comes forth in a disordered rush of images, but in its incoherent phrases the mad imagination pierces through the hollow values of the world to the fundamental nature of man beneath. When all men are seen as gods and fiends, it is no longer possible to think of being more sinned against than sinning. When Lear said that, at the beginning of the storm, he found in the storm the justice of the gods before which *other* sinful men should tremble. But now he sees that the man who wields the whip should bare his own back to receive it. Again one scene links with another to reveal Lear's spiritual progress.

Having discovered that human nature, stripped of its outward trappings, is everywhere the same, Lear can have no use now for social distinctions, and it becomes possible for the father in the scene which immediately follows, instead of requiring obeisance from his child, himself to kneel to her. Even those natural staples of the social order, parental prerogative and filial duty, pale in a light which has revealed the naked human being. All that matters now is contrition and forgiveness. But so long as he was mad the old self still struggled with the new. Though he could preach patience to Gloucester, he was still calling for no quarter to his enemies when Cordelia's messengers found him. It is only when his madness leaves him that he is delivered from his former passions. And as these fall away from him there are still new discoveries to be made. For his vision of the universal depravity of man had the one-sidedness, if also the clarity, of delusion. Something else that is in human nature is waiting to reveal itself as he wakes into Cordelia's embrace. It is a wonderful conception of Shakespeare's that the same sleep as ends Lear's madness should have this awakening, as though fury must be exhausted before love can be known. And it is Cordelia's love that finally releases his spirit from Goneril's and Regan's power. When they turned him from their homes he showered curses upon them and cried to heaven for revenge. When he madly pursued justice, he wanted to 'arraign Goneril' and 'anatomize Regan'; but reunited with his other daughter, he is unaffected by them. It is Cordelia who asks, 'Shall we not see these daughters and these sisters?', but Lear's reply is the fourfold 'No, no, no, no.' This is another of those apparently simple things which in the context of the play acquire great depth of meaning.

Secure in Cordelia's love, Lear can be content in prison, his spirit free and unassailable. Detached from all the strivings of the world, he can be unmoved by 'court news', 'who's in, who's out', and the transient glory of the 'great ones / That ebb and flow by th' moon.' This is the state of mind at which the king who began in pomp and power arrives. For Shakespeare's play the usual ending of the story has become impossible. Its Lear could have no satisfaction in that restoration of throne and kingdom which preceding versions granted him. He aspired towards a vaster vision, in which earth's majesty and misery, its justice and injustice, and even unnatural daughters, sink into insignificance.

So, although this play exhibits at its maximum intensity that descent from prosperity to wretchedness which we recognize as the pattern of tragedy, accompanying the hero's fall, and counterpointed against it, is an upward journey of the spirit. *Hamlet*, I think, suggests something of this in that new tranquillity of spirit, that new submission to providence which the hero shows towards the end after his return to Denmark. But in no other tragedy is the inner development of the hero, through painful and bewildering experience to a new serenity of mind, presented with such fullness as in *King Lear*. Because Lear's suffering has brought him to 'see better', to know himself more than 'slenderly', because the descent in his fortunes is accompanied by an ascent in understanding and so in spiritual power, along with all the pity and the fear goes a sense of regeneration.

Yet, while I join with all who have stressed Lear's regeneration, one can hardly agree with Bradley that the play might be called 'The Redemption of King Lear'.[9] For it is not upon this note that Lear's tragedy ends, though some have wished it might. Nowhere more poignantly than in the last scene of *King Lear* is the tragic truth brought home to us that the journeys of man's spirit are inseparable from the weakness of the flesh and the anguish of the heart. Shakespeare does not permit Lear to retire to some new life in prison. Nor is there a transfiguration into some other state of being such as Eliot seems to envisage for the heroes of his plays. Though we have heard much in recent criticism of Lear's purgatorial experience, this is not a religious drama but an intensely human one. If Lear's new insight brings an under-standing of himself and of the nature that is his, it cannot detach him from his human plight. And it is with the human feelings that belong to it that he must suffer one last affliction. The joy he has attained to has come to him through Cordelia's love and it stays with him as long as she is alive. But Edmund does not repent in time to save her and the heavens to whose judgement Albany ascribed her wicked sisters' deaths do not now intervene. Their ways remain inscrutable. Lear had thought to take upon himself the 'mystery of things', to view all in some vast perspective as from some vantage-point of the gods. Yet it is not as God's spy but with the passions of a man that he 'killed the slave that was a-hanging' her; and, as he enters with Cordelia dead in his arms, there are still some last flickers of the rage he hurled against the storm:

> Howl! howl! howl! O ye are men of stones.
> Had I your tongue and eyes, I'd use them so
> That heaven's vault should crack.

Instead of taking on himself the 'mystery of things' as he had wished to do, he is brought back to the unanswerable questions –

> Why should a dog, a horse, a rat have life
> And thou no breath at all?

– and to the stark fact of mortality:

>   She's gone for ever.
> I know when one is dead, and when one lives.

But even this, as the feather seems to stir, he finally does not know. With the certainty of her death alternates a hope that she may yet live. 'Thou'lt come no more', he repeats, 'Never, never, never, never, never.' And then upon the reiteration of this blank finality come the words that would undo it. 'Look on her, look, her lips.' If we are right to interpret this as showing that Lear thinks Cordelia breathes, it may be, as Bradley holds, that he dies in an ecstasy of joy – though a joy based on illusion.[10] Are we to say, then, as some have done, that Lear in one last error of deluded sight dies as he has lived? This seems to ignore that the Lear who joys in Cordelia's love is a different man from the one who made her a stranger from his heart. Or are we to say, with R.W. Chambers, that Lear's illusion is the symbol of a higher truth concerning the victory of love?[11] The supposed stirring of Cordelia's lips does not obliterate for us the fact of her death, and Lear's cries of joy, though they may supersede, cannot dispel the desolation of that fivefold 'Never' still echoing in our minds. What I think we must say of Lear's death is what Edgar has said of Gloucester's:

> his flaw'd heart,
> Alack, too weak the conflict to support,
> 'Twixt two extremes of passion, joy and grief,
> Burst smilingly.

What in the one case is narrated in the other is exhibited – the heartbreak through the extremes of emotion. What Lear retains to the end, when so much has been stripped from him, are the elemental human feelings of love and sorrow, and, if you like, the illusions of his human frailty. What Lear has discovered about man and his world, much though it is and including love as well as cruelty, is what it lies within human experience to know. The ultimate mysteries of life and death elude him. From the joys and pains of his human condition only his own death can release him. The truth the play leaves with us, and what Lear has finally learnt – though this again is said of Gloucester – is that 'Men must endure / Their going hence even as their coming hither.'

3

MACBETH

As I already hinted in my opening lecture, the plot of *Macbeth* exhibits one fundamental point of difference from those of the three great tragedies which we take to have preceded it. In them the heroes, to put it crudely, are brought to suffering and calamity through the machinations of the villains. Claudius has killed Hamlet's father and will later plot to kill him; Iago schemes Othello's ruin; Lear's daughters, having got possession of his kingdom, turn him out into the storm. Whatever the degree of the hero's own responsibility for his downfall, in all these plays the villains are necessary as the instigators of the events which lead to it and thus make the tragic action. But in *Macbeth* the villain who commits the initial crime is the hero himself. Macbeth inaugurates the train of disaster when he, no less than Claudius, murders his good kinsman and his king. The antagonist has become the protagonist; we see the action from the other, from the evil, side.

Yet it is not simply that the situation has been turned round to present its contrary aspect. In being turned round it has become a different, and a more complex, situation. For it is not simply that we now regard events from the viewpoint of the killer instead of the avenger, the agent of evil instead of its victim. *Macbeth* is not *Richard III*. Dr Johnson said that every reader rejoices at Macbeth's fall;[1] but, if rejoicing were all we felt, we who know our Aristotle would not call it a tragedy at all.[2] If the events are to impress us as tragic, our sympathies must still be drawn to the man who suffers the fall from happiness to wretchedness. We cannot say of Macbeth's death, as is said of Goneril's and

Edmund's, that it 'touches us not with pity'.[3] Even though he is himself the perpetrator of evil, we must see him also as its victim. It is not that the protagonist and antagonist have changed places; they have become the same.

In *Macbeth* therefore it is less easy to express the tragic action in terms of an external conflict which opposes the good man to the bad. The plot of *Hamlet* can be summarized, superficially at least, in an account of the schemes and counter-schemes of Hamlet and Claudius; in *Othello*, though we watch how Othello comes to destroy both what he loves and himself, we are always aware of Iago's designing and hostile hand. But in *Macbeth* the very nature of the conflict compels an emphasis upon that inner drama which takes place in the hero's mind. It is there essentially that the struggle between good and evil is waged. And this, I take it, is the interest that the subject had for Shakespeare at this stage of his dramatic career.

Perhaps you will bear with me if I recapitulate a little. In the tragedies of Shakespeare's maturity, good and evil are, as we have seen, always conceived as having their seeds together in nature.[4] That which in Othello inspires his love of Desdemona also enables his jealousy to take root, so that while he begins as a noble warrior he becomes the victim of delusions in which evil takes possession of his mind and drives him to destruction. The dualism of Hamlet has many aspects. The avenger of a murder, he is also a manslayer upon whom vengeance has to be taken. Called to a noble deed which will set wrong right, he finds himself contaminated by that nature which in his own mother has subjected the 'discourse of reason' to the bestial appetite; and, when he reproaches himself for neglect of his duty, he attributes it to his having allowed his 'godlike reason' either to 'fust ... unused' or to become frustrated by that scrupulous thought which he calls cowardice. In *King Lear* that opening scene in which the King gives away his kingdom images, I suggested, his denial of the good and surrender to the base impulses of humanity.[5] That the cruelty he suffers is born of his own flesh is impressed upon us when – if I may vary my example – he himself calls Goneril 'a disease that's in my flesh', 'a plague sore, or embossed carbuncle / In my corrupted blood'. What the play shows us is this corruption at work through his wild passions, then purified by self-abasement. *King Lear* no less than *Macbeth* has its centre in this inner spiritual conflict. Yet in *King Lear* the spiritual conflict was provided with its external counterpart by the fable Shakespeare used. Lear's passions are embodied in his daughters, who stand symmetrically opposed upon the stage in that formal opening scene. And, though the good and evil sisters never meet again until their dead bodies are brought together at the end, their armies fight against one another, and we are always aware of them balanced against one another to shape and poise the action, like the angels and devils of some morality play. Is it perhaps a natural development of Shakespeare's tragedy, with its vision of good and evil, that he should now choose a subject in which angel and devil combine within a single human figure? This, I think, is what gives *Macbeth* its intensity and, in contrast to the multiplicity of figures in *Hamlet* and *King Lear*, its concentration.

In Macbeth, more obviously than in any of the other tragic heroes, we see growing together man's noble aspiration and his tyrannous selfishness in all its malign force. This is Shakespeare's profoundest study of the power of evil to destroy the soul which gives it birth. That is not to say that the play marks a growing pessimism in Shakespeare or indeed any philosophic change in his outlook. Rather it gives scope for the further imaginative exploration of the nature of evil, as Shakespeare now, with remarkable psychological penetration, follows out the successive crises in an individual mind. But the coalescence of hero and villain in *Macbeth* does present some new dramatic problems. In the first place, the sympathy of the audience has to be enlisted for one whom they recognize as criminal; in the second the conflict between good and evil, which centres now in an interior drama, must still, if it is to be acted out upon a stage, be exhibited to some degree in an external struggle between different persons. In fact I suppose no stage spectacles are more haunting than the witches and Banquo's ghost, which give a visible form to Macbeth's terrors and seem to show mysterious powers operating outside himself, alluring or pursuing him. And these apparitions are also supported on the human plane by those secondary figures in the story whom Shakespeare builds up into a prominence beyond the suggestions of his source. Lady Macbeth, as well as the witches, gives evil an external presence so that it seems to have an existence independent of Macbeth. It is notable that both the witches and Lady Macbeth first appear in the play alone, before Macbeth encounters them; if in different ways they are linked with him as though part of him, they are also creatures outside him from whom the good in him can recoil. On the other side, the need to oppose good to evil leads to the magnification of the roles of Macbeth's virtuous adversaries when Malcolm and Macduff rise to fight against him. It is particularly interesting to notice in the structure of the play how, so long as Macbeth can still be thought of as a noble warrior, his wicked wife is a very conspicuous figure; but as he develops from good to bad she becomes less necessary. After her commanding presence at the banquet, where she seeks to annul the effect of Banquo's ghost – 'You look but on a stool' – we see and know nothing of her until the scene of her sleepwalking. But, as *she* ceases to be prominent, correspondingly, on the other side, the figure of Macduff increases in importance, so that together they supply the place of an antagonist for Macbeth; each side of Macbeth's nature is matched against one of these two. We can hardly call Lady Macbeth an antagonist, but Macduff of course *is* that in the second half of the play. I shall have more to say about each of them later. For the moment it is enough that Macbeth's collaboration with his wicked wife in the murder of Duncan and his enmity to the good Macduff who avenges it may be said to frame the exterior action. Yet the shift of emphasis from Lady Macbeth to Macduff only brings out more clearly how the interest of the tragedy is in Macbeth's own course.

In this at least it may be said to resemble *King Lear*. For, in *King Lear*, it seems reasonable to see a comparable shift in the hero's relations with the secondary characters. After the exposition of the opening scene, Goneril and Regan are conspicuous in the first part of the play, Cordelia in the second. Macbeth first conspires with his wife, then fights against Macduff; while Lear first suffers from his cruel daughters and then is united with the other. In both these later tragedies the hero's relation with the other characters marks his own development. The focus is on the hero himself. Strange though it may seem, I think this is more so with them than it is with *Hamlet*. For in *Hamlet* the hero's internal drama and his campaign against the villain, though both command our interest, do not fully coalesce. This is one way of stating the difficulty that criticism has often felt about *Hamlet*: does the Prince matter more than the play? I think it was an endeavour to make him not matter more that led Professor Waldock to minimize the importance of Hamlet's delay;[6] and T.S. Eliot, in calling *Hamlet* an artistic failure, held that there was a discrepancy between Hamlet's emotions and their cause.[7] Though I think the discrepancy disappears if we fully appreciate Hamlet's own conception of his task, we may still see that in *Hamlet* the internal and the external conflicts are less closely integrated than in *King Lear* and *Macbeth*, where the plot itself is an expression of the hero's spiritual development. This may be an indication of an advance in Shakespeare's tragic art. What is interesting in a comparison between the two later tragedies, and what makes them complementary to one another, is that the hero's development runs a contrary course. In *King Lear* we watch Lear's spiritual regeneration from a state of enslavement to his passions to the point where he has subdued them. But what by contrast we behold in *Macbeth* is the evil subduing the good in Macbeth's nature and bringing him to ruin, not only physical but moral. This is the course of the action that I shall have to try to trace.

If I am right in supposing that Macbeth's overthrow, unlike that of Goneril and Edmund, touches us with pity, this must surely be because we have been made aware of the nobility in Macbeth's nature and have come to see it defeated by the baseness. Bradley doubted whether Macbeth could be called noble.[8] Yet 'noble' is the epithet chosen for him by Duncan when he rounds off the impression we are given of Macbeth in the second scene of the play before the hero himself has yet appeared.

And it is of course to establish this initial nobility that Shakespeare gives us thus early the account of Macbeth's prowess against the King's enemies. 'Brave' Macbeth – this is the first epithet applied to him in the play, to be speedily followed by 'valiant' and 'worthy' – is presented as the bridegroom of Bellona, the goddess of war. This tribute to the godlike in him is amply justified, before we even see him, by the tale of his almost miraculous deed when, confronting the King's foe, he 'unseam'd him from the nave to th' chaps'. The character of the victim here is important: 'merciless' in a 'damned quarrel', he was one in whom 'the multiplying villainies of nature' swarmed. So that Macbeth, 'valour's minion', disdaining Fortune, as only the great can do, is shown as a man splendid against wrong. He is not only a heroic figure: he is heroic in the cause of virtue. There is not much time for us to see him on this pinnacle before the decline begins. But the vision must be given us and it must stay with us throughout. Shakespeare has made it unforgettable; but he has also done something else. Before we have this description of Macbeth, or know anything of what he is, we have first the witches arranging to gather on the stormswept heath, 'there to meet with Macbeth'. These weird beings, ominous of doom, wait for him 'when the battle's lost and won', in the moment therefore of his victory. Before he is placed upon his pinnacle of glory, their shadow is cast over it. Macbeth's entry in the third scene is thus prepared for with Shakespeare's characteristic dramatic skill. We are keyed up with expectancy, but in divided hope and fear. We have been led to expect a majestic hero, but we know the witches are in wait. 'Fair is foul, and foul is fair', they said; and Macbeth's first words echo theirs: 'So foul and fair a day I have not seen.' So that already there seems to be an affinity between them which may induce a shudder of apprehension. And it is of course precisely now, in the moment of our first seeing him, noble and triumphant, that the evil begins to work in him. I find nothing in the text to suggest that Macbeth and his wife have already discussed their crime together, and critical speculation on the point is irrelevant; for in this scene, when Macbeth first receives the witches' greeting, we actually see the deed being born in his mind. He starts and seems to fear – we have Banquo's word for this; and the effect of it is the greater because it contrasts with the reaction of Banquo, who does not fear. He regards the witches with matter-of-fact disdain, while over Macbeth they cast their awful spell. 'My *noble* partner', says Banquo, 'seems rapt'; and he repeats this later as Macbeth stands in a sort of trance. 'Look how our partner's *rapt*.' It is also Macbeth's word in the letter to his wife – 'I stood *rapt* in the wonder of it.' Macbeth gives his mind to the witches' mysterious prophecies with a fascinated urgency. 'Stay ... tell me more'; and, when they have vanished, 'Would they had stayed.' When Banquo asks if he and his companion have 'eaten on the insane root / That takes the reason prisoner', this is a further light on Macbeth's state. His reason – the godlike reason, as Hamlet calls it – succumbs to an insane appetite. Then when, directly after, Macbeth learns that he is Thane of Cawdor and the first of the witches' prophecies is fulfilled, there comes into his mind a 'suggestion / Whose horrid image doth unfix my hair'. What this is is not yet defined. We are as yet in the stage of 'horrible imaginings', the thought is as yet 'fantastical', but the fantasy, in this moment of its birth, is one of murder. It is part of Macbeth's agony throughout the play that his thought leaps ahead to foresee the horror he is creating.

> Why do I yield to that suggestion
> Whose horrid image doth unfix my hair ...
> Against the use of nature? Present fears
> Are less than horrible imaginings,
> My thought, whose murder yet is but fantastical,
> Shakes so my single state of man.

We may note that what is happening in Macbeth is 'against the use', or wont, of nature, and that Macbeth's 'state of man' is shaken or, to use the words of Brutus when a comparable crime is being born in *his* mind, suffers an insurrection. The singleness of the state of man is disturbed by the rebellion of that other creature in his dual being. If we care ourselves to look forward, we shall see how, when he turns in dread from the contemplated deed, he says, 'I dare do all that may become a man', to which

Lady Macbeth can only retort that when he proposed the enterprise he must have been a beast.

After this wonderful passage, which shows Macbeth's mind reeling before the image of a future crime, we pass at once to Duncan speaking of 'a gentleman on whom I built / An absolute trust'. He is saying this of the Thane of Cawdor, who has just been executed, but we cannot help the suspicion that this reference to trust betrayed may also come to apply to the new Thane of Cawdor, whose entry before Duncan has finished speaking ensures that the irony shall not be missed. The subject invites irony throughout these early scenes and Shakespeare uses it to great effect. Duncan greets Macbeth as the 'worthy' man he still is and Macbeth replies by speaking of the 'service' and 'loyalty' he owes his king. If there is irony in this, there is of course no insincerity, for he has not yet surrendered to his horrible imaginings. But we have had a glimpse of them and even as Duncan talks to him we see Macbeth giving them a larger hospitality. In a brief aside he bids the stars to hide their light so that the 'black desires' which he fears to look on may nevertheless flourish. Meantime Duncan, still calling Macbeth 'worthy' and 'valiant' and finally his 'peerless kinsman', trustfully prepares to strengthen the bond between them by going to stay at Macbeth's house.

It is of course at this fateful moment that we are first introduced to Macbeth's wife. Her function in the play I see as twofold. First, she is the temptress, who lures Macbeth on to the deed. This is the part she has in Holinshed, who tells us that Macbeth's 'wife lay sore upon him to attempt the thing, as she that was very ambitious, burning in unquenchable desire to bear the name of queen'. Shakespeare transforms the pettiness of this by making her ambitious less for herself than for her husband, and by giving her regal language. The crown is for her the 'golden round', and the deed which is to get it is 'this night's great business', which will procure for them a future of 'sovereign sway and masterdom'. This is something on a scale which befits Macbeth's heroic valour. But, if Lady Macbeth magnifies the glory of the enterprise, she also intensifies its evil. For Shakespeare makes of her much more than a characterization of the wife who persuades her husband with the force of her woman's resolution. Pouring her spirits into Macbeth's ear, stilling his scruples with the valour of her tongue, she seems to take upon herself the role of Satan. And we remember how as she waits for Macbeth to come she invokes the night to invest itself with 'the dunnest smoke of hell' so that heaven may not peep through the dark in which the deed is to be enveloped. She, no less than the witches, and by her own choice, becomes an instrument of darkness.

Her wilful giving of herself to hell suggests also her second function in the play, though it is one that critics have less often emphasized. We have seen that Shakespeare's art often employs the boldest contrasts in order to achieve dramatic emphasis; and Lady Macbeth not only tempts and drives her husband on, she contrasts with him throughout in their reactions to their crime. The struggle that evil has before it can win mastery in his mind is thrown into relief when he is set against her who is given over to evil absolutely. This comes out strongly in her own speeches. She deliberately stops up in herself those 'compunctious visitings of nature' which make so much of his agony. She recognizes in him those instincts towards good which she seeks to overcome. 'What thou wouldst highly, / That wouldst thou holily.' But for herself, instead of holiness, she wishes to be 'from the crown to the toe topfull / Of direst cruelty'. His nature is 'full o'th' milk of human kindness', but in her woman's breasts where milk should be she wants to have only gall. Denying in herself the tender feelings that belong to womanhood, she cries to be 'unsexed'. The recurrent image of the milk is one of great power, for it is of course by her milk that the natural mother nourishes the life of her child. But Lady Macbeth destroys the life that she should suckle. She is presently to say:

> I have given suck and know
> How tender 'tis to love the babe that milks me.
> I would, while it was smiling in my face,
> Have pluck'd my nipple from his boneless gums
> And dashed the brains out.

This picture of the helpless infant smiling at its mother's nipple vividly presents the natural situation within the description of its ferocious violation. And this violation of the natural relationship suggests the monstrous unnaturalness of what this woman is about. This savagery against one's own offspring is further associated with the murder of Duncan when we remember how Macbeth had called his loyal duties 'children' to the throne; and an image of a babe again appears when he thinks of the virtues of the king he is to kill. He has a vision of angels trumpeting the damnation of his crime and of pity 'like a naked new-born babe'. All heaven and all the natural feelings of humanity towards its children condemn this 'horrid deed', and when he approaches Duncan's chamber 'nature seems dead'. In this way the poetic imagination brings out the fullest significance of the dramatic action. Duncan's murder shatters all those sacred ties which bind nature's parts together. This is what Macbeth so terribly sees and what Lady Macbeth refuses to acknowledge.

It is of course fundamental to Macbeth's tragedy that he has noble promptings and goes against them. The good in him clings to that natural order which the bad in him destroys. In the soliloquy in which he meditates on the assassination, he enumerates all the ties that bind him to the man he plans to kill. He is Duncan's kinsman, he is his subject, he is his host. These are the relationships that the dialogue between them has already stressed – and not the dialogue alone. We have seen the King in state being received at Macbeth's home. Three times he has greeted Lady Macbeth as his fair and honoured 'hostess' and he has taken her hand to be conducted to his 'host'. ('Give me your hand; / Conduct me to mine host.') In our knowledge of what is planning, this simple action, as we see it on the stage, has a dramatic irony of extraordinary intensity. Nor does this exhaust the irony of the King's reception. When Lady Macbeth heard of Duncan's coming, her words were ominous: 'The raven himself is hoarse / That croaks the fatal entrance of Duncan / Under my battlements.' But now, immediately after, when Duncan and his retinue arrive, it is not a raven they see but a 'temple-haunting martlet'. 'Temple-haunting' – the holiness in Macbeth's nature hangs also about his house, where 'heaven's breath / Smells wooingly'. And the martlet nests against the buttresses, making a cradle for its young. Whereas the croaking raven is notoriously a presage of death, the martlet is here associated with birth. The suggestions again are of something naturally benign and life-protecting which Macbeth and his wife are perverting. It is a truism that since the Elizabethan stage lacked scenery and artificial lighting the dramatist had to set his scene in words. But this was not altogether a disadvantage. Certainly no stage carpenter or electrician could show us the dual aspect of Macbeth's castle, abode of trust *and* murder, as powerfully as Shakespeare brings it to our imagination through his poetic juxtaposition of these two birds.

I have tried to suggest a little of Macbeth's moral crisis and of the way in which Shakespeare brings out the profound implications of his crime. The act itself need not detain us, though it is of course dramatically rendered in all the nightmare of its doing. Macbeth sees the dagger with drops of blood; he hears cries from the sleepers round about; and when they call, 'God bless us', he (significantly) cannot say 'Amen'. And, when the deed is done though not discovered, the drunken porter who breaks the tension with his fooling also appals us further with his masquerade as a porter at the gate of hell. That repeated knocking that we hear belongs to the present moment but to all eternity as well.

The contrast that was established between Macbeth and his wife as they moved towards their crime continues after it is done. Lady Macbeth, having deafened herself to moral promptings and stopped the passage of remorse, is a creature without conscience. 'Go get some water / And wash this filthy witness from your hand.' The blood is no more than a physical defilement which perhaps may tell a tale. 'A little water clears us of this deed.' But Macbeth knows differently. The stain of evil cannot be washed from off the soul.

> Will all great Neptune's ocean wash this blood
> Clean from my hand? No, this my hand will rather
> The multitudinous seas incarnadine.

In this wonderful hyperbole with the polysyllabic flow, the stain spreads round the world. The single crime becomes the epitome of all guilt.

The act in which Macbeth has overturned the laws of nature is accompanied by a series of happenings of a similar kind, as though evil has been let loose throughout the universe. Darkness continues into morning; an owl kills a falcon; the King's horses turn against their masters and then eat one another. I need not at this stage stress the significance of this cannibalistic climax. In the language itself the impression of evil is intensified in metaphors of unnatural death. Night 'strangles' the sun, and 'darkness does the face of earth *entomb* / When *living* light should kiss it'.

When the natural order is once overthrown, disorders multiply, both in the universe at large and in the individual being. The progressive degeneration of Macbeth is marked in the crimes which follow when evil is once unleashed. One murder prompts another and as soon as Macbeth has become king he is planning Banquo's death, not needing his wife now as instigator or accomplice. But the increased resourcefulness in evil does not yet lessen its horror for him. It is his fate both to do it and to be revolted in his soul by what he does. The apparition at the banquet is only the most spectacular manifestation of the terror that pursues him. His awareness of what is happening reveals itself in tormenting dreams; his mind is full of scorpions. Yet remorse for what is done pales in the vision of crimes to come which now opens up before him. Yet repetition brings familiarity and familiarity acceptance. Worse even than his terror is his recognition that it will pass. Fear will be conquered by use. In murdering Duncan he knew he had murdered sleep, but after Banquo's murder he can say, 'Come, we'll to sleep.' He has hardly recovered from the shock of Banquo's ghost before we find him at the end of that same scene submitting himself to the inevitable. 'I am in blood / Stepp'd in so far that, should I wade no more, / Returning were as tedious as go o'er.' With his self-appraisal still undimmed, he recognizes the milestones on his journey into vileness; and yet accepts the going forward. And, if there is sometimes a note of weariness or resignation, there is also a desperate daring and new signs of dreadful determination. His words at the end of the banquet scene, 'We are yet but young in deed', are ominous. The climax of this movement comes in his visit to the witches. It is a small point, perhaps, but full of significance, that, whereas at first they waylaid him on the heath, he now seeks them out himself.

With this new initiative in evil goes a hardening of the spirit which reconciles him to the destruction that he causes in the world in pursuit of his own ends. 'For mine own good / All causes shall give way.' When he waited for the news of Banquo's assassination, he cried, 'Let the frame of things disjoint', rather than that he should be left in torment. This disjointing of the frame of things is symbolized when he breaks up the ceremonial banquet 'with most admired disorder'. And this chaos in the society he rules he is willing to extend to the universe itself, 'the frame of things'. One of the most terrible speeches in the play comes when he visits the witches. To get his answer from them he is prepared for them 'to untie the winds and let them fight / Against the churches' – this is a glimpse of nature loosed from law and destroying holy places. He is prepared for the waves to 'swallow navigation up' – this is nature rebelling against man's control, destroying his system and devouring him. The lines that follow give a catalogue of particular disasters united through the act of falling, which is expressed in every verb:

> Though bladed corn be *lodged* [= laid flat] and trees *blown down*;
> Though castles *topple* on their warders' heads;
> Though palaces and pyramids do *slope*
> Their heads to their foundations; though the treasure
> Of nature's germens *tumble* all together.

All the seeds in which nature is forever putting forth life he will see destroyed as they 'tumble all together' into chaos. And this may go on 'even till destruction sicken' (of a surfeit). Here, as with King Lear in the storm, we confront disaster on a universal scale. And this is what began in that first barely definable thought which came into Macbeth's mind when he left the battlefield triumphant and was startled by the witches.

But by now the counter-movement has begun. For the contest is still between good and evil, and as Macbeth moves to the climax of destructiveness, the forces of good are gathering against him. In the structure of the drama it is at this stage, when the hero's own spiritual conflict dies down as his wicked passions achieve their mastery, that the external conflict emerges into prominence. Chief of those who oppose Macbeth are Malcolm, son of the murdered king, the rightful heir who will eventually inherit, and even more conspicuously Macduff, who in the end will kill him.

The importance of Macduff in the design of the play is not to be overlooked. It is significant that, whereas Holinshed first mentions Macduff as one who resisted Macbeth's tyranny, Shakespeare introduces him much earlier – in the same way as he will promote Aufidius, the slayer of Coriolanus, from the place he has in Plutarch. Macduff indeed is made the actual discoverer of the murder he is ultimately to avenge. He makes a first sensational impact on our minds when he rushes from Duncan's chamber crying, 'O horror, horror, horror.' It is he who helps us to recognize the full meaning of the crime by an image of holiness outraged:

> Most *sacrilegious* murder hath broke ope
> The Lord's anointed temple, and stole thence
> The *life* o'th' building.

Although through the middle of the play we do not see Macduff on the stage, from this moment we are not permitted to forget him. He declines to go to Scone for the crowning of Macbeth; he is, of course, absent from the banquet. But his absence is remarked on as a sign of his defiance. There is Macbeth's threat, 'Macduff denies his person / At our great bidding.' 'I will send.' Then the witches expressly warn Macbeth against him and Macbeth plans and executes the murder of his family. But already Macduff himself is, we are told, in England, where he has gone 'to pray the holy King upon his aid'. Such references are like those in *King Lear* to events in France, which drop their promise of Cordelia's return.

At length, directly after the murder of his family, we see Macduff with Malcolm in England in a scene whose purpose is largely to present the contrast between a good reign and a bad. While in Scotland Macbeth makes new orphans every day, in England the king goes about to heal the sick. Drawing upon Holinshed's account of Edward the Confessor, Shakespeare makes use of the legend of the King's Evil, a disease so called because the king was supposed to be able to cure it at a touch. The king does, according to the play, 'a most miraculous work', of 'healing benediction', which he is able to perform through the 'sanctity' which 'heaven hath given his hand'. Nor is this good and pious king alone in contrast with Macbeth. The scene ends by informing us that 'the powers above / Put on their instruments' against Macbeth, who now 'is ripe for shaking'. It is from this blessed realm, and it would seem as warriors of God, that Macduff and Malcolm come to put an end to Macbeth's wicked reign. It is, then, in the guise of a conflict between heavenly and hellish powers that we may see the play's last act, when the forces of Macbeth and Macduff draw together. Finally Macduff will enter with Macbeth's severed head, and with this grim trophy evil is purged from the world. Now, says Macduff, 'the time is free'; and as Malcolm prepares for his own coronation he speaks of the new regime which is to be 'planted'. The metaphor is eloquent; it speaks of new growth and suggests the resurgence of that life whose very seeds Macbeth would have seen tumble in confusion.

In the last act the final degeneration of Macbeth appears in his ferocity. 'The devil damn thee black, thou cream-faced loon' is his greeting to a messenger; and to another – though this one admittedly has said Birnam Wood is moving – 'If thou speak'st false, / Upon the next tree shalt thou hang alive / Till famine cling thee.' Savagery as well as courage is implicit in his comparison of himself to a bear fighting at the stake. The originally sensitive nature has become brutalized. The measure of Macbeth's fall is seen when he who began as 'Bellona's bridegroom' ends as 'this dead butcher'.

As for his wife, who won him to his crime, she still contrasts with him in her contrary development. While his conscience hardens, hers has come to life. That her resolve to cauterize her natural feelings was never entirely successful was perhaps apparent when she could not kill Duncan because he resembled her father in his sleep, and at the discovery of the murder she swooned. (There is of course no warrant for the notion that she faked.) Now, below the level of her will, her remorse breaks out in dreams. A little water has not cleared her of her deed and she washes her hands repeatedly in vain. The poignancy of the sleepwalking scene may soften our judgement of her. Yet the play's last reference to her as a '*fiendlike* queen' finally reconfirms the hellish part that she has played.

But it is the playing out of Macbeth's own drama that holds our thoughts to the end. When Dr Johnson rejoiced at his fall, he added that Macbeth nevertheless retains some of our esteem through his still heroic courage.[9] This I think is so; but what impresses us most about him as he draws to his end, and what compels our pity, is rather his recognition of his own spiritual state. 'I have lived long enough', he says, 'My way of life / Is fall'n into the sere, the yellow leaf.' This is another of those metaphors which unite the individual life with the general course of life in nature. Malcolm may achieve new plantings, but in Macbeth we see growth withered. He has 'supped full of horrors', and satiety even of horror quenches response. 'The time has been', he says, when his hair would have stood on end at a shriek in the night – and we have seen him in such a state of fear. But now 'I have almost forgot the taste of fears.' Suffering ultimately numbs the spirit. In this condition of spiritual exhaustion, there is nothing more to be experienced but death. So he grows 'aweary of the sun'. Like the other tragic heroes – and most of all perhaps like King Lear – he has gone through agony to reach a stage where afflictions can hardly touch him any more. But in this phase he achieves a new breadth of vision and can contemplate his past and present with detachment. He seems to acquire a perspective by which he can survey all life and time laid out before him like a map.

> Tomorrow and tomorrow and tomorrow
> Creeps in this petty pace from day to day

To the last syllable of recorded time;
And all our yesterdays have lighted fools
The way to dusty death.

In this state the impact of particular incidents is dulled in the
sense of the general monotonous rhythm of life. This is most
apparent when we find him unmoved even by the wailing which
announces his wife's death. If she had not died now, 'she should
have died hereafter'. Hamlet, we may remember, at a similar
stage, says of his own death, 'If it be now, 'tis not to come ... If it
be not now, yet it will come.'

But if before his end Macbeth achieves a still, clear vision, even
as Lear and Hamlet do, there is in the vision of the evil hero an
important difference. Hamlet became aware of a divinity that
shapes our ends; Lear felt he could see like God's spy. This is not
at all how Macbeth sees. After his terrible experiences all life falls
into perspective, but he sees no design or purpose in it. 'It is a tale /
Told by an idiot, full of sound and fury' but 'signifying nothing'.
We must not of course make the mistake of supposing that these
much-quoted words express Shakespeare's own philosophy. They
are strictly dramatic. This is the vision of life Macbeth comes to,
and it is appropriate to the kind of career his is. The man who has
embraced evil and let loose cruelty and destruction upon the
world finds in the end that all is meaningless. Whereas Lear
becomes ready to take upon himself the mystery of things, in
Macbeth that mystery is extinguished. The light of things goes
out and all he is left with is a vision of negation. This perhaps we
may say is the final reward of evil. Its destructiveness ends by
destroying the meaning of life itself. This, more than the severed
head which exhibits him as a criminal, suggests the profoundest
aspect of his tragedy.

The tragedy of Macbeth, then, is that of a man who begins
noble, with an aura of heroic valour and full of glorious promise,
but who, not without a harrowing struggle, surrenders to the evil
passions inside him and turns his splendid powers to the work of
destruction. His career ends physically in an ignominious death,
spiritually in a vision of life as 'signifying nothing'. The exhibition

of the tortures of a mind – the frightful imaginings, the terror not merely of the consequence but of the guilt, the anguish of remorse – followed by the dulling of sensibilities and the final spiritual exhaustion – all this makes an intensely human drama. There is nothing surely, even in Shakespeare, more profound in its psychology or more imaginative in its expression. But evil in the individual mind is involved also with tyranny in the kingdom and disorder in society; and by the poetic imagery the human drama is also enlarged to embrace the warring forces which are active throughout the universe. In the hero's personality and career there inheres a conception of good and evil as the fulfilment or the perversion of nature's purposes in the life that nature has created. Finally, the tragic pattern is complete when in the downfall of the great man evil destroys itself, ordered government is re-established and a new life is planted.

4

THE CATASTROPHE IN
SHAKESPEAREAN TRAGEDY

My inaugural lecture must open on a melancholy note. If it had not
been for the death of John Butt I should not have been called upon
to give it. In my deep appreciation of the many kindnesses I have
received since I came to this university I do not forget, as you will
not forget, the sadness which occasioned my coming. Of my
personal memories of Professor Butt, since the time over thirty
years ago when a young lecturer in London lent a still younger
postgraduate student a copy of Swift, this is not the moment to
speak. By the generous warmth of his personality he won your
affection in Edinburgh no less than he gained your esteem by the
inspiration he gave to literary studies in this university and by
those achievements of scholarship which have made his name well
known among all who study English literature whether in
Edinburgh or elsewhere. Of much that we all owe to him it is
right that I should make particular mention of the authoritative
edition of Pope and of the scholarly research now going forward on
Dickens which looks to him as one of its pioneers. To anyone who
succeeds to the chair of English Literature of which Butt was so
worthy an occupant it must be a source of pride, and indeed of
daily gratitude, that so many of the authors with whom he has to
deal are illuminated by the admirable scholarship of those who
have held the chair before him. I think of what the study of Milton
owes to Masson, of Donne to Grierson, of Spenser to Renwick, and
this afternoon I may be permitted a special thought of what the
study of Shakespeare in this century has owed to Dover Wilson. As
I recall to you now some of my illustrious predecessors, I am
inevitably reminded of the words of Donne when he saw

man
Contracted to an inch, who was a span.

Yet the sense of my own insufficiency must not deter me from attempting what is due to the greatness of my subject. I have chosen to devote my inaugural lecture to the writer whose pre-eminence in English literature is undisputed, and to that group of Shakespeare's works which includes the greatest of them. My particular choice of topic concerning Shakespeare's tragedies I like to think might not have lacked the approval of the first holder of this chair. For Blair, in those *Lectures on Rhetoric* that he used to give to his students here two hundred years ago, remarked that in the catastrophe of a tragedy 'we always expect the art and genius of the poet to be most fully displayed'.

~

The catastrophe is of course that part of a tragedy which brings the action to its conclusion. Its one essential principle is that it shall be appropriate to the events which have preceded, that it shall indeed appear to follow from them as a necessary or probable consequence. And, not to neglect the obvious, since Shakespeare's tragic actions are of very different kinds – the revenge for a father, the assassination of a ruler, the murder of a wife, the defeat of a general, the ingratitude of children – the conclusions to which these various actions lead will themselves be of a variety which makes generalization precarious. Such few generalizations as I venture I shall therefore combine with a particular, if necessarily brief, discussion of some individual cases. Nevertheless I think it sometimes possible to discover, in the catastrophes of unlike plays, or in the way they are led up to, correspondences which may suggest a predilection on Shakespeare's part for certain kinds of tragic effect rather than others; and some of these correspondences it may be interesting to note. Comparison, however, will usually reveal significant points of difference which accord with the individual character of each play and may serve to illumine it.

One or two obvious generalizations may be permitted at the outset. With the Elizabethans, though it has not always been so, the ending of a tragedy was normally disastrous; and a disastrous end almost invariably meant the death of the protagonist. The dramatist Fletcher took it for granted that if a play lacked deaths this was 'enough to make it no tragedy';[1] and the author of *Soliman and Perseda*, referring to 'tragedy's discourse', adds by way of explanation: 'And what are tragedies but acts of death?'[2] If this to you, along with Aristotle and Chaucer's Monk, may seem an unsophisticated view, the evidence suggests that Shakespeare did not find it unacceptable. In *Titus Andronicus* Tamora describes a letter which has arranged the murder of Bassianus as 'the complot of this timeless tragedy'; and in *A Midsummer Night's Dream* the master of ceremonies, while his eyes water at the 'tragical mirth' of the workmen's play, is made to confess that

> tragical ... it is;
> For Pyramus therein doth kill himself.

In Elizabethan tragedy death is usually violent. Among the Shakespearean protagonists only King Lear and Timon die by neither sword nor poison; and only in *Timon of Athens* is the catastrophe unspectacular. The Elizabethans, heedless rather than ignorant of classical convention, liked to show their deaths on the stage. And their method has obvious advantages. It ends the action at a high pitch of theatrical excitement; it gives immediacy to the hero in extremis; it permits him a dramatic dying speech; and, in the hands of a skilful dramatist, it may finally exhibit the hero in a way that will confirm, or in some cases complete, our impression of his character. Dr Leavis well observes that, in a 'superb *coup de théâtre*', 'Othello dies belonging to the world of action in which his true part lay.'[3] Coriolanus is hacked down amid a last blaze of wrath. Hamlet appears in the fencing match as the man of courtly accomplishment we have not fully seen before.

However sensational the means by which the catastrophe is brought about, if it is to achieve its maximum effect it must of course be carefully prepared for; and I shall give a little attention to Shakespeare's art of preparation. In a sense no doubt the catastrophe is being prepared for all the time. Shakespeare respects the principle that if a story is to end badly it must end badly from the beginning. His tragic openings would make a study in themselves. Yet, when initial portents have led us on through murder or battle, storm or madness, there is often some particular indication of the catastrophe's approach. In *Richard III* and *Julius Caesar* it is heralded by ghosts. In *Antony and Cleopatra* there is ghostly music. The mad songs of Ophelia and the sleepwalking of Lady Macbeth are ominous. In several plays the hero's death is preceded by the death of a secondary character closely linked with him: as well as Ophelia and Lady Macbeth one may instance Portia, Enobarbus, Gloucester in *King Lear*. Bradley observed that in that part of a tragedy which comes between the crisis and the catastrophe Shakespeare frequently introduces a strain of pathos which gives relief from previous tension.[4] What I myself am more often conscious of is the beginning, perhaps in a quiet and even a meditative manner, of a doleful movement which creates expectancy and carries through to the close. It is not that the secondary deaths themselves precipitate the catastrophe. Usually they do not. Rather they contribute to what might be called the emotional rhythm of the play, inducing in us a sombre or at least a grave and melancholy mood, which adjusts us to the coming of the end. The instance of Portia's death is especially notable. Plutarch tells of this at the end of the 'Life of Brutus' in what is almost an addendum. But Shakespeare, who could well have left it out, makes Portia's death the beginning of a sequence which continues with the fateful decision to march to Philippi, the strangely affecting drowsiness of Brutus's boy, and then the apparition. That Shakespeare attached importance to his account of Portia's death seems clear from his having apparently had two goes at it. In one version Brutus reacts to the news by saying, 'We must die, Messala', and it is interesting, if not surprising, to observe that some reflection on this universal destiny of man, either momentary or prolonged, occurs at a roughly similar point in several plays. That all men must die has naturally been the subject of reflection from the very earliest times. That it is no more than a truism is precisely the dramatic point when Capulet dismisses Tybalt's death with 'Well, we were born to die', and when Gertrude attempts to console Hamlet for his father's death by remarking, 'All that lives must die.' Yet, when this thought occurs just as a play is setting towards catastrophe, it has a peculiar resonance.

> Men must endure
> Their going hence, even as their coming hither,

says Edgar in *King Lear*, and, though these words are not directly applied to Lear, they come just when we hear that Lear and Cordelia have been defeated in battle. It was also a commonplace of consolation that since death had to be endured it did not so much matter when. And this thought too occurs several times in Shakespeare. But again a commonplace may acquire importance from its context. When Brutus learns that his wife is dead, he meditates that 'she must die once', that is to say at some time. And this is clearly what Macbeth means when he responds to the news of *his* wife's death in a line that commentators have strangely found ambiguous: 'She should have died hereafter.' If she had not died now, her death would still have come. 'There would have been a time', he says, 'for such a word.' And the same thought occurs to Hamlet with reference to his own death: 'If it be now, 'tis not to come ... if it be not now, yet it will come.' In each case, I think, this reminder of the common destiny of human beings points forward to the catastrophe, which it prepares us to accept. Yet reflections identical in substance may in different contexts have dissimilar effect. What gives Brutus patience to endure the loss of *his* wife marks for Macbeth his inability to feel the loss of his. The thought which shows Hamlet in a state of preparedness to meet his death leads Macbeth only to a meditation on the futility of life.

It is characteristically in *Hamlet*, a play which has brooded deeply on the nature of man's existence, that the theme of death as his inevitable end receives its most extended treatment. And to *Hamlet* I now turn. For sheer theatrical excitement its catastrophe is surely unsurpassed. The fencing match, designed as a performance by two virtuosos in the art, as the preceding text makes clear, is conducted with full ceremony before a splendid court while death hangs on every thrust. As Hamlet wins the first two bouts and rejects the poisoned wine, a hope that he may yet escape flickers against our deeper certainty that he will not. At length the fatal wound brings a sudden change of tempo, and in the ensuing tumult the four chief personages fall in turn, with the hero last, to permit a dying speech, which death none the less cuts short. But what is more to my present purpose than this satisfying climax is the dramatic art which prepares for it and the dramatist's creation of the context in which the hero's death will be placed. From the moment when Claudius and Laertes hatch their plot against Hamlet, 'under the which he shall not choose but fall', we feel his death to be imminent; and though the long scene of Ophelia's burial keeps the main action in suspense, it holds us all the time to the death motif. That death has various aspects the play has already shown. Polonius has been killed like a rat behind the arras, his corpse has been lugged away and will soon stink if not disposed of. Ophelia's death by contrast, as she drowns singing in the stream, has a sad pathetic beauty which, even through the wranglings of survivors, will continue in the flowers upon her grave. But a grave after all has to be dug, and, if burial has its mourning ritual, Shakespeare does not forget its workaday routine. The humorous vitality of the gravedigger who sings happily at his work boldly shifts the tone. Yet his very songs are about dying and being buried, while the most triumphant of his jokes concerns the perpetuity of the grave: 'The houses he makes lasts till doomsday.' It is just as he is saying this that the hero whose death is already plotted is brought in to overhear, and the skulls that the gravedigger so carelessly throws up prompt Hamlet's meditation on mortality. With this the play now draws upon the accumulated emotions inspired by the Dance of Death, in which for many ages the skeleton had grinned at living men. As Hamlet holds up the skull of Yorick the jester, he sees in it both the end of jesting and the jest that still goes on. The occasion of Ophelia's burial has quite naturally expanded to embrace this universal theme. Yet even as the play takes on this large dimension it still focuses upon the particular man whose coming death concerns us. It is through the jester's grinning skull that we get our only glimpse of Hamlet's carefree boyhood; and his casual talk with the gravedigger brings up the subject of his birth. That the gravedigger came to his present job on the day that Hamlet was born has exercised many scholars on the question of Hamlet's age; but what of course is important is not the precise number of Hamlet's years but the fact that when he entered the world a gravedigger began his occupation. To insinuate this point by way of comic dialogue is in Shakespeare's characteristic manner; but the point will surely stay with us as the action now moves forward and the appearance of the mourners brings Hamlet's intending killer into prominence. When Hamlet draws attention to Laertes as 'a very noble youth' we are ironically reminded of what threatens; and the fight at Ophelia's grave, while it dramatizes, to be sure, the roles of the two combatants in the disastrous story of her love, serves also as a prelude to their other combat, which we still await. The entry of the court fop Osric seems at first a fresh diversion, but, while Hamlet's mockery of Osric introduces a further note of comedy to relax the surface tension, their talk is of the wager, which dangles its menace before us as the moment of decision is still heralded and deferred. And then, upon the news that the court is coming down for the fencing to begin, Horatio's 'You will lose this wager, my lord' strikes ominous. It is now with the action poised upon the brink that the hero who has so long meditated on life and death finally resigns himself to Providence and accepts his mortal destiny. Throughout the long suspense as the catastrophe draws nearer we have been made aware both of the threat that hangs upon the individual life and of that larger pattern to which all life conforms. In perfect adjustment to the fact that death will come and to the possibility that it will come now, Hamlet says, 'The readiness is all.'

Readiness, though in various forms and degrees, is commonly the spirit in which the Shakespearean heroes meet death. Coriolanus, seeing that the consequence of his sparing Rome may be 'most mortal to him', adds: 'But let it come.' It is only the criminal Richard III who fears death, and even he recovers a heroic stance to face all possibilities not merely with resolution but with a superb, if desperate, valour. Shakespeare's protagonists often welcome death – most obviously, though for opposite reasons, Cleopatra, who greets death as reunion, and Timon, who finds 'all things' in 'nothing'. All seem reconciled to dying. For even Lear has it said of him when his body at length collapses:

> He hates him
> That would upon the rack of this tough world
> Stretch him out longer.

After all that they have suffered, death often comes with a feeling of release. For Cleopatra death is 'liberty', for Antony 'sleep', for Hamlet 'felicity', for Brutus 'rest'. Usually, I think, there is a sense of an action completing itself in a way that, after all the pity and the terror, at the last forbids regret. A number of the heroes voice for us this recognition and acceptance of the end. 'Unarm, Eros', says Antony,

> The long day's task is done,
> And we must sleep.

And Brutus:

> I know my hour is come ...
> ... Brutus' tongue
> Hath almost ended his life's history.
> Night hangs upon mine eyes; my bones would rest,
> That have but laboured to attain this hour.

It will not be rest Othello speaks of, but he too perceives with equal clarity the necessary ending of his very different course:

> Here is my journey's end, here is my butt,
> And very sea-mark of my utmost sail.

And even Timon, though his death is not to be shown and its manner is unimportant, has ready his own epitaph, which 'will be seen tomorrow'. All these have reached an extreme point at which life is willingly relinquished. Macbeth of course fights to the last, but when he encounters Macduff, he knows this *is* 'the last'; and he has already said, 'I have lived long enough.'

Yet a consideration of the ending of *Macbeth* reveals that between this tragedy and the others the distance is immense. Between Brutus's 'I know my hour is come' and Macbeth's 'I have lived long enough' there is a world of difference. The one regards an appointed death, the other only a satiety of living. The life that attains its hour conforms in its conclusion to a pattern which has some meaning, but Macbeth looks only to cessation. A history at its finish, a day's task done, a journey's end suggest a course that has been shaped or is shaping. There is a tragedy of 'purposes mistook', but there is another kind of tragedy in which all purpose withers; and this Shakespeare expresses with his usual felicity of metaphor:

> My way of life
> Is fall'n into the sere, the yellow leaf.

Antony and Brutus see the setting of the sun, but Macbeth grows 'aweary of the sun' while it still shines. When *they* look on death as the night that follows day, they acknowledge and accept an ordered universe; but Macbeth arrives at a condition of mind when he wishes 'th'estate o'th' world were now undone'.

It is possible to see here an ending which befits a man who has been led to set his will against the social and moral order and the universal order it reflects. This order Macbeth has triply violated by killing his kinsman, guest and king. Later, seeking deliverance from 'the torture of the mind', he has cried, 'Let the frame of things disjoint.' Still later and still more terribly, he has demanded answers of the witches,

> though the treasure
> Of nature's germens tumble all together

and creation plunge to confusion. But the action that began with the murder of Duncan reaches its conclusion with Macbeth's own destruction when Macduff, who first proclaimed the murder's horror, displays the murderer's severed head. The final movement towards the catastrophe has an unrelenting progress. Alternating scenes afford glimpses of opposing forces preparing for decisive battle. Macbeth is besieged in his castle. The cry of women heard offstage sounds an omen of disaster. Lady Macbeth is dead. And, while Macbeth's enemies close upon him, the false security given him by the witches is stripped away: Birnam Wood appears to come to Dunsinane, and, still fighting furiously for a life he does not hope to save, he finds himself confronted with the man not 'of woman born'. Yet set against this outward action, though involved with it, is the interior drama of Macbeth's mind. The 'horrible imaginings' which precede and the 'terrible dreams' which follow the murder of Duncan lead on to a surfeit of suffering which causes a numbing of the spirit until nothing that now happens to Macbeth can affect him any more. He has 'supped full with horrors' till he has 'almost forgot the taste of fears'. Such apparitions as visit Richard III on the night before his last battle do not appear to Macbeth: the time for Banquo's ghost is past. That cry of women fails to move him – except to the reflection that it would have moved him once. His wife's death brings a reminder of the universal end, and in a moment of expanded vision he surveys the whole of human life. But, whereas Hamlet at a corresponding stage in his play discovers 'a divinity that shapes our ends' and Lear aspires to take upon himself 'the mystery of things', Macbeth sees nothing more than the trivial monotony of existence in the meaningless succession of its days.

> Tomorrow and tomorrow and tomorrow
> Creeps in this petty pace from day to day ...
> And all our yesterdays have lighted fools
> The way to dusty death.

With Macbeth's death the 'estate o'th' world' is not undone but renewed. As Duncan's son prepares for his crowning he speaks of things being newly planted and of doing what is needful 'in measure, time, and place'. But with our satisfaction at the destruction of the destroyer there mingles the awe with which we have witnessed the dying of a soul. Yet it may perplex the understanding of this tragedy to call it, as it has been called, a play about damnation.[5] For when Macbeth murdered Duncan he knew that, setting aside 'the life to come', 'we still have judgement here'. And while his death at the hands of Macduff presents one aspect of that judgement, another aspect of it shows the nothingness that life becomes to him before it is taken from him. And it is in this, I believe, that his deeper nemesis lies.

This is what profoundly distinguishes *Macbeth* from other tragedies of the villain hero – not least the earlier one by Shakespeare. But if *Macbeth* has a dimension which is lacking in *Richard III* this will not obscure from us the degree to which the two plays correspond. Macbeth no less than Richard is slain by a righteous foe. The last words on the one are 'The bloody dog is dead', on the other 'this dead butcher'. In *Richard III* 'peace lives again', in *Macbeth* 'the time is free'. In the justice of their tragic ending the two plays of wicked heroes necessarily stand apart from the others, where what is finally impressed on us is not the justice of the hero's fall but that quality of the man which, in vicissitude and defeat, in error or in failure, calls forth our admiration. Shakespeare's favourite epithet for this quality is 'noble'. It is often used of the tragic hero even by the enemies who have destroyed him. Hamlet is called 'noble' by Laertes as well as by Horatio; Brutus is praised by Antony as 'the noblest Roman of them all'; and, even while remembering the slaughters done by Coriolanus, Aufidius says in the play's last line, 'Yet he shall have a noble memory.' Even of Timon it is said, 'Dead is noble Timon', though the words seem to have been overlooked by the critic who couples this play with *Macbeth* as a tragedy of damnation.[6] Othello can hardly be called noble with Desdemona lying dead before us, but the last words spoken of him are that 'he was great of heart'. It is one generalization about Shakespeare's tragic endings to which there are no exceptions that they all include some posthumous description of the hero, however brief, which governs our ultimate response to him. Often such description is reinforced by the spectacle of the stage. The exhibition of Macbeth's severed head, suggested it is true by Holinshed, confers a final mark of ignominy. In several plays the practical necessity of the removal of the dead is turned to good account by being made the occasion of a last dramatic tribute.

Bear Hamlet like a soldier to the stage;
For he was likely, had he been put on,
To have proved most royal.

Similarly, as Brutus is carried off, Octavius says:

Within my tent his bones tonight shall lie,
Most like a soldier, ordered honourably.

And Coriolanus is to be regarded

As the most noble corse that ever herald
Did follow to his urn.

In *Antony and Cleopatra* Shakespeare develops a hint from
Plutarch in making the bearing off of Cleopatra the symbol not
only of a tragic love but of a triumphant union in death:

She shall be buried by her Antony;
No grave upon the earth shall clip in it
A pair so famous.

Such closing rituals and the eulogies which go with them bring the
tragic action to its appropriate conclusion. They cannot and do not
attempt to epitomize the significance of the conflicts now at an end.
Even such a judgement as that which presents the deaths of Romeo
and Juliet as a scourge for parental hate does not occur in later
plays. Horatio may sum up on 'purposes mistook / Fall'n on
th'inventors' heads', which is certainly one aspect of *Hamlet*; but
even Horatio cannot retell Hamlet's story. And what can now be
said of the tremendous inner drama of *Macbeth*, or of *King Lear*?
Occasionally, however, a final appraisal of the hero may glance back
at the central action of a tragedy in such a way as to suggest, or even
direct, an interpretation of his role. In his final eulogy of Brutus,
Antony refers specifically to his part in the assassination of Caesar:

All the conspirators save only he
Did that they did in envy of great Caesar;
He only in a general honest thought
And common good to all made one of them.

This clearly voices a judgement the play asks us to accept. And there is, I think, one play in which the dramatist seems to take especial care to guide our response to the hero and his doing of his fatal act. I glance now at *Othello*.

The catastrophe of *Othello*, both in conception and execution, shows a dramatic mastery unexcelled even in Shakespeare. In the story that came to him from Cinthio, the Moor, having killed his wife, suffers the revenge of her kinsfolk – and apparently without learning that his suspicion of her was false. But the dramatist perceives that the ending the story demands is that the Moor shall discover his error and kill himself in consequence. The catastrophe therefore depends on a powerful peripeteia, and its onset is of all Shakespeare's, appropriately, the swiftest. The murder of Desdemona is followed on the instant by the arrival of Emilia to discover it; her outcries precipitate the confrontation with Iago and that momentous dialogue which reveals the appalling truth. Othello's two attacks upon Iago and Iago's murder of Emilia sustain the excitement of the action, which nevertheless slows temporarily to exhibit Othello in his torment with his weapon poised for death. When he is – for the second time – disarmed, he would seem to have been frustrated, and the last rapid explanations, half persuading us that all is over, cause a lulling of expectancy in which Othello can begin on a quiet note what we do not yet recognize to be his death-speech. Our attention is artfully diverted from what Othello is to do, so that a death which is expected will nevertheless come on us with the full force of surprise. What our attention is diverted *to* is a review of what has already happened. And the opportunity is taken, at this important moment, for a comment on Othello's jealousy. This is spoken, it is true, by Othello himself in directing Lodovico what he is to report of him to the Venetian senate. But through Othello's directions to Lodovico does not the play also speak to us – no less than when Antony in his dying speech in *his* play instructs Cleopatra, and through her the audience, how they are to think of him (not as one who basely dies but as 'a Roman by a Roman / Valiantly vanquished')? The hero, while still performing his hero's role within the confines of the action, absorbs into it

the function of a Chorus which presents the hero to us. 'Speak of
me as I am', Othello says,

> Nothing extenuate,
> Nor set down aught in malice. Then must you speak ...

The call on our attention could hardly be more insistent, nor
correspondingly the verdict more emphatic.

> Speak of me as I am ...
> ... Then must you speak ...
> Of one not easily jealous, but, being wrought,
> Perplexed in the extreme.

I am well aware that these crucial words, in spite of, or perhaps
because of, the emphasis they receive, have not invariably been
taken at face value. T.S. Eliot thought Othello was making excuses
for himself, 'cheering himself up' by seeing things as they are not,
'dramatizing himself against his environment'; and Dr Leavis
seized on this to make self-dramatization the clue to Othello's
character.[7] But this is a twentieth-century reading, which suits the
taste for deflation in an unheroic age. It would hardly have
occurred to an Elizabethan audience, less predisposed than the
modern reader to probe for concealed motives. And it applies to
an Elizabethan tragedy the criteria of a naturalistic drama. When
in a final speech which reviews his tragic career Othello describes
himself as 'one not easily jealous', to suppose that we are really
to understand the opposite is to impute to Shakespeare a kind of
irony which is alien to the nature and conventions of his art. No
one has said better than Dr Leavis – and in this very essay on
Othello – that if characters in poetic drama speak poetry they are
not thereby poets. By the same token, I think, if characters
in poetic drama adopt dramatic attitudes they are not thereby
self-dramatizing. When Eliot admits that Othello not only takes
in himself but takes in the audience too, he may be thought to
explode his own case.

Othello's review of *his* case not only indicates, as I think, the
impression the play wishes to leave with us but it marks a bold
technical innovation on which the sensational climax will

depend. A résumé of the tragic action is given not, as in *Romeo and Juliet*, when the action is complete, but while we still await its issue; and it is spoken not by an observer but by the hero himself, who, when his account reaches the present, acts out what he describes. Othello continues from his jealousy to the fatal deed it led to, epitomized in an image of a man who threw his priceless pearl away. With the tears the deed calls forth we move from past to present; and these tears, as Othello now sheds them, like 'medicinable gum' from Arabian trees, suggest a healing penitence, which looks forward to atonement. And atonement finds *its* image in the slaughter of an infidel. This incident of the Turk whom Othello once slew in Aleppo seems to take us back into his past; but as he re-enacts it, image becomes actuality, past and present coalesce, and Othello dies in the dual role of killed and killer, both the enemy and the champion of his love.

The catastrophe of *Othello* is as original as it is masterly. But its originality consists to a large extent in striking adaptations of the conventions and devices of the drama. The catastrophe of *King Lear*, the last I shall examine, has an originality of another and deeper kind. In the endings of the other tragedies, *Timon* alone excepted, there is something histrionic, whether the sudden shock of *Othello*, the prolonged suspense of *Hamlet* or the slow majestic ritual of the death of Cleopatra. To die in the high Roman fashion, or like Macbeth with harness on one's back, itself demands a sense of the dramatic, or at least of the heroic; and the art that makes the most of this expresses something in the temper of the Elizabethan age. But Lear has shed that element of pride or egotism that Eliot complains of in the Elizabethan heroes, and the play correspondingly breaks free of traditional dramatic modes. To the scene of Lear's death such a word as 'histrionic' is not so much inapplicable as irrelevant. Unique among the tragic heroes, King Lear does not confront death; he is unaware of his 'journey's end'. There can be no dying speech. And, when he is dead, uniquely there is no word of eulogy or obloquy. The one thing that is now said of him relates simply to his suffering. There are no funeral honours. Heroics are entirely and rhetoric almost absent. Nothing interposes between us and what Wordsworth called 'the essential passions of the heart'; and even the traditional motif of greatness fallen, the contrast between what once was and what now is, though it is interesting to find this present, seeks no aid beyond 'the very language of men':

> I have seen the day, with my good biting falchion,
> I would have made them skip: I am old now.

Yet this novel tragic ending, which so extraordinarily relies on the unadorned expression of the most powerful human feelings, does not deny itself the resources of dramatic art. Lear's entry with Cordelia dead in his arms is in itself perhaps the most moving thing in drama. Yet its impact is still enhanced by the irony of Albany's preceding words, 'The gods defend her', and by the horror of the bystanders, who see an image of the end of the world. The business of the feather and the glass, though it seems the very gesture of nature, is none the less a dramatic rendering of those hopes born out of grief which alternate with Lear's despair; and its theatrical effectiveness is vouched for by later imitation. The scene lacks neither spectacle nor suspense. The whole emotion of it is focused on the sight of Cordelia lying dead, and, against our certain knowledge that she *is* dead, there is still a part of our minds which watches with Lear for a sign.[8] While he gazes on Cordelia, there are also other dead, whom he may but we are not permitted to forget. What Puttenham called 'the shows of the stage' can sometimes say things more eloquently than words. The entry of Lear with Cordelia follows directly upon the bringing in of Goneril and Regan. And the story of Lear and his three daughters comes to its perfect end when all four lie dead together on the stage. As if to make the point clearer, while the three sisters, after they have died off, are all brought on, Edmund, who has received his fatal wound on stage, is simultaneously carried off. The report of his death a little later has but a single line, and the comment it provokes, 'That's but a trifle here', may have more than its surface meaning. Gloucester and his sons have served their dramatic purpose and their story may not now disturb this final tableau.

If we perceive the significance of this tableau, we shall hardly revive the protests at Cordelia's death. Johnson notoriously could not bear it, and even Bradley, though no less severe than Lamb on Tate's sentimental ending, confessed to a wish that Shakespeare might have granted Lear 'peace and happiness by Cordelia's fireside'.[9] It is true that Cordelia's death, occasioned by the accident of a messenger's delay, may not seem to be inevitable by the logic of events. Yet there is a higher logic which belongs to the imagination. And if in this archetypal story of Lear's three daughters, two wicked and one good, but equally sprung from him, the imagination perceives the potentialities of Lear's own human nature, with all the good and evil it generates and experiences, it may be led to an ending in which the deaths of the good and evil sisters must coincide and their father will not survive them. In earlier versions of the story, after the rout of the wicked sisters, Lear regained his kingdom, which Cordelia inherited, though in many of the versions she was afterwards overcome in battle and killed herself in prison. Shakespeare rejects for the good daughter both happiness and self-destruction, and makes her death instrumental in her father's tragedy.

As Shakespeare has refashioned the story Lear and Cordelia are defeated. But Lear, after all his suffering, knows the happiness of Cordelia's love; and so long as he has this he would gladly withdraw from participation in man's strivings to survey them as from some viewpoint of the gods. But what he cannot escape from is his human plight, and with Cordelia's death he is brought back to face the stark fact of mortality – 'She's dead as earth' – and to go on asking man's unanswerable questions:

> Why should a dog, a horse, a rat have life,
> And thou no breath at all?

When he dies believing Cordelia breathes, his death dramatizes what has already been narrated of Gloucester's death, which foreshadows it:

> His flawed heart ...
> 'Twixt two extremes of passion, joy and grief,
> Burst smilingly.

'Men must endure / Their going hence, even as their coming hither.' These words, which I quoted earlier, are actually spoken to Gloucester, and although, as I suggested, their resonance extends beyond their immediate context, we must also note, as is not always done, their particular relevance to it. Gloucester is anxious to die, and has just said, 'No further ... A man may rot even here.' So that, when the play now says, through Edgar, 'Men must endure / Their going hence', the words will suggest not only that men must suffer death but that they must live out their lives to the end. And, whereas Gloucester has seen the end of life as rotting, Edgar adds 'Ripeness is all.' The commentators tend to equate this with Hamlet's 'The readiness is all.' But readiness and ripeness are not the same, as is clear if you try to transpose them. Hamlet may have reached the mature age of thirty, but he will hardly be thought to have 'ripeness', while Gloucester need receive no reflection on readiness – he is too ready as it is. The universal destiny of man, as shown to us in *King Lear*, is not simply that he must die but that he must love and sorrow. What moves us in the ending of this play has little to do with the traditional horror of the grinning skeleton nor with the heroism of facing one's moment when it comes. It is the piercing sight and the familiar language of a human being grieving. Lear's death comes when experience has made him ripe for it; he dies of having lived.

Each tragedy has the ending appropriate to itself. But all the other endings are comparable in one respect. When they speak of a task that is done, a journey that is ended, an hour that is attained, or even of a butcher that is dead, they regard the tragic action as something that is now finishing. The story that Horatio is to tell about Hamlet and the act that Lodovico will with heavy heart relate of Othello refer to things which are now past. It is true that the tragedies always end with a glance towards futurity: indeed they usually provide for the future government of a state. But in doing so they make clear that a happier order is about to be established. *Timon of Athens*, no less than *Macbeth* and *Richard III*, celebrates the coming of peace. At the end of *Coriolanus* Rome is freed from threat of burning. The warring parents of Romeo and Juliet take one another's hands. In *Othello* it is the wronged Cassio who is the new governor of Cyprus. In *King Lear* too power passes to the innocent; but, when Edgar is called on to take over the realm, the words that deliver it to him say that he must 'the gored state sustain'. And the closing lines of the play look neither to suffering ended nor to a new beginning, but rather to continuance. Lear's own story ends with the tableau of his death among his daughters. But when Kent says 'Let him pass' we know that there is a scene which will still go on without him. The rack of this tough world will remain when Lear is no longer stretched on it. There is a little of this in *Hamlet*, when the dying hero leaves Horatio to draw his breath in pain 'in this harsh world'. Yet when the election lights on Fortinbras the sorrow with which he embraces his fortune is for what has given him his fortune, not for the fortune he receives. In *King Lear* the survivors, while they remember the hero who is dead, remind us that they too must die. In all the tragedies we are left with the impression that those who remain are lesser figures than the one who has departed, and in *King Lear* this impression is confirmed explicitly in the last lines of the play:

> The oldest hath borne most: we that are young
> Shall never see so much nor live so long.

But there is no suggestion that what they see and what they bear in their more circumscribed lives will be different in its kind. *King Lear* is the most universal of the tragedies. Its archetypal story, the ancient figure among the warring elements, the vagueness as to time and place which has often been remarked on, the duplication of Lear's case in Gloucester's – all combine to detach the play from that particularity which adheres in a greater or lesser degree to the tragic lives of the Moor of Venice, the Roman triumvir, the Scottish regicide and even the Prince of Denmark. And the catastrophe of *King Lear*, while it shows the passing of a single individual with all the intensity of feeling that goes to a particular man and the vividness of spectacle that marks the conclusion of his story, may also suggest to us, as a lesser generation takes over his kingdom, the continuing condition of humanity in which men must endure, if on a smaller scale, what belongs to the coming hither and the going hence.

5

MUCH ADO ABOUT NOTHING

When *Much Ado About Nothing* was revived at court a few years before Shakespeare's death, the official accounts referred to a play 'called *Benedicte and Betteris*'; and Charles I in his copy of Shakespeare wrote those two names against the printed title. The play was already, it seems, celebrated for two brilliant stage roles, and it is Beatrice and Benedick who, as Peter Alexander puts it, 'give the play its immortality'. 'Take away Benedick, Beatrice, Dogberry', said Coleridge, 'and what will remain?' The trouble of course is that what remains is not the nothing that seems to be implied by the play's main plot. Coleridge was quite unperturbed by this: it simply showed how in Shakespeare the plot existed for the sake of the characters. The plot, he said, was the canvas only, useful apparently as something on which portraits could be painted. And such a view has been remarkably persistent, though with some slackening of metaphor. In our century the story of Hero and Claudio has been seen as 'little more than a background', 'only a framework', as 'the old stock' on which new characters could be 'grafted' and finally as a 'necessary buttress'. A recent study of the play accepts that Hero and Claudio provide 'no more than necessary episodes in a plot whose main purpose is to give life to Beatrice and Benedick'.

Yet this plot so readily dismissed is based on a story told by Ariosto, Bandello, Belleforest, Spenser and a dozen others, and was evidently very popular in Elizabethan times. The first thing that ought to strike us about it is that it belongs to a type that is a great favourite with Shakespeare. We may call it the plot of the rejected bride. The repudiation of a woman by her husband or her intended husband is a central situation in at least half a dozen of Shakespeare's plays. In *The Two Gentlemen of Verona* the heroine seeks out her lover on his travels only to find him serenading another woman. In *All's Well that Ends Well* the prince whom the heroine wins as her prize flatly refuses to have her. But the most frequent kind of rejected bride is the woman who is slandered and repudiated through a false belief in her dishonour. *Much Ado About Nothing* shares this theme with *Othello*, *Cymbeline* and *The Winter's Tale*, the last of which presents the interesting case of the slanderer who is the husband himself. There is a further variant in *Hamlet*, where a prince renounces the woman he has wooed from a false belief less in what she is than in what she might become. In plays on other themes the rejected lady is always liable to turn up in some minor role: Demetrius's Helena is spurned in the wood near Athens, Mariana forsaken at the moated grange; while even in *King Lear*, when the King of France takes Cordelia without a dowry, Shakespeare adds a Duke of Burgundy who declines to.

These stories have of course widely different outcomes: the tragic potentialities of the slandered bride are fully realized in *Othello*. But, more characteristically, the slander is subsequently discredited to provide a happy ending when the estranged couples are reunited, though often only after the woman has been believed to be dead and the man who disowned her has done penance. *Much Ado About Nothing* is one of four plays in which this formula occurs, and five if we count *The Two Gentlemen of Verona*, where Proteus pretends the woman is dead and she swoons in a symbolic death before being restored to him. We may also have the end of the story without the beginning, the woman recovered from seeming death without ever having been rejected. In two plays a wife is lost by shipwreck and takes refuge in a religious house, from which she finally emerges to a marital reunion. And, if we were to count all reunions with people who have been supposed dead, we could find this motif in at least nine plays from *The Comedy of Errors* at the beginning of Shakespeare's career to *The Tempest* at the end. What happens in *Much Ado About Nothing* is revealed as a Shakespearean paradigm: the heroine is courted, betrothed, then slandered and rejected, seems to die, revives and, when the gentleman has done penance, is reunited with him. This is the one play in which all the elements of the paradigm are present; so that when I find its plot being disparaged by knowing reviewers in the Sunday papers as too tiresomely artificial to hold interest, I reflect that this cannot have been Shakespeare's view.

Much Ado, then, presents a marriage arranged, broken off and then remade, the three crucial events – betrothal, rejection, wedding – each having its high moment on the stage. In other plays other emphases are possible, but in this one the rejection itself is made central and supplies the theatrical climax in that wonderful scene in the church which we call Act 4 scene 1 and which thus corresponds, in position as in theatrical excitement, with the trial scene in *The Merchant of Venice* and the deposition scene in *Richard II*. By contrast the deception at the window, the Borachio and Margaret business, is, as the critics complain, cavalierly, even perfunctorily treated. Shakespeare, if it had suited him, could have shown the lover's agony as he watched his lady's seeming infidelity, as is clear from what he does in *Troilus and Cressida* and *Othello*; but what is important in this play is not the hero's distress but the sensation of his consequent act. In the narrative of Bandello the bridegroom simply sends to the bride's home to break the marriage off; and there have not been wanting critics who blame Claudio for not following this example – the same, no doubt, as object to Prince Hal for disowning Falstaff in the public street instead of having a word with him in private. But that is to confuse the demands of life with those of art, which, as Aristotle recognized, seeks to go one better. If you are writing a play, and wish to make the dramatic most of the bride's rejection, where will it make more éclat than at the very altar – as Claudio perfectly well understands? 'In the congregation where I should wed, there will I shame her.' This means, no doubt, that Claudio performs his role as a character in a play better than as a compassionate human being; but that is a limitation of the subject, and one which the dramatist evidently accepts, so that it is beside the point to denounce Claudio, in the words of one book on Shakespeare's comedies, as 'priggish', 'brutal', 'insufferable' and, finally, 'unworthy even of such a Hero as he thinks her to be'. This seems strangely uncomprehending of what he does think her to be, and we can hardly count it against him, or indeed Shakespeare, that he did not foresee the permissive generation. It might be better to note how the scene in the church is carefully prepared for so as to achieve its maximum impact. This is obviously why the thing most stressed about the lady who is to be shamed is her modesty. 'Is she not a modest young lady?' is the first thing Claudio says when he confesses his love; and she herself, when she agrees to help in the trick on Beatrice, says, 'I will do any modest office, my lord, to help my cousin to a good husband.' Who will and will not get a husband has been the talk from the beginning, which gives point to the boast of Beatrice, who knows what to steer clear of, that she can see a church by daylight. But as soon as Claudio is betrothed he is asked when he means 'to go to church'. His later threat that he will shame the lady there is still later echoed by Borachio with the addition, 'and send her home again without a husband'. When the texture of the dialogue has thus created a delightful expectation of what is going to happen to a 'modest young lady' when she comes to church to get a husband, a most artful little sequence holds us on the brink. The bride all unsuspecting is seen dressing for the wedding to the accompaniment of prattle about wedding gowns and even a joke about what will happen to her tonight. And then the constables arrive with the tale that would avert the whole disaster if only they could get it out before the impatient father is fetched away 'to give his daughter to her husband'. The awaited moment inexorably comes, we find ourselves in the middle of the marriage service – 'You come hither, my lord, to marry this lady?' – and the bridegroom, in one resounding monosyllable, drops his bomb: 'No.' Astonishingly the bomb fails to explode, it is passed off as a quibble; and nothing is more theatrically dexterous than the way the dramatist still holds the situation poised until at length the explosion comes:

There, Leonato, take her back again.
Give not this rotten orange to your friend.

The 'modest' bride in her wedding dress is denounced by her intended husband as a wanton, 'a common stale', 'more intemperate' in her blood than 'pamper'd animals / That rage in savage sensuality'. I suppose you may think the colour here laid on a little thick, but what you will surely not dispute is the dazzling virtuosity of an artist seizing the opportunities of his subject. What Coleridge called the canvas appears to be the picture itself.

Yet it is of course only part of the picture, and too simple a thing in itself for an artist of Shakespeare's kind. It is a frequent practice of Elizabethan dramatists to complement one plot with another which reflects or contrasts with it, thus combining the satisfactions of artistic form with a sense of the ambivalences of life. In Shakespeare, though not in his source story, there are *two* gentlemen of Verona; the inconstant lover Proteus is paired with the devoted lover Valentine, the man who forsakes his mistress with the man who is banished from *his*. The shrew who is tamed is provided with a demure sister who is decorously wooed. In *Much Ado* the cousin of the rejected bride, a mere lay figure in Bandello, becomes a rejecter of marriage. The technique seems especially suited to comedy, but it will not escape students of *Hamlet* that the prince whose task it is to avenge his father's murder is himself the murderer of another man whose son will seek vengeance on him.

The analogies give little support to the common view that it was because Shakespeare 'could make so little' of Hero and Claudio that 'he was led to create the other couple who outshine them'.[1] I hope I have shown that it is not exactly little that Shakespeare makes of Claudio's rejection of Hero; and, if he invented another couple to set against them, it must surely have been because they interested him rather than because they did not. While the lovers who look to their marriage are forced apart, another couple who decry marriage are in spite of themselves conjoined. Moreover, what separates one couple is a similar device to that which unites the other. Hero is rejected because Don John tricks Claudio into believing a fabricated tale; and it is because Don Pedro devises a trick whereby Benedick and Beatrice are each made to overhear a fabricated tale that they accept one another. The basic plot of betrothal, rejection, wedding becomes part of a symmetry of antithetical movements from which the design of *Much Ado About Nothing* evolves.

The roles of Beatrice and Benedick are, I take it, no less than those of Hero and Claudio, determined by the plot in which they are required to figure. Certainly the trick Don Pedro plays on them is no less artificially contrived than the one Don John plays on Claudio. Yet for those who mock love to succumb to it is perhaps commoner in human experience than for a bridegroom to denounce his virgin bride as a whore. It is also more amusing, and, since the eavesdropping in the orchard, no less than the rejection in the church, is fully acted out, it brings into the centre of the play a laughter which modifies its tone. Moreover, since the tale that Benedick and Beatrice overhear is one they are happy to accept, they retain at least the illusion of freedom of manoeuvre. Whereas poor Hero and Claudio must passively submit to their story, Benedick and Beatrice can actively collaborate with theirs, and their role of mocking love and marriage supplies inexhaustible matter for their wit. They are free to mock the other couple for the restrictions which the plot imposes upon them. Thus before the ball, when Hero is receiving instructions about a marriage proposal, Beatrice chips in with 'It is my cousin's duty to make curtsey and say, "Father, as it please you"'; and after the ball, when the bride is won, Beatrice prompts Claudio, 'Speak, count, 'tis your cue.' But Beatrice and Benedick also need to be given *their* cue if they are to discover their love, and the stratagem that gives it them enables Hero and Claudio to take part in mocking them. Perhaps we may say that Beatrice and Benedick, like Falstaff in a nearly contemporary play, are not only witty in themselves but the cause of wit in others. The graver episodes involving Hero and Claudio are appropriately in verse; but the witty prose dialogue in which Beatrice and Benedick achieve their intense dramatic life becomes the dominant medium of the play.

The witty style of *Much Ado About Nothing* has been more celebrated than described, and the limited time of a lecture cannot do more but must not do less than give brief illustration. A messenger begins the play with a flourish of verbal patterns:

those killed in battle are 'but few of any sort and none of name' (*few* is balanced with *none*, which alliterates with *name*); Claudio, significantly introduced as early as the fifth speech, has done 'in the figure of a lamb the feats of a lion' (Shakespeare has learnt from the euphuists the art of cross-alliteration: 'in the *f*igure of a *l*amb the *f*eats of a *l*ion'); 'he hath, indeed, better bettered expectation than you must expect of me to tell you how'. This messenger is almost too good for his message, but not, I think, for his function, which is, with the formal artifice of his figured speech, to create a model for the polished society in which courtly lovers and love mockers will move. The ladies and gentlemen themselves, once the tone is set, speak with a more nonchalant grace, but they never lose this rhythm. Phrase balances phrase, a cadence is repeated with pleasing variations, as we progress to a controlled climax – as in Benedick's manifesto: 'That a woman conceived me I thank her; that she brought me up I likewise give her most humble thanks, but ... Because I will not do them the *wrong* to mistrust any, I will do myself the *right* to trust none; and the *fine* is' – with a pun to embroider the end – 'the *fine* is, for the which I may go the *finer*, I will live a bachelor.' An actor can hardly fail with speech like this; the speech pattern dictates its own emphasis.

This is the staple. But what turns speech into dramatic dialogue is the thrust and parry of speakers who are on the alert to score. It was repartee, the quick retort, that Dryden called the greatest grace of comedy. At its best the speaker takes up his opponent's word and sends it back in a new context – as when Beatrice and Benedick begin their merry war: 'What, my dear Lady Disdain! Are you yet living? – Is it possible Disdain should die while she hath such meet food to feed it as Signior Benedick?'

But here we also notice something else. Along with the dexterity of verbal patterning there is a fertility of metaphor and personification, an exuberant inventiveness which seizes on any idea as material from which to create fantastical situations. Disdain thrives by feeding on Benedick. When Benedick mocks the idea of himself as a married man, he sees a picture of himself with horns on his head on an inn sign; and, when Beatrice prays

God to send her no husband, she conjures up the scene: 'I am at him upon my knees every morning and evening.' As she goes on, a quick comparison of beard and blanket gives concreteness to the idea of the male: 'Lord, I could not endure a husband with a beard on his face. I had rather lie in the woollen!' Her uncle interposes an objection – 'You may light on a husband that hath no beard' – but this only supplies new ammunition:

> What should I do with him? Dress him in my apparel and make him my waiting gentlewoman? He that hath a beard is more than a youth, and he that hath no beard is less than a man; and he that is more than a youth is not for me; and he that is less than a man, I am not for him. Therefore I will even take sixpence in earnest of the bearward and lead his apes into hell.

A woman who died an old maid was said to lead apes in hell; but Beatrice cannot cite the proverb without seeing herself in the act, with the keeper of the apes paying her for the job. 'Well then,' says Leonato, quick to score a point, 'go you into hell?'

> No, but to the gate, and there will the devil meet me like an old cuckold with horns on his head, and say, 'Get you to heaven, Beatrice, get you to heaven. Here's no place for you maids.' So deliver I up my apes, and away to St Peter – for the heavens. He shows me where the bachelors sit, and there live we as merry as the day is long.

With what vivacity she projects herself into a succession of imagined situations! And, although her uncle, himself rather more than a feed, tries to trip her up, her agile fancy can always speed away to some high-spirited invention. And all she says, while it seems the quintessence of spontaneity, is of course supremely relevant, since it imprints on our minds the antagonism from which the drama of Beatrice and Benedick must spring.

Nothing is more artful than the way in which the dialogue, as it sweeps along on its seemingly unpremeditated course, is unobtrusively manoeuvring the characters into the positions required of them by the scheme of contrasting plots. The masterly opening scene, which seems little more than an exchange of courtesies with newly arrived guests, yet gets them all into place. After the dialogue has cast its first spotlight upon Claudio and Beatrice's gibes about Benedick have shown the direction of her interest, with a passing jest about Leonato's daughter to bring Hero into prominence, the 'merry war' has its first skirmish. Benedick is still fresh from declaring his antipathy to women when he receives Claudio's confession of love; so that the two are already facing opposite ways, Claudio ready to 'turn husband' if Hero will be his wife, Benedick affirming his vow to 'live a bachelor'. The Prince warns Benedick about the savage bull that bears the yoke at the same time as he promises to win Claudio a bride at the ball. It is while we wait for the ball in which Hero will be won that Beatrice makes her boast of leading apes to hell on her way to an unmarried heaven; and after the ball, when Claudio comes to claim his bride, Benedick makes his exit to avoid 'my Lady Tongue'. Hence the betrothal of one pair takes place on the stage with the other couple divided, and Hero's silence at this moment is remarked on by the tongue which is still descanting on the lack of a husband. This leads easily into the play's next movement, when Don Pedro proposes to get her one and, to fill the time till Claudio can 'go to church', devises his scheme for a match between Beatrice and Benedick. But even as he goes to set about it, his place on stage is taken by Don John and the scheme to break the first match off. Hence the threat is already hanging over the betrothed pair when they play their parts in tricking the others into love. Claudio's pleasure in the success of the trick on Benedick is interrupted by the entry of Don John to play the trick on *him*, and he is told why he should break his marriage off just when Benedick has gone, it seems, to ask for Beatrice's hand. It is surely difficult to say that Shakespeare is interested only in one couple when he takes so much care to interweave the plots as the play moves simultaneously along its two antithetical lines. Even the little ironic scene that shows Hero dressing for the wedding that is not to be does not forget to bring in Beatrice now strangely out of sorts as a result of what she heard about herself, and combines our apprehension about what is to happen to Hero with our amusement at what is happening to her cousin.

What has now to be added about the sensational scene in the church is that it brings not one but both plots to their climax, and the one as a consequence of the other. For after the tumult of the broken marriage, when even her own father has accepted the bride's dishonour, there remain, alone on the stage, two who do not. It is Beatrice and Benedick, the scorners of love, who now express their faith in it, and it is in their united defence of the rejected bride that they declare their love. When Benedick the woman-scorner now goes off in love's service to challenge to mortal combat the friend whose love he has mocked, the dramatic reversals are almost complete. Don Pedro, and possibly we as well, gleefully looked forward to the meeting of Beatrice and Benedick when each was under the illusion of the other's 'dotage'. 'That's the scene that I would see,' he said. But Shakespeare's superb dramatic tact frustrates his and our expectation of such cheap 'sport' and declines to degrade this brilliant pair to comic butts. Embarrassment at their own feelings is submerged in what they feel for someone else. 'Surely I do believe your fair cousin is *wronged* – Ah, how much might the man deserve of me that would *right* her.' Beatrice is still delivering her challenge to the male sex, and with the same verbal snap in retort. But a new serious intonation takes their mutual declaration on to a level where feeling reveals unexpected depths. This does not mean that we may not still smile at them when the mockers of love start behaving like any knight and lady of romance. Indeed they take the initiative in smiling at themselves. The famous command, 'Kill Claudio', electric in the theatre, has a conscious extravagance at once deflated by Benedick – 'Not for the wide world' – before he goes on none the less to obey it. And it is the same fantastic Beatrice who promised at the beginning to eat all the men Benedick killed who now exclaims of Claudio: 'I would eat his heart in the market-place.' So if, as has been said, the mockers are here swept into the romantic story, they bring a glint of their mockery with them. It is Beatrice who sees the preposterousness not, of course, of Hero's rejection, which loses nothing of its dreadfulness, but of the false accusation that has led to it: 'Talk with a man out at a window! A proper saying!' Put like this it may recall to us how tawdry a tale it was as told by Borachio and overheard by the Watch with the result that it is even now the subject of Dogberry's 'excommunication' at the gaol.

Of Dogberry and his henchmen Coleridge notoriously remarked that 'any other less ingeniously absurd watchmen and night-constables would have answered'. But I am not the first to observe that the creative imagination which puts Dogberry on to the stage in all his bumbling self-importance exactly meets the practical dramatic requirement that the truth which must come out must not come out too soon. If Dogberry had had less tediousness to bestow on the bride's father, the bride would have been spared. But Dogberry enables the dramatist and us to have things both ways: we are not denied our due theatrical sensation in the matter of the bride's rejection, but our knowledge that the truth is already on its blundering way out prevents her distress from distressing us too deeply. And already the 'strange misprision in the princes' has been reflected in the no less strange misprisions of the constables and Watch. 'Are you good men and true? – Yea, or else it were pity but they should suffer salvation ... – Nay, that were a punishment too good for them if they should have any allegiance in them.' Their dislocation of words is something more than malapropism; it reflects the topsyturvy world in which the way of detectives with a thief is to let him steal out of their company. The linguistic feats of Dogberry also have their place in parodying the verbal wit of his social superiors; and collectively the Watch are hardly less fertile in imagination than Beatrice herself. It is enough for them to hear talk of a deformed thief for them to bring a man of that name to life. 'I know that Deformed ... a goes up and down like a gentleman ... a wears a lock.' As the play goes on, a communal exuberance further elaborates confusion until we leave the man Deformed wearing not just a dangling lock of hair but a key in his ear to go with it.

The key in the ear, however, if you like to see it so, is a little more than a pun; for it is of course through what is thrust into their ears that the Watch are able to unlock the deception. In most versions of the story the deceivers confess through remorse. But here is perhaps a reason why Shakespeare chose not to show the deception at the window: it is better that we should learn of it from the drunken cavalier who blabs. So the bride who is rejected through what her lover overheard is restored through what the Watch overhear. The nature of the main plot has not only suggested what we may perhaps call the counterplot but also the manner of its own denouement. All the crucial turns in the action of the play are effected by a succession of eavesdroppings; and Benedick and Beatrice and Dogberry, who in stage history and criticism have overshadowed Claudio and Hero, were in a very real sense created by them.

The contrivances and accidents of overhearing supply the recurrent motif of the whole dramatic design; and it is clear that Shakespeare perceived and planned this from the outset. Overhearings and their consequent misunderstandings begin in the first act. When in the first scene Don Pedro offers to woo for Claudio and says, 'I will assume thy part in some disguise / And tell fair Hero I am Claudio', this anticipates what Borachio will do later, and it gives ample opportunity for mishap. In the second scene Antonio's man in the orchard and in the third Don John's man perfuming a room overhear and misreport. Two cases of overhearing already seem perhaps a little much, and I have sometimes wondered if the dramatist meant both to stand. As is not unusual with Shakespeare, while he is still feeling his way into his play a clear apprehension of the main lines of a design goes with little uncertainties in the detail which is yet to be worked out. Leonato's wife, an important figure in Bandello, survives in a couple of quarto stage directions but is never provided with a part; and the mistaken supposition of the father and uncle that the Prince wants Hero for himself, since it promises a contretemps which then does not occur, seems an evident false start. There are also little obscurities in the masked ball itself, assisted it would seem by some confusion in the text.[2] But on the Elizabethan stage it must have been clearer than it is to us who partners whom and which of the dancers are masked. (I take it the ladies are not.) The problem of Margaret's partner (first Benedick then Balthasar in quarto and Folio) invited Dover Wilson's happy hypothesis that she must dance with Borachio, her partner in deception later; but this unfortunately seems incompatible with his role in the rest of the scene. Nevertheless the ball, with its playful disguises and deceits, is an epitome of the whole play. The Prince, wooing for Claudio, duly leads off with Hero; it may be Shakespeare's art which leaves it undisclosed whether she takes him for Claudio or not. Then, after the ladies-in-waiting, whose roles it will be respectively to damage and assist the marriage-making, we have another skirmish in the 'merry war' of Beatrice and Benedick. He exploits his incognito by delivering some home truths, to which she responds in kind when she sees through his disguise while pretending not to. Nevertheless they end by admitting that they 'must follow the leaders', as they do, not only in the dance but in the larger play when they too 'speak love'. The scene ends with Claudio having won his bride, but not before Don John with a lying tale has persuaded him he has lost her. This preliminary mistaking is speedily sorted out but it has its importance as a prefiguring of the graver deception later. What is now sketched out in little will presently be writ large. But, although Claudio is to be thus twice deceived, we are not meant to blame him as being unduly gullible any more than he should be called timid because he does not do his own wooing. If his mistake at the ball makes his later mistake in the church, as has been said, 'more credible', that is surely not because it illumines his character but because it exhibits his role in a pattern which the play will repeat. Claudio's plain statement at the end we should, I think, accept: 'Yet sinned I not / But in mistaking.' And, since his mistakes are not ones he is required or even permitted to learn from, the play hardly encourages us to regard it, along with one recent critic, as a 'controlled experiment' in which Shakespeare investigates the educative processes of love. Perhaps we could regard it as a 'controlled experiment' in fashioning out of a repetition of plot motifs a dramatic design to which the characters, even those who seem to transcend it, must ultimately submit.

There *are* comedies of Shakespeare which reveal a moral structure such as some earnest criticism demands. *The Merchant of Venice* shows the virtue of hazarding all one has; *The Two Gentlemen of Verona* teaches Proteus the importance of constancy. But because *Much Ado About Nothing* is not of this kind it does not mean that its design need lack significance. There are two characters at its centre who have never, I think, received the attention they deserve. One reason why Claudio woos by proxy is that that is what happened in the source story. But an inspired change on Shakespeare's part makes the wooer the Prince himself, the leader of the courteous society that the bride's father entertains. And it is no mere matter of convenience that makes the Prince also the deviser of the stratagem which leads Beatrice and Benedick to marry. The perpetrator of the contrary trick, which leads to Hero's rejection, was in Bandello a rival lover who wanted the bride for himself; but Shakespeare has replaced the jealous lover by the man who is jealous of love, who has only to hear of an intended marriage to seek for a plan to cross it. Don John has typically been regarded as merely a cardboard figure: Hazelton Spencer thought the 'inadequacy of the villain' the one serious flaw in the play; Quiller-Couch complained that the whole intrigue had only a 'feeble spring of motive'. On the contrary, if Don John is regarded not psychologically but emblematically, he is a sinister figure of some force. Of few words and tart looks, in this vivacious company he is the antisocial man. A bastard, significantly enough, he attempts to break the marriage his legitimate brother makes, and thus to frustrate the purposes not just of society but of life. To ask a further motive of Don John is like asking one of the wicked fairy who turns up at the christening with her curse. It will be his role like hers to be defeated in the end, as he has already, again significantly enough, been defeated at the beginning.

The intrigue which springs from the activities of these two brothers, the marriage-maker and the marriage-breaker, and ends in the triumph of the former expresses one of comedy's universal themes. *Much Ado About Nothing* celebrates courtship and marriage, and in them, one might add, those processes of nature which even human folly and stupidity have it in them to assist ('What your wisdoms could not discover these shallow fools have brought to light'). By the additions and adjustments he has made to the source story – in the characters of Beatrice and Benedick and Dogberry, in the roles of the good and bad brothers – Shakespeare has not only wrought from the story a formal dramatic design but has invested it with significance. The design, of course, and the significance are such as bring the story of the rejected bride firmly into the comic ethos; and this again is what some of the play's critics are unable to forgive. They complain of incompatibilities of tone or of what Sir Edmund Chambers called 'a clashing of dramatic planes'. Yet, whatever the neo-classic critics may have thought, we no longer find disharmony in the gravedigger scene in *Hamlet* or the porter in *Macbeth*, and conversely perhaps a comedy may be allowed its sombre moment. As soon as the play begins with the decorum of a war which is over and in which no one who matters has been killed, we know that all will end happily. Reassurance is given by the divertissements of the masked dance in which a pattern of amusing errors leads to a betrothal (contrast the storm on the way to Cyprus in *Othello*); and Dogberry and his fellows erect their conspicuous signpost at the very entrance to the church. The rejection scene, however, in all its outrage, is played for its full value, and it is perhaps important to note that the one person henceforth shielded from mirth and mockery is the bride herself. We cannot say the same of the young men, nor even of the old. The scene in which Don Pedro and Claudio boast that they have been near to having their 'two noses snapped off with two old men without teeth' may well be regarded as callous and has even been called 'painfully silly'; but it functions in the play's design by exhibiting the completeness of the reversal when the plans of the marriage-makers, the Prince and the bride's father, have collapsed and the civilized hospitalities of the opening are replaced by a society at strife. It is also in the service of the design that the jokes about the savage bull, premonitory in the opening, return with the wedding bells, though one may grant the bull roars somewhat stridently in the mutual taunts of the bridegrooms when they are jointly submitting to the yoke. But one of the happiest turns in the whole play comes in Benedick's penultimate speech, when the newly married man tells the princely marriage-maker to get a wife for himself.

There are critics who complain that the last two acts are too heavily weighted with the business of getting the bride to the altar for the second time. With the shallow fools to bring the truth to light, what need Hero to have died? I think it can only be that the story that came from Bandello offered Shakespeare not merely a canvas but the materials for a picture which he felt an urge to complete. The stratagem of the pretended death – yet another instance of a fabricated tale – is proposed by a holy friar (brought in from *Romeo and Juliet* for the purpose), who tells in some of the loveliest lines of the play how it will revive in Claudio's soul 'More moving, delicate, and full of life', the idea of her he loved. It is true that things do not happen quite so simply, and it may be a flaw that they do not: Claudio needs the revelation of the Watch, but once he has that he can say,

> Sweet Hero, now thy image doth appear
> In the rare semblance that I loved it first.

He has of course to do penance, and the scene at the tomb in which he does it makes a solemn moment on the stage, to which the approach of dawn gives an expanded context:

> The wolves have preyed, and look, the gentle day ...
> Dapples the drowsy east ...

The Friar's references to life through death have their echo in the dirge, as also in the words which ring out in Hero's single speech at her wedding: 'One Hero died defiled; but I do live.' In the necessary brevity of these episodes I see nothing perfunctory, only a masterly compression. Nor do I think Shakespeare saw any incompatibility in including within a light-hearted comedy of courtship and marriage the graver joy of life's universal cycle in which darkness is followed by dawn, winter by spring, and things dying with things new-born. Even in Shakespeare's early and middle comedies the heroine's return from supposed death (in *Much Ado* as in *The Comedy of Errors* and *All's Well that Ends*

Well) and the hero's repentance (in *Much Ado* as in *The Two Gentlemen of Verona*) are something more than a convenient theatrical denouement.

One thing that may strike us in *Much Ado* is that the wife of Leonato, who is given two entries but no part, has the remarkable name of Innogen. A decade later Shakespeare would write another play in which the rejected bride herself would be called (as the Folio has it) Imogen and the rejecting husband Posthumus Leonatus. One cannot doubt that a seed was already stirring which would presently blossom in *Cymbeline*. It is in plays like *Cymbeline* and *The Winter's Tale* which reach beyond the comic range that the restoration of the wife to her penitent husband receives fuller and more moving treatment. Before those Shakespeare wrote the tragedy of *Othello*. In *Much Ado About Nothing*, however, he was content to stay within the scope of a courtship comedy. The twofold love-plot in which the couples move through the play in contrary directions yet end alongside at the altar itself proclaims the overthrow of Don John before the messenger reports his capture; and with a word about punishments in store for him, to be devised appropriately by Benedick the married man, the *comedy* of the rejected bride concludes with a wedding dance.

6

AS YOU LIKE IT

A masterpiece is not to be explained, and to attempt to explain it is apt to seem ridiculous. I must say at once that I propose nothing so ambitious. I merely hope, by looking at one play, even in what must necessarily be a very fragmentary way and with my own imperfect sight, to illustrate something of what Shakespeare's method in comedy may be. And I have chosen *As You Like It* because it seems to me to exhibit, most clearly of all the comedies, Shakespeare's characteristic excellences in this kind. This is not to say that *As You Like It* is exactly a representative specimen. Indeed I am going to suggest that it is not. In this play, what I take to be Shakespeare's distinctive virtues as a writer of comedy have their fullest scope; but, in order that they may have it, certain of the usual ingredients of Shakespeare's comedy, or indeed of any comedy, have to be – not of course eliminated, but very much circumscribed. In *As You Like It*, I suggest, Shakespeare took his comedy in one direction nearly as far as it could go. And then, as occasionally happens in Shakespeare's career, when he has developed his art far in one direction, in the comedy which succeeds he seems to readjust his course.

If our chronology is right, after *As You Like It* comes, among the comedies, *Twelfth Night*. And while we may accept that *Twelfth Night* is, as Sir Edmund Chambers says, very much akin to *As You Like It* 'in style and temper', in some important respects it returns to the method and structure of the previous comedy of *Much Ado About Nothing*. Sandwiched between these two, *As You Like It* is conspicuously lacking in comedy's more robust and boisterous elements – the pomps of Dogberry and the romps of

Sir Toby. More significantly, it has nothing that corresponds to the splendid theatricalism of the church scene in *Much Ado*, nothing that answers to those crucial bits of trickery by which Benedick and Beatrice in turn are hoodwinked into love. Even if, as may be objected, they are not hoodwinked but merely tricked into removing their hoods, still those stratagems in Leonato's orchard are necessary if the happy ending proper to the comedy is to be brought about. These ambushes, if I may call them so – they are really inverted ambushes – are paralleled, or should one say parodied, in *Twelfth Night* in the scene where Malvolio is persuaded that he too is beloved. And this ambush too is necessary if, as the comedy demands, Malvolio is to have his sanity called in question and his authority undermined. The slandering of Hero in *Much Ado* also is to have its counterpart in *Twelfth Night*. For the slandering of Hero, with its culmination in the church scene, forces one pair of lovers violently apart while bringing another pair together. And in *Twelfth Night* the confusion of identities holds one pair of lovers – Orsino and Viola – temporarily apart, yet forces another pair – Olivia and Sebastian – with some violence together. A satisfactory outcome in *Much Ado* and *Twelfth Night* depends on such embroilments; and the same is even more true in an earlier comedy like *A Midsummer Night's Dream*. In *As You Like It* I can hardly say that such embroilments do not occur, but they are not structural to anything like the same degree. Without the heroine's masculine disguise Phebe would not have married Silvius any more than in *Twelfth Night* Olivia would have married Sebastian; but the confusions of identity in *As You Like It* have no influence whatever upon the ultimate destiny of Rosalind and Orlando, or of the kingdom of Duke Senior, or of the estate of Sir Rowland de Boys. Yet these are the destinies with which the action of the play is concerned. It is in the defectiveness of its action that *As You Like It* differs from the rest of the major comedies – in its dearth not only of big theatrical scenes but of events linked together by the logical intricacies of cause and effect. Of comedy, as of tragedy, action is the first essential; but *As You Like It* suggests that action is not, if I may adapt a phrase of Marston's, 'the life of these things'. It may be merely the foundation on which they are built. And *As You Like It* further shows that on a very flimsy foundation, if only you are skilful enough, a very elaborate structure may be poised. But the method has its dangers, and, though Shakespeare's skill conceals these dangers from us, *Twelfth Night*, as I said, returns to a more orthodox scheme.

The story which provides the action for *As You Like It* belongs to the world of fairy-tale or folklore. This is a world which supplied the plots of a number of Shakespeare's plays, including the greatest, notably *King Lear*. And fairy-tales have many advantages for the dramatist, among which is their total disregard of practical probabilities. In fairy-tales, for example, evil is always absolute, clearly recognized and finally overthrown; all of which may have something to do with the Aristotelian theory that, while history records what has happened, poetry shows what should happen. Relaxing the more prosaic demands of verisimilitude, the fairy-tale invites the imagination. It can certainly provide a convenient road into the Forest of Arden. And this is not less true for Shakespeare because the road had already been built for him by Lodge.

A man has died and left three sons. Three is the inevitable number, and, though Shakespeare, like Lodge, forgets to do much with the middle one, he is not therefore unimportant. The eldest brother is wicked, the youngest virtuous – and does fabulous feats of strength, notably destroying a giant in the shape of Charles the wrestler, who has torn other hopeful youths to pieces. Orlando therefore wins the princess, herself the victim of a wicked uncle, who has usurped her father's throne. This is the *story* of *As You Like It*. And Shakespeare, making the journey of the imagination far more quickly than Lodge, gets most of it over in the first act. That is what is remarkable. By the time we reach the second act Rosalind has already come safe to the Forest of Arden, by the aid of her man's disguise. From this disguise, as everybody knows, springs the principal comic situation of the play. But such is the inconsequential nature of the action that this comic situation develops only when the practical need for the disguise is past. The course of true love has not run smooth.

But most of its obstacles have really disappeared before the main
comedy begins. It only remains for the wicked to be converted, as
they duly are at the end, all in comedy's good but arbitrary time,
when the wicked eldest brother makes a suitable husband for the
second princess. Or a most *un*suitable husband, as all the critics
have complained. But this, I think, is to misunderstand. Instead
of lamenting that Celia should be thrown away on Oliver, he
having been much too wicked to deserve her, we should rather
see that Oliver's getting this reward is a seal set on his conversion,
and a sign of how good he has now become.

The first act of *As You Like It* has to supply the necessary
minimum of event. But, Quiller-Couch notwithstanding, this
first act is something more than mechanical.[1] It is for one thing a
feat of compression, rapid, lucid and, incidentally, theatrical. In
fifty lines we know all about the three brothers and the youngest
is at the eldest's throat. In three hundred more we know all about
the banished Duke and where and how he lives, and the giant has
been destroyed before our eyes. But there is more to the first act
than this. Before we enter Arden, to 'fleet the time carelessly, as
they did in the golden world', we must be able to contrast its
simple life with the brittle refinement of the court. This surely
is the point of some of what 'Q' called the 'rather pointless chop-
logic'; and also of the courtier figure of Le Beau, a little sketch for
Osric, with his foppery of diction and his expert knowledge of
sport. Le Beau's notion of sport provokes Touchstone's pointed
comment on the courtier's values: 'Thus men may grow wiser
every day: it is the first time that ever I heard breaking of ribs was
sport for ladies.' This *is* the callousness one learns at a court ruled
by a tyrannous Duke, whose malevolent rage against Rosalind
and Orlando not only drives them both to Arden but completes
the picture of the world they leave behind.

This first act, then, shows some instinct for dramatic
preparation, though we may grant that Shakespeare's haste to
get ahead makes him curiously perfunctory. He is in two minds
about when Duke Senior was banished; and about which Duke is
to be called Frederick; and whether Rosalind or Celia is the taller.
He has not quite decided about the character of Touchstone. I do

not think these are signs of revision. They simply show Shakespeare plunging into his play with some of its details still but half shaped in his mind. The strangest of these details is the mysterious middle brother, called Fernandyne by Lodge but merely 'Second Brother' in *As You Like It*, when at length he makes his appearance at the end. Yet in the fifth line of the play he was already christened Jaques; and Shakespeare of course afterwards gave this name to someone else. It seems clear enough that these two men with the same name were originally meant to be one. As things turned out, Jaques could claim to have acquired his famous melancholy from travel and experience; but I suspect that it really began in the schoolbooks which were studied with such profit by Jaques de Boys. Though he grew into something very different, Jaques surely had his beginnings in the family of De Boys and in such an academy as that in Navarre where four young men turned their backs on love and life in the belief that they could supply the want of experience by study and contemplation.

Interesting as it might be to develop this idea, the important point of comparison between *As You Like It* and *Love's Labour's Lost* is of another kind. And to this I should like briefly to refer before I come to discuss the main part of *As You Like It*. *Love's Labour's Lost* is the one play before *As You Like It* in which Shakespeare sought to write a comedy with the minimum of action. Four young men make a vow to have nothing to do with a woman; each breaks his oath and ends vowing to serve a woman. That is the story; far slighter than in *As You Like It*. Yet, in contrast with *As You Like It*, the careful and conspicuous organization of *Love's Labour's Lost* distributes its thin action evenly through the play. And the characters always act in concert. In the first act the men, all together, make their vow; in the second the ladies, all together, arrive and the temptation begins. The climax duly comes, where you would expect it, in a big scene in Act 4, when each in turn breaks his vow and all together are found out. *Love's Labour's Lost* is the most formally constructed of all the comedies. When the ladies and gentlemen temporarily exchange partners, this is done symmetrically and to order.

Indeed the movement of the whole play is like a well-ordered dance in which each of the participants repeats the steps of the others. But this is exactly what does *not* happen in *As You Like It*, where the characters do *not* keep in step. When they *seem* to be doing the same thing they are really doing something different, and if they ever echo one another they mean quite different things by what they say – as could easily be illustrated from the little quartet of lovers in the fifth act ('And so am I for Phebe. – And I for Ganymede. – And I for Rosalind. – And I for no woman'), where the similarity of the tune they sing conceals their different situations. The pattern of *As You Like It* comes not from a mere repetition of steps, but from constant little shifts and changes. The formal parallelisms of *Love's Labour's Lost* are replaced by a more complex design, one loose enough to hold all sorts of asymmetries within it.

But of course the effect of variations upon a theme instead of simple repetitions is not new in *As You Like It*. It is the tendency of Shakespeare's comedy from the start. In *Love's Labour's Lost* itself the courtly gestures of the four young men are burlesqued by those of a fantastic knight, and while the four young men are vowing not to see a woman, Costard the clown is 'taken with a wench'. Moreover, one of the four, though he goes through the movements with the others, has some trouble to keep in step, and is always threatening to break out of the ring. Even when he makes his vow with the others, he knows that necessity will make him break it. As he joins in their purposes he knows them to be foolish and he mocks at ideals which he at the same time pursues. Human activity offers itself to the dramatist in a large variety of forms, and the same individual can play contradictory parts. The drunken tinker in *The Taming of the Shrew* does not know whether he may not really be a noble lord. Although Shakespeare did not invent this situation, it was just the thing to appeal to him. For he knew that a man is very easily 'translated'. In the middle of his fairy play he put a man with an ass's head. In perhaps the most remarkable encounter in Shakespeare the daintiest fairy queen caresses a man turned brute, who, with a fairy kingdom around him, can think only of scratching his itch. When the animal appears in a man it may terrify his fellows; it may also attract to it his finest dreams and fancies, corrupting them, or be uplifted by them to a vision of new wonder. Shakespeare of course does nothing as crude as *say* this. He knows as well as the Duke in Arden that sermons may be found in stones, but much better than the Duke that it is tedious to preach them, a thing, incidentally, he does not permit the Duke to do. What Shakespeare characteristically does in his comedy is to set together the contrasting elements in human nature and leave them by their juxtaposition or interaction to comment on one another.

In *As You Like It* the art of comic juxtaposition is at its subtlest. It is to give it fullest scope that the action can be pushed up into a corner, and the usual entanglements of plotting, though not dispensed with altogether, can be loosened. Freedom, of course, is in the hospitable air of Arden, where convenient caves stand ready to receive outlaws, alfresco meals are abundantly provided, with a concert of birds and running brooks, and there is no worse hardship than a salubrious winter wind. This is 'the golden world' to which, with the beginning of his second act, Shakespeare at once transports us, such a world as has been the dream of poets since at least the time of Virgil when, wearied with the toilings and wranglings of society, they yearn for the simplicity and innocence of what they choose to think man's natural state.[2] It is of course a very literary tradition that Shakespeare is here using, but the long vogue of the pastoral suggests that it is connected with a universal impulse of the human mind, to which Shakespeare in *As You Like It* gives permanent expression. But this aspect of the play is merely the one that confronts us most conspicuously. There are many others. *As You Like It* has been too often praised for its idyllic quality alone, as though it were some mere May-morning frolic prolonged into a lotus-eating afternoon. A contrast with the ideal state was necessitated by the literary tradition itself, since the poet seeking an escape into the simple life was expected to hint at the ills of the society he was escaping from. That meant especially the courts of princes, where life – it was axiomatic –

was at its most artificial. And the vivid sketching in of the courtly half of the antithesis is, as I have shown, an important function of *As You Like It*'s maligned first act. With the first speech of the banished Duke at the opening of the second act, the complete contrast is before us; for, while introducing us to Arden, this speech brings into sharp focus that first act which has just culminated in the usurper's murderous malice. 'Are not these woods / More free from peril than the envious court?' Though the contrast is traditional, it comes upon us here, like so many things in Shakespeare, with the vitality of fresh experience. The Forest of Arden comes to life in numerous little touches of the countryside, and the heartless self-seeking of the outer world is concentrated into phrases which have the force of permanent truth. The line that 'Q' admired – 'And unregarded age in corners thrown' – might have come from one of the sonnets, and when Orlando observes how 'none will sweat but for promotion' we recognize the fashion of our times as well as his. As the play proceeds, it is easy enough for Shakespeare to keep us ever aware of the forest, what with Amiens to sing for us, the procession home after the killing of the deer, an empty cottage standing ready for Rosalind and Celia, surrounded by olive-trees beyond a willow stream, and a good supply of oaks for Orlando or Oliver to lie under. It cannot have been quite so easy to keep us in touch with the court life we have now abandoned; but nothing is neater in the construction of the play than those well-placed little scenes which, by dispatching first Orlando and then Oliver to the forest, do what is still required by the story and give the illusion that an action is still going briskly forward, while at the same time they renew our acquaintance with the wicked world. After the first scene in the ideal world of Arden and a sentimental discourse on the deer, there is Frederick again in one of his rages, sending for Oliver, who, an act later, when we are well acclimatized to the forest, duly turns up at court. Then occurs a scene of eighteen lines, in which Shakespeare gives as vivid a sketch of the unjust tyrant as one could hope to find. The tyrant prides himself upon his mercy, punishes one man for his brother's sins, and finds in his victim's excuses further cause of offence. Oliver's plaint that he had never loved his brother brings the instant retort, 'More villain thou. Well, push him out of doors.' As this eruption dies down, there appears in the Forest of Arden the cause of all the trouble quietly hanging his verses on a tree.

The contrast between court and country is thus presented and our preference is very plain. Yet as a counterpoise to all this, there is one man in the countryside who actually prefers the court. Finding himself in Arden, Touchstone decides: 'When I was at home, I was in a better place.' It is no doubt important that he is a fool, whose values may well be topsy-turvy. But in one word he reminds us that there are such things as domestic comforts. And presently we find that the old man whom society throws into the corner is likely in the 'uncouth forest' to die of hunger and exposure to the 'bleak air'. There is clearly something to be said on the other side; the fool may anatomize the wise man's folly. And there is also Jaques to point out that the natural life in Arden, where men usurp the forest from the deer and kill them in their 'native dwelling-place', while deer, like men, are in distress abandoned by their friends, is as cruel and unnatural as the other. When Amiens sings under the greenwood tree and turns 'his merry note unto the sweet bird's throat', inviting us to shun ambition and be pleased with what we get, Jaques adds a further stanza to the song which suggests that to leave your 'wealth and ease' is the act of an ass or a fool. Most of us, I suppose, have moods in which we would certainly agree with him, and it is a mark of Shakespeare's mature comedy that he permits this criticism of his ideal world in the very centre of it. The triumphal procession after the killing of the deer, a symbolic ritual of the forester's prowess, is accompanied by a mocking song, while the slayer of the deer is given its horns to wear as a somewhat ambiguous trophy.

It is Jaques, mostly, with the touch of the medieval buffoon in him, who contributes this grotesque element to the songs and rituals of Arden. Like Touchstone he is not impressed by Arden, but unlike Touchstone he does not prefer the court. Indeed, as we have seen, he is able to show that they are very much alike, infected by the same diseases. No doubt his is a jaundiced view of life, and it is strange that some earlier critics should have thought it might be Shakespeare's. Shakespeare's contemporaries would hardly have had difficulty in recognizing in Jaques a variant of the Elizabethan melancholy man – the epithet is applied to him often enough – though I remain a little sceptical when I am told by O.J. Campbell that, from the first moment they heard Jaques described, the Elizabethans would have perceived 'the unnatural melancholy produced by the adustion of phlegm'.[3] Whatever its physiological kind, the important thing about his melancholy is that it is not the fatigue of spirits of the man who has found the world too much for him, but an active principle manifesting itself in tireless and exuberant antics. Far from being a morose man, whether he is weeping with the stag or jeering at the huntsman, he throws himself into these things with something akin to passion. His misanthropy is a form of self-indulgence, as is plain enough in his very first words:

JAQUES
More, more, I prithee, more.
AMIENS
It will make you melancholy, Monsieur Jaques.
JAQUES
I thank it. More, I prithee, more. I can suck melancholy out of a song.

His own comparison with a weasel sucking eggs suggests what a ferocious and life-destroying thing this passion is. Shakespeare's final dismissal of Jaques is profound. Far from making Celia a better husband than Oliver, as George Sand apparently thought, he is the one person in the play who could not be allowed to marry anyone, since he can have nothing to do with either love or generation. His attempt to forward the nuptials of Touchstone and Audrey serves only to postpone them. He is of course the one consistent character in the play in that he declines to go back with the others to the court that they have scorned. Yet how *can* he go back when the court has been converted? Jaques's occupation's gone. And he will not easily thrive away from the social life on which he feeds. It is notable that the place he really covets, or affects to, is that of the motley fool, licensed to mock at society, indulged by society but not of it. Yet, seeking for a fool, he has only to look in the brook to find one; and it is the romantic hero who will tell him so.

Shakespeare, then, builds up his ideal world and lets his idealists scorn the real one. But into their midst he introduces people who mock their ideals and others who mock *them*. One must not say that Shakespeare never judges, but one judgement is always being modified by another. Opposite views may contradict one another, but of course they do not cancel out. Instead they add up to an all-embracing view far larger and more satisfying than any one of them in itself.

Now when Orlando tells Jaques that he may see a fool by looking in the brook, this is not the first time that Jaques and Orlando meet; and the relations between the two of them are worth a moment's glance. Their first encounter occurs in public when the Duke and his retinue are met for one of their forest repasts. Jaques has just been eloquent about the vices of mankind and is justifying the satirist who scourges them, when he is confronted with the romantic hero in his most heroic attitude, rushing into the middle of the scene with drawn sword,[4] crying, 'Forbear, and eat no more.' But Jaques is not the man to be discomposed, even when a sudden interruption throws him off his hobby-horse. When he has inquired, 'Of what kind should this cock come of?', the heroic attitude begins to look extravagant. The hero stands his ground: 'Forbear, I say: / He dies that touches any of this fruit'; at which Jaques nonchalantly helps himself to a grape, saying, 'An you will not be answered with reason (raisin), I must die.' Heroism now appears thoroughly deflated, or would do if Jaques were attended to by the company at large. The hero is in fact saved by the Duke's 'civility'; and their talk of 'gentleness' and 'nurture' even throws back into perspective Jaques's recent attack upon society. The situation as a whole retains its equilibrium. And yet as a result of this little incident we are bound to feel that the romantic hero is very vulnerable to the ridicule of the satirist, until their duel of wit in the following act readjusts our view by allowing Orlando his retort.

There is a formal point to notice here, easy to miss but full of meaning. The wit combat between Jaques and the hero is matched an act or so later – there is no strict regularity about these things – by a similar wit combat between Jaques and the heroine. On each occasion Jaques is worsted and departs, leaving Rosalind and Orlando to come together. In fact the discomfiture of Monsieur Melancholy by one or other of the lovers is the prelude to each of the two big love scenes of the play. And this arrangement makes a point more prettily than any action-plot involving Jaques could do. The mocking words of Jaques's farewell are in each case illuminating: 'Farewell, good Signior Love'; and 'Nay, then, God be wi' you, an you talk in blank verse.' The gibe at blank verse is not an incidental or decorative jest. It makes it clear that, however we judge of them, the melancholy spirit of Jaques and the romantic emotion of Rosalind and Orlando cannot mingle. Shakespeare dismisses the melancholy man before he gives the lovers their scope. And in this I follow his example.

So far I have dealt only with the immigrants to Arden. There is of course a native population. The natural world of the poet's dreams has always been inhabited by shepherds, who from the time of Theocritus have piped their songs of love. And Rosalind and Celia have been in the forest for only twenty lines when two shepherds appear pat before them. In an earlier comedy perhaps these might have been a similar pair singing comparable love-ditties. But in *As You Like It* – Shakespeare making the most of what is offered him by Lodge – they are a contrasting pair. One is young and one is old, one is in love and one is not. The lover is the standard type. But the notion of love has undergone a change since classical times and the shepherds of Renaissance pastorals have all been bred in the schools of courtly love. So young Silvius is the faithful abject lover who finds disdain in his fair shepherdess's eye and sighs 'upon a midnight pillow' – Shakespeare always fixes on a detail in which a whole situation is epitomized. There are of course many other lovers in the play, but the story of Silvius and Phebe is of the pure pastoral world, the familiar literary norm against which all the others may be measured. First against Silvius and Phebe are set Rosalind and Orlando, and the immediate result of this is that Rosalind and Orlando, though they clearly belong to the pastoral world, seem much closer to the ordinary one. Indeed, since Silvius and Phebe relieve them of the necessity of displaying the lovers' more extravagant postures, Rosalind and Orlando are freer to act like human beings. Rosalind need only play at taunting her adorer while allowing her real woman's heart to be in love with him in earnest. In an earlier comedy like *The Two Gentlemen of Verona* the heroes themselves had to undergo those 'bitter fasts, with penitential groans, / With nightly tears and daily heart-sore sighs', and these are what, as H.B. Charlton says, may make Valentine look a fool. But, with Silvius to take this burden from him, Orlando can really be a hero, performing the traditional hero's fabulous feats, and upon occasion may even be a common man like ourselves. He has, for example, the very human trait of unpunctuality: he is twice late for an appointment. And, although on one occasion he has the perfect excuse of a bloody accident, on the other he has nothing to say, beyond 'My fair Rosalind, I come within an hour of my promise.' Such engaging casualness is of course outside Silvius's range. Although Orlando has his due share of lovers' sighs and is indeed the 'unfortunate he' who hangs the verses on the trees, in so human a creature these love gestures appear not as his *raison d'être* but as an aberration. A delightful aberration, no doubt – 'I would not be cured, youth,' he says – but still an aberration that can be the legitimate subject of our mockery. Lying contemplating his love under an oak, he seems to Celia 'like a dropped acorn', and both the ladies smile at his youthful lack of beard. But Orlando is robust enough to stand their mockery and ours, and Shakespeare's superb dramatic tact arranges that Orlando shall draw our laughter towards him so that he may protect the fragile Silvius from the ridicule that would destroy *him*. Rosalind alone is privileged to make fun of Silvius; and that because, searching his wounds, she finds her own. The encounters which do not occur have their significance as well as those which do: Touchstone is only once, and Jaques never, allowed a sight of Silvius before the final scene of the play.

Silvius has not to be destroyed or the play will lack something near its centre.

If in a pastoral play the ideal shepherd is satirized it must be indirectly. But that he is, through his complete unreality, a likely target for satire has been commonly recognized by the poets, who have therefore had a habit of providing him with a burlesque counterpart to redress the balance and show that they did know what rustics were like in real life. As Gay was to put it in his proem to *The Shepherd's Week*, the shepherd 'sleepeth not under myrtle shades, but under a hedge'; and so when Gay's shepherd makes love it is in a sly kiss behind a haycock to the accompaniment of the lady's yells of laughter. This may have been the method of Shakespeare's William, for, far from inditing verses to his mistress, William is singularly tongue-tied; though he is 'five and twenty' and thinks he has 'a pretty wit', the biggest of his eleven speeches is only seven words long. And his partner is just as much a contrast to the shepherdess of pastoral legend. She thanks the gods she is not beautiful, does not even know the meaning of 'poetical', and her sheep, alas, are goats.

Shakespeare, then, presents the conventional pastoral, and duly burlesques it. But, with a surer knowledge of life than many poets have had, he seems to suspect that the burlesque as well as the convention may also miss the truth. Do shepherds really sleep under hedges? In order to be unsophisticated, must they be stupid too? So among his varied array of shepherds, Silvius and Ganymede and William, Shakespeare introduces yet another shepherd, the only one who knows anything of sheep, whose hands even get greasy with handling them. It does not matter that Shakespeare got the hint for Corin from Corydon in Lodge. For Lodge found Corydon in literature, and for Corin Shakespeare went to life. Lodge's Corydon, though he may make the king smile with his clownish salutation, has evidently been bred at court himself. Would he ever else accost a lady in distress in strains like these:

> If I should not, fair damosel, occasion offence, or renew your griefs by rubbing the scar, I would fain crave so much favour as to know the cause of your misfortunes.

Shakespeare's Corin speaks at once of grazing and shearing and an unkind master; and when he talks about the shepherd's life he shows that he knows the value of money and that fat sheep need good pasture. His greatest pride is to see his ewes graze and his lambs suck. This is the note of his philosophy, and, if it has its limitations, it is far from despicable and is splendidly anchored to fact. His attitude to love is that of the fully sane man undisturbed by illusions. Being a man, he has been in love and can still guess what it is like; but it is so long ago he has forgotten all the details. How little he belongs to Arcadia may be discovered from Sidney, whose shepherd-boy went on piping 'as though he should never be old'. In *As You Like It* perpetual youth is the happiness of Silvius, and his fate. *That* much of the difference between Silvius and Corin is apparent from the short dialogue of twenty lines which first introduces them together to us.

In Corin, Shakespeare provides us with a touchstone with which to test the pastoral. Corin's dialogue with the Touchstone of the court, dropped into the middle of the play, adds to the conventional antithesis between courtier and countryman a glimpse of the real thing. Our picture of the court as a place of tyranny, ambition and corruption is no doubt true enough. But its colours are modified somewhat when Touchstone gives us the court's plain routine. For him, as he lets us know on another occasion, the court is the place where he has trod a measure, flattered a lady, been smooth with his enemy and undone three tailors. Though Touchstone seeks to entangle Corin in the fantastications of his wit, his arguments to show that the court is better than the sheep farm have a way of recoiling on himself. What emerges from the encounter of these two realists is that ewe and ram, like man and woman, are put together and that though the courtier perfumes his body it sweats like any other creature's. In city or country, *all* ways of life are at bottom the same, and we recognize a conclusion that Jaques, by a different route, has helped us to reach before.

The melancholy moralizings of Jaques and the Robin Hood raptures of the Duke, though in contrast, are equally the product of man's spirit. There has to be someone in Arden to remind us of the indispensable flesh. It was a shrewd irony of Shakespeare's to give this office to the jester. Whether he is wiser or more foolish than other men it is never possible to decide, but Touchstone is, as well as the most artificial wit, the most natural man of them all; and the most conscious of his corporal needs. After the journey to the forest Rosalind complains of a weariness of spirits, to which Touchstone retorts, 'I care not for my spirits, if my legs were not weary.' And when he displays his wit at the expense of Orlando's bad verses, saying, 'I'll rhyme you so eight years together', he remembers to add 'dinners and suppers and sleeping-hours excepted'. A 'material fool', as Jaques notes. This preoccupation with the physical makes Touchstone the obvious choice for the sensual lover who will burlesque the romantic dream. So Touchstone not only deprives the yokel William of his mistress, but steals his part in the play, making it in the process of infinitely greater significance. However, Shakespeare from the beginning cast Touchstone for this burlesque role, though he may not have seen at first what form the burlesque would take. When Silvius first exhibits his love to us, and reminds Rosalind of hers, Touchstone completes the trio on his discordant note:

> I remember, when I was in love I broke my sword upon a stone and bid him take that for coming a-night to Jane Smile; and I remember the kissing of ... the cow's dugs that her pretty chopt hands had milked.

This sort of extravagance – in the burlesque-chivalrous vein – is not, I think, developed; but an indecent jest about a peascod does point forward to the animal lust which propels him towards Audrey, and his amour with her forms the perfect contrast to the three idealized courtships of the play. If we need a formal juxtaposition of the two kinds of love to point the matter further, I note that it is just when Rosalind has met Orlando in the forest and Orlando has promised to woo her 'by the faith of [his] love' and 'with all [his] heart' that we see Touchstone courting the goat-girl, regretting that fair women should be honest and talking of sexual desire.

The fool is not only a material touchstone; he is also the timekeeper of the play. At least, in the forest, where 'there's no clock', he carries a timepiece with him; and it provokes the reflection: 'It is ten o'clock ... 'Tis but an hour ago since it was nine, / And after one hour more 'twill be eleven.' The people of Arcadia will do well to take note of this, but, if all you can do with your hours is to count them, this undeniable truth may seem a trifle futile. Touchstone, to do him justice, goes on: 'And so, from hour to hour, we ripe and ripe, / And then, from hour to hour, we rot and rot.' He dares to speak in Arcadia, where one can never grow old, of Time's inevitable processes of maturity and decay. By this the ideal life of the banished Duke is mocked, and, since Touchstone's words are repeated by Jaques with delighted and uproarious laughter, the mockery is double. Yet, in accordance with the play's principle of countering one view with another, there are two things that may be noted: first, that in a later scene Touchstone, who sums up life as riping and rotting, is compared by Rosalind to a medlar, which is rotten before it is ripe; and second, that it is at this very point, when the ideal life is doubly mocked, that the Duke administers to the mocker Jaques a direct and fierce rebuke, charging the mocker of the world's vices with having lived a vicious life himself.

The satirist, of course, is far from silenced; it is now that he ridicules the romantic hero, and presently he delivers his famous speech on the seven ages of man, brilliantly summing up the course of human life, but omitting to notice anything in it that is noble or even pleasant. However, as has often been observed, though the seven ages speech ends with a description of man's final decrepitude – 'sans teeth, sans eyes, sans taste, sans everything' – it has not yet left the speaker's tongue when an aged man appears who is at once addressed as 'venerable'. There is always this readjustment of the point of view. Senility and venerableness – are they different things or different ways of looking at the same? Certainly the entry of the venerable Adam does not disprove what Jaques says; Shakespeare seeks no cheap antithesis. 'Sans teeth' – Adam himself has admitted to being toothless, Orlando has called him 'a rotten tree', and his helplessness is only too visible when he is *carried* on to the stage. Yet he *is* carried, tenderly, by the master whom he has followed 'to the last gasp, with truth and loyalty'. Here is the glimpse of human virtue that the seven ages speech omitted. And then it is upon this moving spectacle of mutual affection and devotion that Amiens sings his song, 'Blow, blow, thou winter wind, / Thou art not so unkind / As man's ingratitude.' Placed here, this lovely lyric, blend of joy and pathos, has a special poignancy.

The arrangement of the play depends upon many such piquant but seemingly casual juxtapositions. *As You Like It* contemplates life within and without Arden, with numerous shifts of angle, alternating valuations and variations of mood. As for action or incident – life in the Forest of Arden does not easily lend itself to those. I have suggested that Shakespeare does something to supply this want by a glance or two back at what is happening at court. And departures from the court are matched by arrivals in the forest. For events, of course, even in Arden do sometimes occur. Orlando arrives dramatically, even melodramatically. Presently Rosalind learns that he is about. A little later on they meet. Later still Oliver arrives and is rescued from a lioness. Shakespeare still keeps up a sense of things going on. But the manner of the play, when once it settles down in the forest, is to let two people drift together, talk a little, and part, to be followed by two more. Sometimes a pair will be watched by others, who will sometimes comment on what they see. Sometimes of course there is a larger group, once or twice even a crowded stage; but most often two at a time. When they part, they may arrange to meet again, or they may not. Through the three middle acts of the play, though there are two instances of love at first sight (one of them only reported), it is rare that anything happens in any particular encounter between these people of the sort that changes the course of their lives, anything, that is to say, that goes to make what is usually called a plot. Yet the meetings may properly be called 'encounters', because of the impact the contrasting characters make on one another and the sparkle of wit they kindle in one another. What is important in each meeting is our impression of those who meet and of their different attitudes to one another or to one another's views of life, an impression which is deepened or modified each time they reappear with the same or different partners. As I describe it, this may all sound rather static, but such is the ease and rapidity with which pairs and groups break up, re-form, and succeed one another on the stage that there is a sense of fluid movement. All is done with the utmost lightness and gaiety, but, as the lovers move through the forest, part and meet again, or mingle with the other characters in their constantly changing pairs and groups, every view of life that is presented seems, sooner or later, to find its opposite. Life is 'but a flower in spring time, the only pretty ring time', but for the unromantic Touchstone there is 'no great matter in the ditty' and he counts it but time lost – his eye no doubt still on his timepiece – 'to hear such a foolish song'. A quartet of lovers avowing their love is broken up when one of them says: 'Pray you, no more of this; 'tis like the howling of Irish wolves against the moon.' And the one who says this is she who cannot tell 'how many fathom deep' she is in love. Dominating the centre of the play, playing both the man's and woman's parts, counsellor in love and yet its victim, Rosalind gathers up into herself many of its roles and many of its meanings. Around her in the forest, where the banished Duke presides, is the perfect happiness of the simple life, an illusion, much mocked at, but still cherished. She herself, beloved of the hero, has all the sanity to recognize that 'love is merely a madness' and that lovers should be whipped as madmen are, but admits that 'the whippers are in love too'. Heroine of numerous masquerades, she is none the less always constant and never more true than when insisting that she is counterfeiting. For she is an expert in those dark riddles which mean exactly what they say. Though things are rarely what they seem, they may sometimes be so in a deeper sense. What is wisdom and what is folly is of course never decided – you may have it 'as you like it'. Or, as Touchstone rejoined to Rosalind, after her gibe about the medlar, 'You have said; but whether wisely or no, let the forest judge.'

It may be possible to suggest that the forest gives its verdict. For if *As You Like It* proclaims no final truth its ultimate effect is not negative. Longing to escape to our enchanted world, we are constantly brought up against reality; sanity, practical wisdom sees through our illusions. Yet in *As You Like It* ideals, though always on the point of dissolving, are forever re-creating themselves. They do not delude the eye of reason, yet faith in them is not extinguished in spite of all that reason can do. 'I would not be cured, youth.'

7

TWELFTH NIGHT

What I shall try to do in this lecture is to examine some features of Shakespeare's comic art in one particular example. It may seem temerity enough to have chosen *Twelfth Night*; but, since after all a dramatist, even Shakespeare, is made as well as born, and it is interesting to see, if indeed one ever can, how his art perfects itself, I shall also venture from time to time some comparison between *Twelfth Night* and one of the earlier comedies of Shakespeare which led up to it.

In a book on *Twelfth Night* published four years ago Dr Leslie Hotson suggested that the play was written to compliment an Italian nobleman, Virginio Orsino, Duke of Bracciano, in a court entertainment given for him on Twelfth Night 1601, and that it was after this Orsino that one of the principal characters was named. I am not sure that the Italian Orsino would have felt complimented by seeing himself portrayed as a handsome and poetical but ineffective lover, and I do not think that Queen Elizabeth would have witnessed the play with delight if she had agreed with Dr Hotson that the Lady Olivia in the play was intended to represent her. But, even if *Twelfth Night* were the play with which the Queen entertained the Italian Duke, it would not be necessary to suppose with Dr Hotson that Shakespeare wrote it in ten or eleven days.[1] It is true that the Lord Chamberlain made a memorandum to arrange with the players 'to make choice of' a play that would be 'most pleasing to her Majesty' on this occasion,[2] but 'to make choice of a play' is not quite the same thing as instructing the players to get up a new one.

The most interesting thing of course is that, in however short a time Shakespeare ultimately wrote this play, he had in a sense been composing it during most of the previous decade. It was several years before the Twelfth Night entertainment of 1601 – certainly not later than 1594 – that Shakespeare first wrote a play about identical twins who were separated from one another in a shipwreck and afterwards mistaken for one another even by the wife of one of them; and it was at a similarly early stage in his career that Shakespeare wrote another play about a woman who served her lover as a page, and who in her page's disguise carried messages of love from her lover to another woman. When Shakespeare makes these things happen in *Twelfth Night* he is, in fact, combining the plots of *The Comedy of Errors* and *The Two Gentlemen of Verona*. He does not, however, combine them in equal degree. The heartsick heroine who in page's disguise takes messages of love to another woman provided little more than an episode in the complicated relations of the two gentlemen of Verona; but in *Twelfth Night* this episode has grown into the central situation from which the play draws its life. On the other hand, the confusion of twins which entertained us for five acts of *The Comedy of Errors* appears now as little more than an adroit device to bring about a happy ending. These shifts of emphasis show clearly enough the direction that Shakespeare's art of comedy has taken. When Sebastian appears in *Twelfth Night* we see that Shakespeare can still delight in the jolly mix-up of mistaken identities, not to mention their consequence of broken pates, but his plot now gives chief attention to the delineation of romantic love. This is more than just a preference for one situation rather than another: it means that a plot which turns on external appearances – a resemblance between men's faces – gives way to an action which involves their feelings. In *The Comedy of Errors*, though the physical resemblance between twins is no doubt a fact of nature, the confusion is really the result of accidental circumstances and is as accidentally cleared up. But in *Twelfth Night* the confusion is in the emotions and no denouement is possible until the characters have grown in insight to the point where they can acknowledge the feelings that nature has planted in them. Thus *Twelfth Night* exhibits in its action one of the fundamental motifs of comedy: the education of a man or woman. For a comedy, as everyone knows, is a play in which the situation holds some threat of disaster but issues in the achievement of happiness; and those comedies may satisfy us most deeply in which danger is averted and happiness achieved through something that takes place within the characters. Orsino and Olivia come to their happy ending when they have learnt a new attitude to others and to themselves.

This, I take it, is what is also meant to happen in *The Two Gentlemen of Verona* in the much misunderstood conclusion of that play. Proteus, significantly named for his fickle nature, has vexed the critics by coming into a happiness he seems to have done nothing to deserve. But the point is that, when his best friend has denounced him as a 'treacherous man' and his mistress has rebuked him for his changeableness, he can penitently say, 'O heaven, were man but constant he were perfect.' This has struck some as complacent; but it is not to be taken lightly. For it means that Proteus has now learned the value of constancy, the very virtue he conspicuously lacked. This is what the play set out to teach him and it is only when he has learned it that he can say, 'Bear witness, Heaven, I have my wish for ever', expressing simultaneously a sense of the happiness he is granted and a vow of constancy in future. It is true that in *The Two Gentlemen of Verona* Shakespeare did not allow himself scope to develop all the implications of Proteus's fickleness and reform; but such a story of treachery, if fully explored, might strike too deep for comedy. *Twelfth Night* has no unfaithful lover. But it cannot escape notice that Orsino's love is repeatedly compared to the sea – vast, hungry, but unstable, while his mind appears to Feste like an opal, a jewel of magical but ever-changing colours. The changeable man is there, but he has undergone a subtle transformation, and to notice this is, I think, of far more importance than to object, as Charlotte Lennox did in the eighteenth century, that Shakespeare in *Twelfth Night* has ruined the story of Bandello which she regarded as 'undoubtedly' Shakespeare's source.[3] Shakespeare, she objects, deprives the story of probability because he neglects to provide his characters with acceptable motives. Viola, she says, 'all of a sudden takes up an unaccountable resolution to serve the young bachelor-duke in the habit of a man'. And, since Viola has not even the excuse of being in love with the duke to start with, this goes 'greatly beyond the bounds of decency'. But if Shakespeare had wanted to make Viola assume her man's disguise because she was already in love with Orsino he did not need Bandello to teach him; he had already tried that situation with Julia and Proteus, and it had necessarily involved Proteus in that heartless infidelity from which Orsino is to be spared. The emotional situation of *Twelfth Night* is of a much less obvious kind.

The most important source for *Twelfth Night*, one might therefore say, is *The Two Gentlemen of Verona*. For it is only by a paradox of scholarship that the word *source* is usually restricted to material that an author draws on from someone else's work. But that there were other sources for *Twelfth Night* I readily admit.[4] Charlotte Lennox knew of one in Bandello. And long before that one of Shakespeare's own contemporaries had pointed to another. When John Manningham saw *Twelfth Night* in 1602, he said in his Diary that it reminded him of an Italian play called *Gl'Inganni* (or *The Mistakes*). There were at least two plays of this title that Shakespeare might have used, and in one of them the heroine, on disguising herself as a page, assumed the name Cesare, which may well be why Shakespeare's Viola elects to call herself Cesario. There was also another Italian play called *Gl'Ingannati* (or *The Mistaken*), in which the master told the page, 'You are a child, you do not know the force of love', and Shakespeare's Orsino of course is always similarly reminding Cesario of his uninitiated youth. So the nineteenth-century scholar, Joseph Hunter, perhaps influenced by the fact that he discovered it, found in this play *Gl'Ingannati* 'the true origin' of Shakespeare's. Collier, however, asserted that it was from an English tale by Barnabe Riche, called *Apolonius and Silla*, that Shakespeare drew his plot. Furness was equally certain that he did not, but, as he hoped that Shakespeare had never looked into Riche's 'coarse, repulsive novel',[5] perhaps this also was not quite an impartial judgement.

For my part I find no difficulty in agreeing with those modern scholars who assume that Shakespeare was familiar with all these versions of a story in which a woman disguised as a page pleads her lover's suit with another woman, who then falls in love with the page. But that Shakespeare read up these plays and novels for the express purpose of writing his own play is perhaps another matter. The similarities between Shakespeare and these others are certainly interesting; yet to point out similarities will usually end in drawing attention to their difference. For instance, *Twelfth Night* seems to echo Riche's tale when Olivia, declaring her unrequited love for Cesario, says she has 'laid' her 'honour too unchary out'.[6] But in Riche the lady said that she had 'charely preserved' her 'honour'. The phrasing is reminiscent; but Riche's lady boasts of her honour after she has sacrificed her chastity, while Shakespeare's Olivia reproaches herself for being careless of her honour when her chastity of course is not in question. Riche's lady is anxious lest she has lost her reputation in the eyes of the world, Olivia lest she has fallen from her own high ideal of conduct. Without accepting Furness's view that any reference to the act of sex is coarse and repulsive, we may easily find it significant that Shakespeare leaves it out. His delineation of Olivia's love for the page, in contrast to most of the earlier versions, omits all the physical demonstrations. The usual way when the lady falls in love with the page is for her to astonish him by falling on his neck and kissing him. In Secchi's play of *Gl'Inganni* the relations between them reach the point where the woman page is expected to play the man's part in an actual assignation and she gets out of it by the cunning substitution of her brother. In the play of *Gl'Ingannati*, which comes closer to Shakespeare, the lady takes the brother by mistake, but he goes to bed with her just the same. In Riche's story this incident has consequences, which force the lady so chary of her honour to demand marriage of the page, who can only establish innocence by the disclosure of *her* sex. Shakespeare appropriates this convenient brother as a husband for Olivia, but since he could easily have invented Viola's twin, and in *The Comedy of Errors* had, one might say, already tried him out, this debt is not a profound one. What is more remarkable, the similarity as usual embracing a contrast, is that when Olivia mistakes Sebastian for Cesario she takes him not to bed but to a priest. Olivia no less than Orsino is kept free of moral taint. And this is no mere matter of prudishness. The reckless abandonment of scruple shown by all these earlier lovers – both by the gentlemen who desert their mistresses and by the ladies who fling themselves upon the pageboys – cannot coexist with the more delicate sentiment which gives *Twelfth Night* its character. In Shakespeare, even the twin brother, prop to the plot as he may be, shares in this refinement. When Olivia takes charge of Sebastian's person, what he gives her is less his body than his imagination. He is enwrapped, he says in 'wonder'. And it is his capacity to experience this wonder that lifts him to the level of the other lovers in the play, so that he becomes a worthy partner for Orsino's adored one and Viola's adorer.

Now if *Twelfth Night* is the greatest of Shakespeare's romantic comedies, it is partly because of its success in embodying these feelings of wonder in the principal persons of the play. Stories of romantic love owe something of their perennial appeal, we need not be ashamed to admit, to the taste for tales of pursuit and mysterious adventure, as well as to what psychologists no doubt explain as the sublimation of the natural impulses of sex. But the devotion which the romantic lover bestows upon a woman as pure as she is unattainable may also symbolize the mind's aspiration towards some ever alluring but ever elusive ideal. In the traditional romantic stories the course of true love does not run smooth because of obstacles presented by refractory parents or inconvenient rivals, who have to be overcome or made to change. This is the case in *A Midsummer Night's Dream*. There are perhaps subtler situations, where the obstacles exist in the very nature of the protagonists, who must themselves be made to change. This is variously the case in *The Taming of the Shrew* and *Love's Labour's Lost*, where in their very different ways Katherina and the young gentlemen of Navarre are, to begin with, recalcitrant to love. But a still subtler situation may arise with characters who are from the beginning full of devotion to an ideal of love while mistaking the direction in which it should be sought. This, I take it, is the case with Orsino and Olivia. Orsino, with whom *Twelfth Night* begins and who draws us from the start into the aura of his imagination, is in some ways the most perfect of Shakespeare's romantic lovers simply because he is so much more. This is easily appreciated if we compare him with his earlier prototypes in *The Two Gentlemen of Verona*. He is, as I have suggested, the inconstant Proteus transformed. But he is also the other gentleman, the constant Valentine. He is

> Unstaid and skittish in all motions else
> Save in the constant image of the creature
> That is beloved.

So, simultaneously volatile and steadfast, he combines in a single figure those aspects of man's nature which in the earlier comedy had been systematically contrasted and opposed.

In Valentine, of course, we recognize the typical victim of the passion of courtly love. He tells us himself how he suffers

> With bitter fasts, with penitential groans,
> With nightly tears and daily heartsore sighs.

That these groans and sighs survive in Orsino is clear when Olivia asks 'How does he love me?' and the messenger replies,

> With adorations, with[7] fertile tears,
> With groans that thunder love, with sighs of fire.

The danger of such a hero is, as Professor Charlton has remarked, that, in fulfilling his conventional role, he may to the quizzical eye seem a fool. Shakespeare guards against this danger by anticipating our ridicule; but his mockery of Valentine and Orsino is quite different in kind. The romantic Valentine is given an unromantic servant who pokes broad fun at his conduct: 'to sigh like a schoolboy that has lost his A.B.C.; to weep like a young wench that had buried her grandam; to fast like one that takes diet', and so forth. But Orsino, instead of a servant who laughs at him for loving, has a page who can show him how to do it. 'If I did love you in my master's flame', says Cesario, I would

> Make me a willow-cabin at your gate
> And call upon my soul within the house

till all the hills reverberated with the name of the beloved. This famous willow-cabin speech, often praised for its lyricism, is of course no less a parody of romantic love than are Speed's gibes at Valentine. The willow is the emblem of forsaken love and those songs that issue from it in the dead of night apostrophizing the mistress as her lover's 'soul' – they are easily recognizable as the traditional love-laments. But the parody, though it has its hint of laughter, is of the kind that does not belittle but transfigures its original. So it comes as no surprise when Olivia, hitherto heedless of sighs and groans, suddenly starts to listen. To the page she says, '*You* might do much', and these words are her first acknowledgement of love's power. Orsino, content to woo by proxy a woman who immures herself in a seven-year mourning for a dead brother, may have the glamour of a knight of romance but he is *not* quite free from the risk of absurdity. He seems, they tell us with some justice, in love not so much with a woman as with his own idea of love. But what they do not so often tell us is how splendid an idea this *is*. His very groans go beyond Valentine's; they were said, it will have been noticed, to *thunder*, and his sighs were *fire*. If he indulges his own emotions, this is in no mere dilettantism but with the avidity of hunger.

> If music be the *food* of love, play on,
> Give me *excess* of it, that, *surfeiting*,
> The *appetite* may sicken and so die.

This wonderful opening speech suggests no doubt the changeableness of human emotion: 'play on ... / That strain again! It had a dying fall ... Enough, no more! / 'Tis not so sweet now as it was before.' But if the spirit of love is as transitory as music and as unstable as the sea, it is also as living and capacious. New waves form as often as waves break; the shapes of fancy, insubstantial as they are, make a splendour in the mind, and renew themselves as quickly as they fade. So Orsino's repeated rejections by his mistress do not throw him into despair. Instead he recognizes, in her equally fantastic devotion, a nature of surpassingly 'fine frame' and he reflects on how she *will* love when the throne of her heart shall find its 'king'. How too will *he* love, we are entitled to infer, when his inexhaustible but as yet deluded fancy shall also find the true sovereign it seeks. This of course it does at the end of the play when he exchanges all his dreams of passion for the love of someone he has come to know. In the play's last line before the final song he is able to greet Viola as 'Orsino's mistress and his fancy's queen'.

Before this consummation Orsino and Viola have only one big scene together, and in view of all that depends on it it will need to be a powerful one. Again it finds a model in *The Two Gentlemen of Verona*, where already there is a scene in which a man declares his love for one woman in the hearing of another woman who loves *him*. The technique is in each case that of a scene that centres upon a song, which makes a varying impact upon the different characters who hear it. In *The Two Gentlemen of Verona* a song of adoration to a mistress is presented by a faithless lover and is overheard by the women he has deserted, while her heartbreak goes undetected by her escort, who calmly falls asleep. This is admirably dramatic, but its irony may seem a trifle obvious when set beside the comparable scene in *Twelfth Night*. The song here is one of forsaken love and it is sung to two constant lovers. Most artfully introduced, it is called for by Orsino, whose request for music sustains the role in which he began the play; and the way in which he calls for the song characterizes both him and it before its opening notes are heard. It is to be an old and antique song, belonging to some primitive age, the kind of song chanted by women at their weaving or their knitting in the sun. It will appeal to Orsino in its simple innocence, or, we may say if we wish, by its ideal immunity from fact. So the rational mind can disengage itself from the sentiment in advance, and as soon as the song is ended its effect is counteracted by the jests of the clown who has sung it and the practical necessity of paying him. Yet the sentiment of the song remains to float back and forth over the dialogue which surrounds it as Orsino and Viola tell us of their love. The contrast here is not, as in *The Two Gentlemen of Verona*, between the faithful and the faithless, the heartbroken and the heartwhole. It is between one who is eloquent about an imaginary passion and one who suffers a real grief in concealment. Orsino appropriates the song to himself, yet it is Viola who hears in it 'a very echo to the seat / Where Love is throned'. Orsino is still sending messages to one he calls his 'sovereign', but *his* throne, we may say, is still unoccupied. For his splendid fantasies are as yet self-regarding. When Viola objects, 'But if she cannot love you, sir?', he dismisses this with 'I cannot be so answered.' Yet when she simply retorts, 'Sooth, but you must', he receives his first instruction in the necessity of accommodating his fantasies to practical realities. And soon he begins, however unwittingly, to learn. As Viola tells the history of her father's daughter, though he does not see that she is speaking of herself, he finds himself for the first time giving attention to a sorrow not his own. 'But died thy sister of her love, my boy?' he asks. To this Viola can only reply, 'I know not'; for at this stage in the drama the issue is still in the balance, though Orsino's new absorption in another's plight will provide us with a clue to the outcome. In the very act of sending a fresh embassy to his mistress his thoughts are momentarily distracted from his own affair. When it is necessary for Viola to prompt him – 'Sir, shall I to this lady?' – though he rapidly collects himself, we know that his development has begun.

In the emotional pattern of the play Viola represents a genuineness of feeling against which the illusory can be measured. As the go-between she is of course also at the centre of the plot. It is her role to draw Orsino and Olivia from their insubstantial passions and win them to reality. But her impact upon each of them is inevitably different. Orsino, whom she loves but cannot tell her love, responds to her womanly constancy and sentiment; Olivia, whom she cannot love but has to woo, is to be fascinated by her pageboy effrontery and wit.

Now in all the stories of the woman-page who woos for her master and supplants him, the transference of the mistress's affections must be the pivot of the action. In *The Two Gentlemen of Verona*, of course, the lady fails to fall in love with the page at all, which is really a little surprising of her, since she had done so in Shakespeare's source. It is almost as though Shakespeare were reserving this crowning situation, in which the mistress loves the woman-page, for treatment in some later play. At any rate, in *Twelfth Night* he takes care to throw the emphasis upon it from the first. Viola is got into her pageboy clothes before we are halfway through the first act. The plausibility of this, notwithstanding Mrs Lennox and Dr Johnson, is not the question. What matters is that the encounter of the lady and the page, upon which the plot is to turn, shall be momentous. And there is no encounter in Shakespeare, not even that of Hamlet with the ghost, which is more elaborately prepared for. Olivia's situation is referred to in each of the first four scenes before she herself appears in the fifth. Out of her love for her dead brother she has abjured the sight of men. This is the plain fact as a plain sea captain tells it to Viola and us. But in the more embroidered description of one of Orsino's gentlemen we may detect perhaps a hint of the preposterous:

> like a cloistress she will veiled walk
> And water once a day her chamber round
> With eye-offending brine.

In the fanciful Orsino this inspires adoration; but how it may appear to a less poetical nature we may gather from the first words of Sir Toby Belch: 'What a plague means my niece to take the death of her brother thus?' All these varied views are insinuated naturally into the dialogue, but their cumulative effect is to give Olivia's situation in the round and to make us curious to see her for ourselves. When after all this she appears, curiosity is not satisfied but intensified; she is not, I think, what we expected. Instead of the veiled lady sprinkling her chamber with tears there enters a mistress commanding her household, and her first words are 'Take the fool away.' Equally unexpected is the fool's retort, 'Do you not hear, fellows? Take away the lady.' This great dame is called a fool by one of her own attendants, who then goes on to prove it:

CLOWN
> Good madonna, why mourn'st thou?

OLIVIA
> Good fool, for my brother's death.

CLOWN
> I think his soul is in hell, madonna.

OLIVIA
> I know his soul is in heaven, fool.

CLOWN
> The more fool, madonna, to mourn for your brother's soul being in heaven. Take away the fool, gentlemen.

Now this is excellent fooling, but Shakespeare's incidental gaieties have a way of illuminating important matters and our conception of Olivia is one of them. It is only a fool who calls her a fool, but, as the fool himself has suggested, a fool 'may pass for a wise man', while those who think they have wit 'do very oft prove fools'. The question of Olivia's folly remains open. It is kept alive below the surface of the quipping dialogue which entertains us while Olivia defends the fool and is thanked by the fool in characteristically equivocal terms. 'Thou hast spoke for us, madonna, as if thy eldest son should be a fool.' One could hardly say more than that. Yet the suggestion that her eldest son might be a fool is at best a left-handed compliment. The fool is quick to right it with a prayer that Jove may cram his skull with brains, but it seems that Jove's intervention may be necessary, for – as Sir Toby enters – 'one of thy kin has a most weak pia mater'. The chances of brains or folly in the skull of any son of Olivia seem then to be about equal. But what is surely most remarkable is the notion of Olivia's ever having a son at all. We have been made to associate her not with birth but with death. The weeping cloistress, as Orsino's gentleman put it, was seasoning a 'dead love', and what plagued Sir Toby about this was that care was 'an enemy to life'. Yet the fool seems to see her as available for motherhood. The remarks of a fool – again – strike as deep as you choose to let them – that is the dramatic use of fools – but Olivia interests us more and more.

By now the page is at the gate. Indeed three different messengers announce him. Sir Toby of the weak pia mater is too drunk to do more than keep us in suspense, but Malvolio precisely catalogues the young man's strange behaviour, till we are as curious to see him as is Olivia herself. 'Tell him he shall not speak with me,' she has insisted; but, when this changes to 'Let him approach', the first of her defences is down. Our interest in each of them is now at such a height that the moment of their meeting cannot fail to be electric.

How different all this is from what happened in *The Two Gentlemen of Verona*, where only a single soliloquy prepared us before the page and Sylvia just came together pat. But it is interesting to see how the seeds strewn in the earlier play now germinate in Shakespeare's mature inventiveness. When the page came upon Sylvia, he did not know who she was and actually asked her to direct him to herself. This confusion gave a momentary amusement and the dramatic importance of the encounter was faintly underlined. But, as Sylvia at once disclosed her identity, this little gambit came to nothing. In *Twelfth Night*, however, Cesario only pretends not to recognize Olivia so as to confound her with his raillery. 'Most radiant, exquisite and unmatchable beauty,' he begins, and then breaks off to enquire whether the lady before him is the radiant unmatchable or not. As he has never seen her, how can he possibly tell? This opens up a brilliant series of exchanges in the course of which the familiar moves of the conventional courtship are all similarly transformed. In *The Two Gentlemen of Verona* Proteus was simply following the usual pattern of suitors when he instructed the page,

> Give her that ring and therewithal
> This letter ... Tell my lady
> I claim the promise for her heavenly picture.

To be fair, even in this early play the conventional properties, the ring, the letter and the picture, each made a dramatic point: for Sylvia recognized the ring as that of her rival and so refused to accept it, while she tore the letter up; and, if she compliantly handed over her portrait, she was careful to add the comment that a picture was only a shadow and might appropriately be given for a fickle lover to worship. But in *Twelfth Night* the letter, the picture and the ring are changed almost out of recognition. Shakespeare's superbly original invention allows Orsino to dispense with them; yet they are all vestigially present. Instead of bearing missives, the page is given the task of acting out his master's woes, and so instead of the lover's own letter we are to have the page's speech. This cunningly diverts attention from the message to the messenger, and the effect is still further enhanced when even the speech never gets delivered apart from its opening words. Instead there is talk about the speech – how 'excellently well penn'd', how 'poetical' it is – and are you really the right lady so that I may not waste the praise I have taken such pains to compose? Olivia in turn delights us by matching Cesario's mockery, but, as we watch them finesse about how and even whether the speech shall be delivered, their mocking dialogue says more than any formal speech could say. In fact the very circumventing of the speech brings them to the heart of its forbidden theme. And so we come to the picture. There is of course no picture, any more than there was a letter; but the convention whereby the lover asks for a picture of his mistress is made to provide a metaphor through which the witty duel may proceed. Olivia draws back the curtain and reveals a picture, they talk of the colours that the artist's 'cunning hand laid on', and Cesario asks for a copy. But the curtain Olivia draws back is her own veil, the artist is Nature, and the copy of Nature's handiwork will come as the fruit of marriage – again the suggestion that Olivia could have a child. The cloistress who dedicates herself to the dead is reminded of the claims of life. She waves them aside for the moment by deftly changing the application of the metaphor. Certainly there shall be a copy of her beauty; why not an inventory of its items? As she catalogues them – 'two lips, indifferent red ... two grey eyes, with lids to them' – she ridicules the wooer's praises; but at the same time, it may not be too much to suggest, she robs her womanhood of its incipient animation. Yet the cloistress has removed her veil and presently there is the ring. Orsino again sent no ring, but that need not prevent Olivia from returning it. And with this ruse the ring no less than the picture takes on a new significance. By means of it Olivia rejects Orsino's love but at the same time declares her own. And as Malvolio flings the ring upon the stage it makes its little dramatic éclat.

Shakespeare's portrait of Olivia has usually, I think, been underrated. The critics who used to talk about Shakespeare's heroines fell in love with Viola, and actresses have naturally preferred the bravura of her essentially easier role. Besides there is the risk of the ridiculous about a woman who mistakenly loves one of her own sex. But the delicacy of Shakespeare's handling, once more in contrast with that of his predecessors, steers the situation right away from farce and contrives to show, through her potentially absurd and undisguisedly pathetic plight, the gradual awakening of that noble nature which Orsino detected from the first. We have still permission to laugh at her. The fool, reminding us that foolery like the sun shines everywhere, flits between Orsino's house and hers. But when he is called the Lady Olivia's fool he makes one of his astonishing replies. 'No indeed, sir. The Lady Olivia has no folly.' It is true that his remark is as usual double-edged. 'She will keep no fool, sir, till she be married.' Her present exemption, it would seem, lies in her not having yet secured the husband she is seeking. But, when the fool now tells us that the Lady Olivia has no folly, we are forcibly reminded that he began by proving her a fool. It seems clear she is making progress. The comic artist only hints this with a lightness which the heavy hand of the critic inevitably destroys; but is there not the suggestion that, when Olivia ceases to mourn the dead and gives herself to the pursuit of the living, she has advanced some small way towards wisdom?

There is one character in the play who, unlike Olivia and Orsino, is unable to make this journey. And that brings me to the subplot. For it will already be apparent that I do not agree with a recent paper in the *Shakespeare Quarterly* which makes Malvolio the central figure of the play.[8] The mistake is not a new one. The record of a court performance in the year of the First Folio actually calls the play *Malvolio* and there are other seventeenth-century references, beginning with Manningham in 1602, which go to show that the sublime swagger with which Malvolio walks into the box-hedge trap to emerge in yellow stockings was largely responsible, then as now, for the play's theatrical popularity. The distortion of emphasis this implies is a tribute to Shakespeare's invention of the most novel situation in the play, but, if I venture to suggest that it does no great credit to his audience, no doubt some one will rise up like Sir Toby and ask me, 'Dost thou think because thou art virtuous there shall be no more cakes and ale?' All I think is that the cake-and-ale jollifications are very jolly indeed so long as they stay, whether in criticism or performance, within the bounds of a subplot, which the whole technique of the dramatic exposition marks them out to be. These more hilarious goings-on make an admirable counterweight to the more fragile wit and sentiment of which the main plot is woven; but attention is firmly directed to the love story of Orsino, Olivia and Viola before Sir Toby and Malvolio are heard of, and the courtships are well in progress by the time we come to the midnight caterwaulings. So the love delusions of Malvolio, brilliant as they are, fall into perspective as a parody of the more delicate aberrations of his mistress and her suitor. Like them Malvolio aspires towards an illusory ideal of love, but his mistake is a grosser one than theirs, his posturings more extravagant and grotesque. So *his* illusion enlarges the suggestions of the main plot about the mind's capacity for self-deception; and, if, as Lamb maintained,[9] it gives Malvolio a glory such as no mere reason can attain to, still 'lunacy' was one of Lamb's words for it and it is to the madman's dungeon that it leads.

Malvolio's fate, like Falstaff's, has been much resented by the critics. But drama, as Aristotle indicated and Shakespeare evidently perceived, is not quite the same as life, and punishments that in life would seem excessive have their place in the more ideal world of art. In the ethical scheme of comedy, it may be the doom of those who cannot correct themselves to be imprisoned or suppressed. Olivia and Prince Hal, within their vastly different realms, have shown themselves capable of learning, as Malvolio and Falstaff have not.

The comparison between Olivia and Malvolio is one that the play specifically invites. He is the trusted steward of her household, and he suits her, she says, by being 'sad and civil'. This reminds us that it was with her authority that he descended on the midnight revels to quell that 'uncivil rule'. Have you no manners, he demands of Sir Toby and his crew; and his rebuke is one that Olivia herself will echo later when she calls Sir Toby a barbarian fit to dwell in 'caves / Where manners ne'er were preached'. But, if Olivia and Malvolio are united in seeking to impose an ordered regimen on these unruly elements, that does not mean, though I have found it said, that they share a doctrine of austerity.[10] Indeed, the resemblance between them serves to bring out a distinction that is fundamental to the play. It is clearly marked for us on their first appearance. Significantly enough, they are brought on the stage together and placed in the same situation, as if to attract our attention to their contrasting reactions. The first remark of each of them is one of dissatisfaction with the fool, and the fool's retaliation is first to prove Olivia a fool and then to call Malvolio one. But Olivia is amused and Malvolio is not. 'I marvel your ladyship takes delight in such a barren rascal.' What Olivia delights in, Malvolio finds barren. 'Doth he not mend?' she says, suggesting that the fool is getting wittier. But Malvolio rejoins, Yes, he is mending by becoming a more perfect fool – 'and shall do till the pangs of death shake him'. Olivia too has given her thoughts to death, but whereas she mourns the dead, prettily if absurdly, Malvolio threatens the living in words which betray a cruel relish. This is his first speech in the play and it carries a corresponding emphasis. There are already signs that Olivia may be won from death to life, but the spirit of Malvolio can only be destructive. To say this is again to put it more portentously than it is the nature of comedy to do, but it is Olivia, not Malvolio, whom the comic dialogue invites to have a son, with brains in his skull or otherwise.

The difference in their natures appears in various subtle ways, and I will cite just one example. When Olivia sends after Cesario with the ring, the message that she sends is:

If that the youth will come this way tomorrow,
I'll give him reasons for't.

But Malvolio, who bears the message, translates it thus: 'be never so hardy to come again in his affairs, unless it be to report your lord's taking of this'. It is true that Malvolio cannot know, as we do, the secret meaning of the ring, but that hardly leaves him guiltless when he replaces 'if' by 'unless' and a positive by a negative: 'If that the youth will come', 'be never so hardy to come ... unless'. An invitation has become a warning off.

As the action proceeds, Olivia opens her heart to the new love that is being born within her, but Malvolio is only confirmed in that sickness of self-love of which she has accused him. At the height of his love-dream, his imaginings are all of his own advancement – 'sitting in my state', 'in my branched velvet gown', 'calling my officers about me' as I 'wind up my watch or play with my – some rich jewel'.[11] When he showed resentment at the fool, Olivia reproached Malvolio for his lack of generosity and now his very words freeze every generous impulse – 'I frown the while', 'quenching my familiar smile with an austere regard of control'.[12] This is not the language of Olivia. She speaks of the impossibility of quenching those natural feelings which rise up within her, and which we are made to recognize even in the comicality of her predicament:

Cesario, by the roses of the spring,
By maidhood, honour, truth and everything,
I love thee so that maugre all thy pride,
No wit nor reason can my passion hide.

So Olivia, notwithstanding her mistakes, is allowed to find a husband while Malvolio is shut up in the dark.

The ironic fitness of Malvolio's downfall is dramatically underscored in every detail of his situation. When he dreamed of his own greatness he pictured Sir Toby coming to him with a curtsey and he told Sir Toby to amend his drunkenness: it is now his bitterest complaint that this drunken cousin has been given rule over him. When he rebuked the tipsy revellers, he began,

'My masters, are you mad?', and their revenge upon him is to make it seem that he is mad himself. Particularly instructive is the leading part taken in his torment by the fool he began the play by spurning. The fool taunts him in the darkness of the dungeon and he begs the fool to help him to some light. It is to the fool that the man contemptuous of fools is now made to plead his own sanity. But his insistence on his sanity – 'I am as well in my wits, fool, as thou art' – leaves the matter in some ambiguity, as the fool very promptly retorts: 'Then you are mad indeed, if you be no better in your wits than a fool.' And Malvolio ends the play as he began by being called a fool. And, if at first it was only the fool who called him so, now it is his mistress herself. Even as she pities him for the trick that has been played on him, 'Alas, poor fool' are the words that Shakespeare puts into her mouth.

What then is folly and what wisdom, the comedy seems to ask. The question first appeared in that early cross-talk with the fool which brought Olivia into contrast with Malvolio even while we were awaiting her reception of Cesario. So that the manner in which Malvolio's story is begun clearly puts it into relation with the main plot of the wooing. And of course it is only appropriate that scenes of romantic love should be surrounded by a comic dialogue which gaily tosses off its hints about whether these characters are fools. For the pursuit of the ideal life is not quite compatible with reason. And, as another of Shakespeare's comedies puts it, those who in imagination see more than 'reason ever comprehends' are the lover, the poet and the lunatic. So where does the noble vision end and the madman's dream begin? The greatness and the folly that lie in the mind of man are inextricably entangled and the characters in *Twelfth Night* have each their share of both. Malvolio's moment of lunacy may be, as Lamb suggests, the moment of his glory. Yet Malvolio, so scornful of the follies of others, would persuade us that his own are sane. His sanity is indeed established, but only to leave us wondering whether sanity may not sometimes be the greater folly. What the comedy *may* suggest is that he who in his egotism seeks to fit the world to the procrustean bed of his own reason deserves his own discomfiture. But Olivia, who self-confessedly abandons reason, and Orsino, who avidly gives his mind to all the shapes of fancy, are permitted to pass through whatever folly there may be in this to a greater illumination. Although what they sought has inevitably eluded them, it has nevertheless been vouchsafed to them in another form.

Yet it is the art of Shakespeare's comedy, and perhaps also its wisdom, to make no final judgements. The spirit of the piece, after all, is that of Twelfth Night, and it is in the ideal world of Twelfth Night that Malvolio may be justly punished. Perhaps we should also remember, as even the Twelfth Night lovers do, to pause, if only for a moment, to recognize his precisian virtues. Olivia agrees with him that he has been 'notoriously abused' and the poet-lover Orsino sends after him to 'entreat him to a peace', before they finally enter into the happiness to which 'golden time' will summon them. 'Golden time' – the epithet is characteristically Orsino's. It is only the wise fool who stays to sing to us about the rain that raineth every day.

PART 2

ESSAYS ON *HAMLET*

8

HAMLET AND OPHELIA

In the interpretation of *Hamlet* criticism has found many problems; but none has proved more puzzling than the hero's treatment of Ophelia in the so-called 'nunnery scene'. Dr Johnson saw in this Hamlet's 'useless and wanton cruelty' to one who was young and beautiful, harmless and pious. But Professor Dover Wilson defends Hamlet at some length by explaining how he must regard Ophelia as a jilt and a dissembler. It is usual to stress her playing the decoy, and to speak of her 'betraying' Hamlet. Sir Edmund Chambers may stand for many who deplore her weakness. Others have seen her as a light o' love; Dame Rebecca West tells us roundly that 'she was not a chaste young woman'; and there used to be a theory, favoured by some nineteenth-century German critics and still occasionally revived, that she was actually Hamlet's mistress. Yet Professor G.R. Elliott praises her 'religious strength' and perceives in her the symbol of 'the Christian charity ... which Hamlet needs'. Professor Leo Kirschbaum, on the other hand, regards her as pitifully out of her depth in Hamlet's 'spiritual milieu'.[1] Amid such diverse opinions I feel nearly as bewildered as Ophelia herself. They do not encourage me to hope that anything I say about the problem will be universally acceptable; but at least they may excuse my wish to re-examine it.

The nunnery scene has its origin in the early versions of the Hamlet story. In Saxo and Belleforest, when Hamlet pretends to be mad, in order to test the genuineness of his madness the King employs a beautiful woman to try her charms upon him. This is the beautiful woman's role, and in Saxo and Belleforest it is the whole of it. In Shakespeare, however – with or without the precedent of the lost English play of *Hamlet* – this single episode has become the middle of a story which has also a beginning and an end. And it is the beginning and the end which give the middle its significance.

The beginning of the story is that Hamlet loves Ophelia; and the character of his love is plainly told us by Ophelia herself in three short speeches to her father, who demands to know 'the truth'. Hamlet has made many 'tenders of his affection', 'in honourable fashion', and with 'holy vows of heaven'. Whatever doubts may be cast upon them, now or later, the memory of those 'holy vows of heaven' will stay with us throughout the play. Yet the end of Ophelia's story, when she drowns hanging garlands on a willow, is a death emblematic of forsaken love; and the flowers that should have decked her bride-bed are strewed upon her grave. It is now that we get from the Queen the most explicit statement of what Hamlet's love had looked to: 'I hoped thou shouldst have been my Hamlet's wife.' But that this was also Hamlet's hope we may gather from those 'holy vows' at the beginning and the love so far beyond a brother's that he now at the end declares: 'I loved Ophelia. Forty thousand brothers / Could not ... Make up my sum.' Ophelia is the woman Hamlet had wished to marry. Yet the disastrous end of initial hope has come about through an encounter in which he has stormed at her to get her to a nunnery. This encounter is clearly the moment of crisis in Hamlet's relations with Ophelia; and that is why, if we would appreciate Ophelia's function in the play, we must try to understand its meaning.

The dramatic impact of the nunnery scene is very great; and the more so since it is most artfully prepared for. Remarkably enough, until it occurs, almost at the middle of the play, we are never allowed to see Hamlet and Ophelia meet, though we have known from the first that they inevitably must. This long deferment holds us in suspense, while everything is being done to enhance our curiosity and ensure that, when they do meet, their encounter will have the maximum effect.

Preparation begins from the moment that Hamlet's love is introduced. The first reference to it is when Ophelia's brother warns her to 'fear' Hamlet's 'trifling' with her chastity. This is before we hear anything of 'holy vows', which her father at once suspects of commending 'unholy suits'. The suspicions of Ophelia's father and brother arouse our apprehension that the course of love will not run smooth, and, with Shakespeare's flair for opening up a dramatic situation, this very scene, which tells of Hamlet's love, has Ophelia promising to give her lover up.

For her obedience to her father Ophelia has been much blamed. This was not, it is observed, the way of Juliet and Desdemona, who defied their fathers in the cause of love. But the simple answer to this is that Ophelia is in a different play – and a play to which the conventions of romantic love-story, where fathers exist in order to be circumvented, have singularly little relevance. The first premiss of *Hamlet* is that sons must avenge their fathers; and a play which required sons to avenge and daughters to flout their fathers would be in danger of moral chaos. Nor ought respect for a father prove so hard to tolerate. The sixteenth century enjoined it, Shakespeare certainly approved of it, and instances of it are occasionally met with even at the present day. The natural bonds of the family are as strong for Ophelia as for Hamlet, as the play will show. It is not unimportant that the first words it gives Ophelia to speak assure her brother she will write to him; and, when this admirable sister shows herself an obedient daughter by ceasing communication with Hamlet, we should not be surprised and should certainly not reproach her but should look forward to developments.

Developments are swift. For the next we see of Ophelia is when she enters terrified by Hamlet's strange apparition in her closet. The 'doublet all unbraced', ungartered stockings, and the rest Polonius immediately recognizes as the symptoms of love-madness, and they are in the play in order that he shall. But what Polonius sees as madness we are invited to regard as feigning. For Hamlet has already warned us that he will 'put on' some 'strange or odd' behaviour; and, though the scholars tell us that two months have intervened, for an audience, who go by playing time, it is no longer ago than it takes to speak a mere eighty lines of verse since Hamlet made the promise which now seems to receive its Q.E.D. Yet this first account of 'strange or odd' behaviour disturbs us with its hints of something more mysterious and profound. That sigh of Hamlet's, which Polonius ascribes to a distracted lover and we to a feigned madman, 'did seem to shatter all his bulk / And end his being'. More has happened to Hamlet, as we know, than Ophelia's denying him. Yet it cannot be an accident that this first evidence of his so ambiguous madness is connected with Ophelia. Her description of how he went from her, finding his way 'without his eyes' and bending their light upon her to the last, haunts us. It is a parting reluctant yet of a spell-like compulsion; and it gives, of course, an image and foreshadowing of that later parting, which the nunnery scene will enact.

The closet episode, with its complex of suggestions, leaves us tantalized. And its effect is not diminished when we now find all the court in alarm about Hamlet's 'transformation' and Polonius arriving to expound his theory of it. To tell the court what Ophelia told him would be natural, but in drama tiresomely repetitive. So instead he reads a letter. We need not ask, as the commentators do, when Hamlet could have written this letter or Ophelia received it. What matters is its introduction at this point. Though this has been disputed, it is certainly a love-letter, but as certainly a strange one. The author of Shakespeare's sonnets could obviously have done better by Hamlet had he wished. The art of the letter, I take it, is neither to confirm nor yet dispel the notion of love-madness. It sustains mystification; and the touch of comedy in Polonius's fussy self-importance can be used to relax tension without surrendering suspense. Indeed comedy acquires an edge of irony as expectation grows that Polonius is due to be confounded. The more he insists that all is clear, the more we feel that all is yet to be explained. When he comes to his plot to confront Hamlet with Ophelia, we eagerly await the promised meeting.

There is ample excuse for the bad quarto to move on to it at once. But the authentic text of the second quarto shows Shakespeare still postponing it. Yet, if we are still to be denied the expected encounter with Ophelia, what better could we have instead than an encounter with her father, who boasts of reading Hamlet's riddle? This will more than satisfy us for the moment by beginning his confounding, while raising interest even higher in what is still to come. When Hamlet enters for Polonius to 'board' him, this is the first time that we see him since the 'transformation' of which we have heard so much. Immediate demonstration is essential, and is delightfully provided when Polonius's too pointed query, 'Do you know me, my lord?', wins the instant retort, 'You are a fishmonger.' Applied to Polonius in its literal sense, the word has a shattering incongruity, which its cant use for a wencher, if we know it, may redouble. Polonius disclaims it, Hamlet talks of the rarity of an honest man, goes on to a dead dog, and ejects 'Have you a daughter?', thereby introducing with an agreeable shock the very topic the play requires them to discuss. All this confirms Polonius in his view that Hamlet is 'far gone', and on Ophelia's account, but permits us to suppose that Hamlet, like Touchstone and other licensed fools, is using his folly like a stalking-horse under cover of which to shoot his wit. Yet the role of the fool is one that Shakespeare often uses to hint at more than sanity can state, and, with the line already blurred between the feint of madness and a genuine disturbance, we get glimpses through the mad talk of what is stirring deep in Hamlet's mind. Polonius's daughter comes into the dialogue in a context highly charged. Fishmongers were popularly associated with loose women, whether as their fathers or procurers, and 'honest' has a second meaning, with which women are concerned. A sudden leap brings us to polluted procreation. 'If the sun breed maggots in a dead dog, being a good kissing carrion –'. 'Carrion', too, has a second meaning, and from kissing and breeding to the woman who may do these a train of thought is clear. It is a pity Warburton perplexed it by emending to 'a *god* kissing carrion', which Johnson thought a 'noble' reading and which some scholars still defend. 'A good kissing carrion', like a good eating apple – to cite a parallel which I think was Percy Simpson's – is one well suited for the purpose. The dead dog which the sun embraces is prolific. The analogy with Polonius's daughter is not perhaps a pretty one; but at least

it will be plain why Hamlet says, 'Let her not walk i'th' sun.'
Knowing that Polonius is planning to 'loose' his daughter to the
Prince, we may find the warning apt. That 'conception is a
blessing' Hamlet punningly acknowledges; but with the maggots
of the dead dog in mind we may have our reservations, and we
must be ready for Hamlet's recoil. 'As your daughter may
conceive – friend, look to't.' The warning given to Polonius is to
guard his daughter from the destiny of her womanhood. This
must be still in Hamlet's mind when on Polonius's next
appearance he addresses him as Jephthah. For Jephthah too
had a 'fair daughter', as Hamlet indeed tells us by quoting a
popular ballad. What he does not tell us, but what the completed
ballad would, and what in any case we ought to know, is that
Jephthah sacrificed his daughter while she was still a virgin. And
though Polonius, along with most Shakespearean commentators,
fails to see this point it does something to explain why Hamlet,
when he meets Ophelia, directs her to a nunnery. The Jephthah
allusion by itself would be enough to refute that queer theory that
Ophelia was Hamlet's mistress. What the play suggests is not
that Hamlet seduces her but that he condemns her to virginity.
This is what the nunnery scene does.

When now at last the lovers meet, for the first time in the play,
we are keyed up with expectancy. We know that Ophelia has first
accepted and then rejected Hamlet's love addresses. We know that
Polonius believes this has driven Hamlet mad. We share
Polonius's view that Hamlet's strangeness is connected with
Ophelia. But I think we do not share his view of what the
connection is. When Ophelia now repeats her rejection of
Hamlet's love, on the stage before our eyes, by giving him back
his lover's gifts, the moment is supremely tense. Yet, whatever we
expect from this, it will hardly be what happens. For the first
astonishing thing about their conversation, though insufficiently
remarked on, is that the expected roles of the lovers are reversed.
Ophelia, to be sure, has denied Hamlet access to her; but it is she,
not he, who speaks of the 'many a day' since they have met. And,
though she returns Hamlet's gifts, it is not she but he who now
repudiates their love. He does not complain of getting his gifts

back; he says he never gave them. It is not the receiver but the giver of the gifts who proves 'unkind', so that, instead of his reproaching her with inconstancy, she reproaches him. This runs so much counter to what Polonius, at least, would have led us to expect that many regard it as duplicity on Ophelia's part. Professor Dover Wilson, for example, says, 'She, the jilt, is accusing him of coldness towards her.'[2] But this is to ignore that Hamlet has just disowned the tokens of his love. It is not Ophelia only, it is the play itself which now presents the estrangement as of Hamlet's making. When Hamlet says, 'I never gave you aught', I cannot think it just for Professor Dover Wilson to put the stress on *you* – 'I never gave *you* aught' – as though Hamlet charges a fickle Ophelia with having become another person. Her reply shows that she has not. It is true that some have heard in it the tones of calculation. Interpretation can be very subjective; and I am aware of that risk in my own. Yet I am fairly certain that a character in an Elizabethan play is not to be judged insincere for speaking in a rhyming couplet. The woman who returns the gifts is the same as first spoke of Hamlet's love. For her the gifts are 'remembrances', and when he chooses to deny them she recalls the 'words of so sweet breath composed / As made the things more rich', whose 'perfume' now is 'lost'. What *we* may recall is that her brother told her at the beginning to esteem Hamlet's love like a 'violet', with a 'perfume' 'sweet not lasting'. The ironic echo is poignant; and there will shortly be another. Her father warned her at the beginning, 'Do not believe his vows'; but now it is Hamlet himself who says, 'You should not have believed me.' The theory, whether Polonius's or ours, that what is troubling Hamlet is Ophelia's unkindness can hardly explain *this*. If the gifts that she holds out to him seem at first to image *her* denial of love, they stay on the stage between them as the sign of *his*.

What, then, of the usual theory that Hamlet treats Ophelia as he does because she has betrayed him? Making Hamlet in our own image, we require him to resent her stopping the addresses she at first was ready to receive; but, if he does, he never lets us know. The ways of madness, real or feigned, are legitimately extraordinary. Yet Hamlet's madness is at the dramatist's service, and, if it serves him by being extraordinary, it must also be extraordinary in a significant way. And what I find both extraordinary and significant is that Hamlet reproaches Ophelia not for refusing his love but for having once accepted it under the illusion that he gave it. We are perhaps at liberty to suppose that Ophelia's repelling him has contributed to this extraordinary behaviour; but that is something the play now chooses not to stress. What I think it comes to is that Ophelia's repelling Hamlet is a necessary part of the dramatic plot, which Shakespeare manipulates with his customary dramatic skill. With Polonius's help it provides the occasion for the nunnery scene. But the use that is made of that occasion when it arrives suggests that Hamlet's imagination, and that of the dramatist who creates him, is involved with something deeper. And the conversations with Polonius have given dark hints of what it is.

Now certainly Hamlet distrusts Ophelia. In one of his sudden, bewildering questions he asks her, 'Are you honest?' If we think Ophelia has played him fast and loose, the question may seem pertinent. It comes just when she has returned his gifts. But it also comes just when she has shown how much she cherished them. This is what makes it particularly cruel. To Ophelia, whose beauty he has praised, Hamlet now maintains that beauty and honesty do not go together.

The power of beauty will sooner transform honesty from what it is to a bawd than the force of honesty can translate beauty into his likeness.

Ophelia's danger is apparent. Hamlet told her father to keep her from the sun; he tells her to 'admit no discourse' to her beauty. I take this to be less an accusation than a warning. But Ophelia has no fears of herself. She appears to believe that a woman's love may be pure. What Hamlet thinks about this, already glanced at in his talk about the carrion in the sun, about kissing, conception and breeding, will now be more explicit. 'Why, wouldst thou be a breeder of sinners?' This question editors always punctuate in a way that seems to me mistaken. The 'why' is not, I think, an interrogative ('Why wouldst thou ...?'), as though Hamlet seeks a reason for a curious predilection on Ophelia's part. I take 'why' as an interjection. It is a favourite with Hamlet and conveys expostulation. 'Why, wouldst thou be a breeder of sinners?' There is one means other than Jephthah's to save Ophelia from this fate. And I note that it is just at this point that Hamlet first bids Ophelia to get her 'to a nunnery'.

Hamlet's objection to Ophelia, then, is that she is a woman, and a woman he has loved. He has come to know what women are, and Ophelia has to be shown. He does not accuse her of having betrayed him; he implies that she inevitably will. He lays out for her her character; but the sins for which he reviles her – unfaithfulness, dissimulation, wantonness – are less her own than the sins of all her sex. To the woman he had hoped to marry he delivers a diatribe against marriage, insisting that there shall be no more of it.

Yet there are two parties to marriage, and we must surely think, as Hamlet does, of both. His protest, 'Wouldst thou be a breeder of sinners?', when regarded merely as denunciation of Ophelia, as it often is, is interpreted in too limited a sense. Though Hamlet sees in Ophelia the nature of a woman and all the sins that belong to it, his first speech to her in this scene – and that means in the play itself – refers not to her sins but to his.

> Nymph, in thy orisons
> Be all my sins remembered.

This is sometimes taken as sarcasm; but Johnson, with good reason, thought it a 'grave and solemn' address; and, if sarcasm it is, like other of Hamlet's sarcasms it hides something underneath. That Hamlet has in mind his condition of sinful man will presently appear when he refers to the human stock from which he springs. The Queen had hoped that Ophelia's virtues would restore her ailing son; but Hamlet knows that virtue itself cannot eliminate his taint. Is that not why he could not love, and why Ophelia should not have received the love he offered? In one significant speech these thoughts all come together:

> You should not have believed me; for virtue cannot so
> inoculate our old stock but we shall relish of it. I loved you
> not.

Is it not because he is what he is that she should not have believed
him? It is now, when she twice confesses that she has, that he
breaks out, 'Get thee to a nunnery. Why, wouldst thou be a
breeder of sinners?' Though he has asked her if she is honest and
will presently proceed to her sins, it is again of his own sins that
he first speaks.

> I am myself indifferent honest, but yet I could accuse me of
> such things that it were better my mother had not borne me.

She should not have believed him, and she must not.

> What should such fellows as I do crawling between earth and
> heaven? ... Believe none of us. Go thy ways to a nunnery.

Far from valuing his love too little, she has valued it too well. So
he not only denies his own love; he would also extinguish hers. It
is not only herself that the nunnery is to save her from. If Hamlet
cannot marry Ophelia, it is equally important that she must not
marry him.

The nunnery scene, then, dramatizes with the utmost force
and vividness Hamlet's parting from Ophelia and some complex
reasons for it. The end of their interview confirms what the
beginning of it suggested, that it is not Ophelia who has
abandoned him but he who abandons her. Five times he bids her
to a nunnery, and three times says 'Farewell', finally going off in
rage while she is left solitary on the stage, 'deject and wretched', to
recall once more those 'musicked vows' of which she has 'sucked
the honey' and which we have just heard him disown. The scene
has shown us that she has treasured Hamlet's love; it suggests that
she has returned it; and may I not now add that she loves him
still? The grief that she expresses is less for her plight than for his.
When he poured abuse upon her, she prayed Heaven to restore
him; and she says less of herself forsaken than of his noble mind

now wrecked. The critic who pronounces her soliloquy 'all surface and starch'[3] may judge less well than Coleridge, who saw in it the exquisite unselfishness of love.[4] I do not think the play which gives her this soliloquy means to present Ophelia as a loose woman or a traitor.

But what are we to say about her famous lie? When Hamlet suddenly asks her, 'Where's your father?', and she replies, 'At home', we gasp. For those who see her as the betrayer, this is the climax of her treachery. Kittredge, however, in a very interesting note, defends it as her only possible answer. She could hardly say, 'My father is behind the arras.' The lie is forced upon her, and we could add that she tells it plainly and without equivocation. But I do not find such arguments entirely satisfactory; for the play, had it wished to, could have saved her from her lie by sparing her Hamlet's question. Her answer is as staggering as the question, and that is one reason why Ophelia must give it. It forces upon our attention, and in the most sensational way, what we may by this time be in danger of forgetting, that Polonius is not 'at home', but close at hand. The crux, of course, is whether Hamlet is supposed to know this too. There is a well-known stage tradition for Polonius to betray his presence at this point, usually by peering through a curtain; and a common interpretation is that Hamlet seizes his opportunity to catch Ophelia out, and that his manner to her consequently changes from now on. His manner must be what the actor makes it, and, if the actor exhibits mounting fury, the text will give him some support. But the text shows Hamlet making no more reference to Ophelia's lie than he has done to her repelling of his suit. I remember again that the ways of a suspected madman may be strange; but I may still observe that Hamlet does not say that women are liars, who betray their lovers to their fathers, and plot with their enemies against them. It is the critics who say this. What Hamlet says is that women are wantons, who give themselves faces God did not, and make cuckolds of their husbands – all of which has little to do with the lie Ophelia has just told but much to do with what he has been saying to her before. He has already put her honesty in question, maintained that beautiful women cannot be expected to stay chaste, and warned her against breeding sinners. He goes on to warn her against marriage. He has already recommended a nunnery twice; he now does so three times more. I have come across the proposal that when he first says, 'Get thee to a nunnery', he should speak the words with tenderness, as though anxious for her safety, and then, on discovering Polonius and the trick, he should change his tone to anger; and the scene could obviously be played in that way. But that the nunnery is first a literal one and then becomes a brothel,[5] and that the actor's voice and gesture can convey this, is something I take leave to doubt. When the nunnery, at whatever stage, becomes a brothel, it becomes, I suspect, a red herring.

The question, 'Where's your father?', interrupts the dialogue in Hamlet's characteristically disconcerting way; but it does not deflect its course. That others before me have perceived this is evident from the practice of some producers of making Hamlet detect Polonius much earlier in the scene – when he asks Ophelia if she is honest, or even when she first offers to return the gifts. But this does not much improve matters, since, as we have seen, the route which brings us to the nunnery has come via Jephthah's daughter from the carrion in the sun. If Hamlet is aware of Polonius's trick at all, must he not be aware of it from the outset? Professor Dover Wilson has some logic on his side in deciding that Hamlet must overhear Polonius propose it, and he invents a new stage direction to enable him to do so. Elizabethan play texts being what they are, their stage directions are often insufficient. But they are only insufficient when they fail to indicate some action which the dialogue necessitates or implies. And an editor who supplements them must be careful not to lead the dialogue when the dialogue should lead him.

Now in the matter of overhearing on the stage the Elizabethans had conventions, and an instructive article by Helen Gardner has shown us what they were.[6] Shakespearean eavesdroppers declare themselves to us as such, as indeed dramatic effect requires and as Polonius and Claudius very elaborately do. They explain that they will be 'behind an arras' to 'mark the encounter' of Hamlet and Ophelia; and when the encounter is over Polonius says, 'We heard it all.' But Hamlet is less helpful. He does not say, 'I heard it all.' He leaves Professor Dover Wilson to infer this. In the converse situation, when a character who is spied on has knowledge of the spies, he must likewise make it clear to us. And that is another dramatic duty which Hamlet fails to perform. Whatever we may think of the trick now being played on him, I find no evidence that Hamlet ever thinks, or knows, of it at all.

To the conventions which Miss Gardner has expounded, I should like to add another, best seen in an example. In *Henry IV* there is an episode in which Prince Hal and Poins arrange to spy on Falstaff with his whore. And no sooner have they taken up their places than Doll Tearsheet obligingly enquires, 'What humour's the Prince of?', with the result that the listeners hear something about themselves. Am I to suppose, as some indeed have done, that they are recognized by Doll Tearsheet, who deliberately leads Falstaff on? I am glad to find that the learned Variorum editor says that I need not. In fact Doll asks about the Prince not because she knows, but because the audience know, that the Prince is within earshot. She requires no further motive for her question; the design it serves is not the speaker's but the play's. And dramatic convention readily permits this. Hamlet's question is no doubt less simple: while fixing on the unseen listener, it also exhibits the workings of Hamlet's mind. But the dramatic convention is fundamentally the same. Indeed it is precisely this convention that allows Hamlet to remind *us* of Polonius's presence and still be his surprising, incalculable self. Those critics and producers who make Hamlet discover where Polonius is provide him with so crude a reason for his question as to destroy half of its effect. That Polonius shall hear what Hamlet says is less Hamlet's purpose than the purpose of the play in which he figures.

It is to assist this purpose of the play that Ophelia must tell her lie. When she says her father is 'at home', Hamlet is able to retort, 'Let the doors be shut upon him, that he may play the fool nowhere but in's own house.' Whatever Hamlet has in mind by this, it is certain that the dramatist has more. For the play will show how Polonius, by not keeping to his own house, by playing the fool once more behind an arras, comes to grief. The fate of the second unseen listener is also now anticipated. We know that Hamlet must ultimately kill the King; and he gives us here the promise that he will. 'Those that are married already, all but one, shall live.' But again, what the play requires is not that Hamlet shall know, but that we shall know, that the King is there to hear it.

The opportunity for such dramatic piquancies was far too good for an accomplished dramatist to miss. But, as Shakespeare's art exploits it, there is more than a brief thrill. The situation of Ophelia at the moment of her crisis is combined and involved with the other situations out of which Hamlet's tragedy develops. While Hamlet is announcing to Ophelia her fate, he foreshadows the fates of Polonius and the King; while he is bidding her to the nunnery, he reminds us of his duty of revenge. And the marriage that will not now take place is linked with one that has taken place already. The conjoining of these situations here is but one sign of the play's intense imaginative coherence. It is in the context of Hamlet's revenge and his mother's marriage that Ophelia's story is shaped, and it is of course within the larger drama of Hamlet's revenge and his mother's marriage – though I can speak of these but briefly – that Hamlet's relations with Ophelia have their deepest significance.

Before we know anything of Hamlet's vows to Ophelia, or indeed of Ophelia's existence, his revulsion from his mother's marriage is deeply impressed upon us. It is the marriage of one who, having hung upon a loving husband, accepts the embraces of his brother, posting with 'wicked speed' to 'incestuous sheets'. The Ghost that comes to tell Hamlet of his father's murder enlarges also on his mother's filthy lust; and these awful revelations will still be in our minds when we hear of Hamlet in Ophelia's closet looking like one 'loosed out of hell / To speak of horrors'. His distracted state, which Polonius ascribes to disappointed love, is connected by the Queen with her 'o'er-hasty marriage'. 'Frailty, thy name is woman!' was Hamlet's bitter comment on what his mother's marriage showed him, and, when at length we find him with Ophelia, it is of woman's frailty that he speaks and the sins that it engenders. The play represents him in the nunnery scene turning from Ophelia in anger and despair, and at once goes on, in its big central scene, where all its various actions intertwine, to show him for the first and only time with his mother and Ophelia together. The primary purpose of the play-within-the-play is no doubt to 'catch the conscience of the King'; but it also makes assault upon the conscience of the Queen. The imaging of her worthless love Hamlet watches, as the dialogue is at some pains to emphasize, from a place at Ophelia's feet. He draws Ophelia's attention to how cheerfully his mother sits by her new husband with her first one but just dead; and it is when the dumb-show has presented the fickleness of a royal wife that he taunts Ophelia with the brevity of woman's love. The re-enacting of his mother's story is framed by his bitter jests to Ophelia, which make her who has received his holy vows the object now of every lewd insinuation. For her share in this dialogue Ophelia's character has suffered much at the commentators' hands; but an examination of the dialogue will show, I think, that the obscene equivocations are all in Hamlet's part. The worst that we can say of her is that she appears to understand them. The explication of them, which editors forbear to give, I need not supply. It will be enough to say that they run all the time upon the sexual organs and their use in copulation. A final thrust about how women take their husbands is Hamlet's last word to Ophelia in the play.

To his mother he will speak further. For the play scene is presently to be followed by a scene between Hamlet and his mother, just as it was preceded by a scene between Hamlet and Ophelia. These two scenes, in which he denounces each of them in turn, balance one another in the structure of the play, and set the marriage which is not to be against the marriage which is in being. In the interview with his mother Hamlet makes no mention of Ophelia; but the patterning of a play may often suggest to us what the dialogue cannot make explicit. It is impossible that we should not think of her. If 'hell' can mutiny 'in a matron's bones', Hamlet bursts out, the virtue of a youthful love may 'melt' in its own 'fire'. How should Ophelia be honest? Hamlet's mother has transformed marriage. She has done an act that

> takes off the rose
> From the fair forehead of an innocent love
> And sets a blister there, makes marriage vows
> As false as dicers' oaths, O, such a deed
> As from the body of contraction plucks
> The very soul.

For the rose of love Hamlet sees the blister of the harlot; with the soul gone out of marriage, grossness alone remains. There must be no more marriage.

It is ironic that Gertrude, who feared that Hamlet's 'distemper' had to do with her marriage, should have hoped that Ophelia's virtues might help to cure him of it. It is still more ironic that the Queen at Ophelia's graveside shold confess her hope that Ophelia should have been Hamlet's wife. And the description of the lovelorn maiden drowning beneath the willow acquires an extra poignancy from the fact that Gertrude speaks it. It is not usual for dramatists to make a royal personage the nuntius, and it cannot be an accident that Shakespeare does so here. Instead of asking whether the speech is out of character, or labelling it, with Kittredge, more lyrical than dramatic, should we not rather appreciate this sharp dramatic point?

In the dramatic ordering of the play the connection between Gertrude and Ophelia is everywhere implicit. Why is it to the King and Queen that Ophelia must sing her mad songs? But I must leave Ophelia for a moment to say something more of Hamlet.

By what his mother is he feels himself contaminated. Her union with her husband's brother, revolting as it is as a violation of natural law, is made still worse by the antithesis between the brothers. They are compared by Hamlet, when he first cries out upon the marriage, to Hyperion and a satyr. Before we know about the murder, the dead and living brothers may already appear in the imagination as something more than themselves. The god in man has died unmourned, and the beast usurps his place. The task imposed upon Hamlet, that of avenging his father, we may see, as I have suggested elsewhere, as the reassertion of the god by the destruction of the beast.[7] The strongest bonds of nature compel Hamlet to respond to the call of his father's spirit, but, with his uncle ruling his father's kingdom and married to his mother, he finds himself in a world of grossness; and, though his soul condemns it and he would isolate himself from it, he knows himself a part of it. He swears that the Ghost's commandment 'all alone shall live' within his brain 'unmixed with baser matter'. But from his lot of man the 'baser matter' can never be eliminated, as he does not long forget. He dedicates himself to his task, saying, 'I will go pray'; but even as he does so he adds, 'for my own poor part', and, thinking of 'so poor a man as Hamlet is', he knows that his noble mission is also his curse. When he shows his mother the pictures of her two husbands, he describes to her a wondrous man on whom 'every god did seem to set his seal', and whose 'empire' a 'vice of kings' has stolen. But hardly has he said this than his father's spirit, whom he has sworn to remember, reappears to warn him of forgetfulness. The 'tardy son' is chided for the deed he has neglected; while the corpse of Polonius lies there to show what he has done instead. The revenge plot, like the marriage plot, is a double one. The destined avenger of a father's murder becomes in a secondary action the killer of another's father and dies as the object of another son's revenge at the moment when he achieves his own. This paradox in the action of the play gives great dramatic tension to its catastrophe; but it also enlarges the whole revenge situation to symbolize that mysterious duality in man's nature upon which Hamlet continually reflects. It reveals to us how the same man may fulfil both parts, how he who is called to right wrong is also capable of perpetrating it. Hamlet requites Claudius for his crime; but he shares something of his guilt. When Hamlet at length resolves to kill the King he knows that it is 'perfect conscience' to remove 'this canker of our nature'. But is it not because the canker belongs to 'our nature' that the play cannot permit Hamlet to kill the King until the moment of his own death?

Hamlet's sense of the contamination in his nature, and in that larger nature of which his is a part, inspires in him a loathing for all the processes of life, of growth, of generation, and sexual union itself. In everything that engenders or nourishes life he sees the evil principle at work. The 'old stock', though virtue be grafted on to it, will still impart its taint. The world is a garden, but 'unweeded', possessed by 'things rank and gross in nature'; and he implores his mother not to 'spread the compost on the weeds / To make them ranker'. She, forgetting her union with the godlike man, sits cheerfully by her bestial husband's side, and lives

> In the rank sweat of an enseamed bed,
> Stewed in corruption, honeying and making love
> Over the nasty sty.

Though Hamlet sees the god in man, he also sees how the beast everywhere transforms him. If he concedes that 'conception is a blessing', he thinks of the sun uniting with the carrion to bring forth living pollution. It is this sense of the pollution of life that destroys his joy in its loveliness. In the beauty of Ophelia he looks for the impurity of woman; in her innocent conversation he discovers sexual nastiness; and from the love that begins in 'holy vows' he foresees unholy issue. His renunciation of Ophelia expresses in the action of the play Hamlet's rejection of the beauty and nobility of life because of what must be inseparable from it.

We may see Ophelia as a decoy whom Polonius places in Hamlet's way; but what Hamlet sees, I think, is a temptress placed there by Nature. He puts the temptress behind him, but the violence with which he does so may suggest how vulnerable he feels himself to be. Remembering those eyes that bent their light upon Ophelia to the last, we know that what drives him from her has to struggle with what draws him to her. But, though love would draw them together, he says, 'We will have no more marriage.'

So Ophelia is left in the state of Jephthah's daughter. And if we recall, as Dowden did, that Jephthah's daughter, before she went to her death, spent two months bewailing her virginity, this may help to explain to us what Ophelia too will do. In forms given to her by madness, she sings of what she has not known. Her drowning under the willow, as I said, is emblematic. Where she sought to hang her garlands, 'an envious sliver broke'. And she is buried with those 'maimed rites' which Hamlet has to watch. But, though a 'churlish priest' may begrudge them, she has, as the play insists, her 'virgin crants', her 'maiden strewments'; and as she is laid in the earth there is the wish that from her 'unpolluted flesh' 'violets' may 'spring'.[8]

Is it perhaps ironic that these words are spoken by Laertes, the brother who began her story by warning her to guard her chastity from Hamlet? That early scene in which she tells of Hamlet's love establishes her relationship with the father her lover will kill and the brother who will avenge him. In beginning the preparation for the nunnery scene, it also begins the design which links her fate with theirs. Polonius, who suspects Hamlet's love, afterwards brings his daughter to him; and Hamlet exhorts her to the nunnery and treats her father as a fool. When Hamlet has killed her father, the lamentations of forsaken love and sorrow for her father's death inextricably mingle in her disordered mind. 'She speaks much of her father', they say. And she says, 'My brother shall know of it.' Her brother indeed comes to avenge his father, but has first to follow his sister to her grave – which he does with a curse for the doer of the 'wicked deed' which has brought her to it. At Ophelia's grave Hamlet at last declares his love, and he and Laertes, as her lover and her brother, fight – in anticipation of their final contest, in which, as avengers of their fathers, both noble and both guilty, they will kill yet forgive one another.[9] Ophelia has died in her virginity. She has escaped life's contamination; she has also been denied its fulfilment. The pathos of her austere funeral preludes the catastrophe, upon which, however, she also sheds the brief fragrance of her innocence.

9

FORTINBRAS AND LAERTES AND THE COMPOSITION OF *HAMLET*

Some years ago, in discussing *Hamlet,* I observed that the role of Fortinbras appears to undergo a change as the action of the play works itself out.[1] The point is not one which has received much attention from the critics,[2] who, when they have concerned themselves with Fortinbras, have usually regarded him as a whole and consistent character. Yet, since nothing is unimportant which may throw light on the workings of Shakespeare's imagination in the process of dramatic composition, I believe that this matter of Fortinbras's transformation merits a little scrutiny. And, since the two roles will be found to impinge on one another, a consideration of Fortinbras must involve Laertes too.

Presumptuous as it may be to suppose that one can ever look into Shakespeare's mind in the act of composition, yet the plays themselves will often reveal something of how the material of the drama is being shaped and patterned. In particular a first act, concerned as it is to prepare lines for future development, may give clues to what the dramatist perceives as the opportunities of his subject. In the old story of Hamlet, as it came down from Saxo through Belleforest and an earlier Elizabethan play, it is clear that Shakespeare saw the focus of interest in the revenge of a son for his father's murder. The tremendous climax of his first act comes with the revelation of the murder to the son by the father's ghost, and it is a climax which was being prepared from the very opening words.

The play's first scene creates expectancy by the agitation of the soldiers on the watch, intensifies it by not one but two appearances of the Ghost, and then at the end makes the first reference to 'young Hamlet', who must be told about the Ghost, they say, because 'This spirit, dumb to us, will speak to him.' Before we even see the hero of the play he is known to us as the son of a dead king and the intended recipient of a message from his ghost. The second scene, at court, then introduces him, a solitary figure in mourning black, and his position as a son is what is emphasized as soon as he is addressed:

> KING
>> But now, my cousin Hamlet, and my son ...
>> How is it that the clouds still hang on you?
> HAMLET
>> Not so, my lord; I am too much in the sun.

In this quibbling retort Hamlet repudiates the new king's attempt to claim him as *his* son and affirms his allegiance to his father. His refusal to be consoled for his father's loss makes the burden of the dialogue which follows. What Shakespeare is stressing here then is the bond between son and father; and the other situations which Shakespeare associates with Hamlet's serve to stress it still more. For Hamlet, though conspicuous from the beginning of the scene, is yet held back for its climax: he is the last in a series of three young men with whom the new king has to deal, and it will become apparent that Fortinbras and Laertes here lead up to Hamlet because their situations are designed to reflect his. Fortinbras, whom we have already had an account of in the first scene, can now be disposed of briefly and still does not appear. Yet he concerns the King and us as the son of a man killed by Hamlet's father who is now in arms to recover 'lands lost by his father'. Before a word is uttered by or to Hamlet, Fortinbras thus supplies an instance of what the son of a dead father might do. The young man we come to next is in a different case; he seeks no more than leave 'to return to France'. But, when his suit is granted and then Hamlet's wish to go back to Wittenberg is opposed, these two are already set in contrast. Not less important, however, than the King's consent to Laertes' suit is the manner of his giving it. He is favourably inclined before he even knows what the suit is – because of what the throne of Denmark owes to Laertes' father;

Laertes is asked if he has his father's leave to go, and Polonius's single speech is to say that he has given it him. The one thing we shall remember from this little episode is that Polonius and Laertes are father and son. And this is what the next scene continues to impress on us when it dramatizes Laertes' actual departure. The son requests and twice receives his father's blessing, and is kept on stage before us by a famous speech of fatherly advice. The critics may debate whether Polonius's 'precepts' are wise or only meanly prudent, as also whether Claudius has shown himself a gracious monarch or only a smooth-tongued hypocrite; but what the theatre audience will be sure of is the matter of family relationships. Hence, in a play so firmly centred on a son's call to avenge his father, no one need be surprised, when Polonius is killed, that Laertes should reappear to avenge *him.*

It is less inevitable, though not therefore less significant, that Fortinbras again provides a prelude for him. Fortinbras arrives on the Danish stage for the first time in Act 4 scene 4, Laertes returns to it after a three-act absence in Act 4 scene 5. Now, as the plot gathers complications, these two, juxtaposed with Hamlet in the second scene of the play, are at length to move across his path. Ruth Nevo has recently observed how, in now bringing into 'effective prominence' the 'important contrast between the three avenging sons', *Hamlet* accords with a formal principle of Shakespearean tragedy whereby, after the hero's situation has reached its crisis in the third act, it is given significant perspective by means of ironic variations in the fourth.[3]

It is of course as unhesitant, unquestioning men of action that Fortinbras and Laertes both contrast with Hamlet. But (unlike the young men in an artificial comedy like *Love's Labour's Lost*) they complement rather than duplicate one another. The patterns of antithesis in which they figure are different and effected in different ways. First Hamlet watches Fortinbras leading his army to action and is given a long soliloquy to lament the comparison with himself. Fortinbras risks death for a 'fantasy' of honour while he himself in his so much more substantial cause – 'a father killed, a mother stained' – lets 'all sleep'. The sight of a prince stirred by 'divine' ambition, who 'Makes mouths at the invisible event', raises self-reproachful thoughts of the neglect of man's 'godlike reason' or the cowardice of heeding the 'event'. No such explicit comment is necessary to point the significance of Laertes. His situation of seeking vengeance for his father's death instead of the reconquest of his lands brings him closer to the hero, as the play indeed, by its order, seems to acknowledge; and his every word and gesture stresses by implication what Hamlet does not do. After Hamlet in the soliloquy on Fortinbras has impressed on us that his deed is still 'to do', Laertes bursts into the presence shouting 'Where is this king?' As he demands of the King himself, 'Give me my father ... How came he dead? ... I'll be revenged / Most throughly for my father', it can hardly fail to occur to us that this is such a challenge as Hamlet might have, but has not yet, made. Hamlet has reflected on the conscience that makes 'cowards of us all', but Laertes consigns conscience 'to the profoundest pit'; Hamlet knows how a man may quail in 'the dread of something after death', but Laertes dares 'damnation'. After Hamlet has failed to kill the King at prayer, Laertes boasts himself ready to cut his foe's throat in church. Even his noisiest rhetoric may be dramatically piquant:

> That drop of blood that's calm proclaims me bastard,
> Cries cuckold to my father, brands the harlot
> Even here between the chaste unsmirched brow
> Of my true mother.

For we can hardly hear Laertes speak these words without recalling that Hamlet could not say them. We have heard him accuse *his* mother of 'such an act' as 'sets a blister' on 'the fair forehead of an innocent love'.

～

This last instance may also serve to remind us that the antithetical pattern of revengers has at its foundation Hamlet's entire predicament and him in it. It is not wholly or simply a matter of contrasting characters, as criticism is a little liable to suggest. Bradley points out that among the characters in *Hamlet* we find 'two, Laertes and Fortinbras, who are evidently designed to throw the character of the hero into relief ', and adds that 'even in the situations there is a curious parallelism; for Fortinbras, like Hamlet, is the son of a king, lately dead, and succeeded by his brother; and Laertes, like Hamlet, has a father slain, and feels bound to avenge him'.[4] Yet this seems to place the emphasis the wrong way round. Shakespeare does not create characters to serve as foils to Hamlet and then devise situations to exhibit them. Nor is the parallelism of situation 'curious' (unless in the matter of Fortinbras's uncle); for without it Fortinbras and Laertes would have no *raison d'être*. It is as the sons of fathers who have been killed that they are brought into the play at all, and whatever characters they respectively acquire they acquire through the performance of their roles.

Neither of them figures of course in the story as it was told by Saxo and Belleforest. Whether or not they were Shakespeare's own invention is concealed from us by the failure of the older play about Hamlet to survive; the question is one which has elicited contradictory views.[5] I have my own opinion, which may later become apparent; but perhaps in a large perspective it does not supremely matter. What does is to see the play of *Hamlet*, as it takes shape in Shakespeare's imagination, with or without the assistance of some dramatist predecessor, acquiring both a principle of form and a significance of idea that the original story lacked. Yet, although the original story knew nothing of other sons than Hamlet, it could supply predicaments in which other sons could be placed. For Hamlet's father was not the only man in the story to be killed. There was the King of Norway overcome in armed combat, and there was the counsellor killed hiding in the Queen's chamber. For a dramatist intent on the theme of a son revenging his father it was an invention as economical as brilliant to allow these other slaughtered men to leave sons behind them too. But this means that the dramatist accepted for these new-created sons the situations which the story laid down for them in advance. It is not enough for us to say with Bradley that Fortinbras 'is the son of a king, lately dead' and that Laertes 'has a father slain, and feels bound to avenge him'. It is equally essential that Fortinbras's father was killed by Hamlet's father and that Laertes' father was killed by Hamlet himself. Certainly the situations of these other aggrieved sons will reflect Hamlet's and will give opportunity for those character contrasts which Shakespeare has so notably – and notedly – exploited; but it is not less important that Fortinbras and Laertes, if they are to come into the play at all, must enter it as Hamlet's enemies.

For Laertes in particular this destiny is inescapable. The dramatist who introduces him, so naturally yet so pointedly, as Polonius's son obviously knows that it will be his role to seek the hero's life. And this is a role which, once added to the story, must profoundly modify the hero's own. For it becomes Hamlet's role not only to call his uncle to account but to be called to account himself. The dramatic complexity of Hamlet's situation reflects the moral complexity of his being wronger as well as wronged. If criticism has insufficiently remarked this, it may be because Shakespeare's Hamlet, for all that he says about the revenge he is commanded to, is less explicit about the one that he must suffer. When he sees Laertes' cause as the image of his own, he does not add – though the play, through his quarrel with Laertes, does – that the image may be inverted. Yet when the body of Polonius is before him he clearly grasps his dual role:

> Heaven hath pleased it so,
> To punish me with this and this with me.

And it is a dual role which Shakespeare must have envisaged for him from the start. This, I venture to suggest, is what made him interesting to Shakespeare. For, instead of the orthodox comment that Laertes 'is put into the play to exhibit the primitive avenger Hamlet is temperamentally unfitted to be',[6] it might be nearer the truth to say that putting Laertes into the play unfits Hamlet to be the primitive avenger. Granted his dual role, he must acquire a dual nature as one capable of good and evil, and if the drama is to express this through the medium of his own speech he must become aware of it himself. So it is not entirely strange if he has much to say about the condition of man, 'crawling between earth and heaven', partaking of both god and beast. To define Hamlet's role is not of course – as it may be with Laertes – to define his character, the most discussed of all the characters of literature, still less to explain how this eloquent, profound, many-sided and enigmatic character grew in Shakespeare's mind. But the dual role I see as the genesis of Hamlet's character and this is where I think the clue to its understanding must lie.

~

The role of Laertes, then, though simple, is in its consequence dramatically momentous. That of Fortinbras is both less momentous and more ambiguous. Though the story offers him the role of a dead king's son, it puts him in a situation where he less faithfully images Hamlet. He seems to begin life, it is true, as the play's third avenging son, but he has important disqualifications for this part. His father's deathsman being already dead, unless he should pursue a vendetta against his son and heir, he lacks a personal antagonist; and of the three bereaved sons in the play he is the only one whose father met his death in honourable combat. Shakespeare no doubt recognized these drawbacks, and sought not to diminish but to capitalize them. Far from seeking to provide Fortinbras with a just grievance, he emphasizes that he had none. His father was defeated in fair fight and the 'pactes' which governed this in Belleforest become in Shakespeare 'a sealed compact / Well ratified by law and heraldry', which not only enhances King Hamlet's chivalry and valour but puts a would-be avenger quite firmly in the wrong. Nor is there any suggestion that Fortinbras might have sought redress for his father's defeat by a return contest with the victor's son. The aim allotted to Fortinbras is not to requite his father's death but to recover what he has forfeited. In Belleforest this was a treasure-ship; the shift to royal lands transforms what might have been a personal quarrel into a matter of armies and kingdoms. It is an important function of the Norwegian prince in Shakespeare to give an international background to the troubles of the Danish court. He becomes the foe less of Hamlet than of Denmark. Yet, if Fortinbras is thus not cast for such an avenger as Laertes was

inevitably to be, the circumstance that brings him into the play –
the combat between the kings – must still set the two princely
sons in opposition. If Norway is to leave a son behind him,
'young Fortinbras' will be the counterpart of 'young Hamlet'.
Shakespeare indeed matches them by the use of the same epithet
and invites us to compare them from the first.

Fortinbras has the dubious advantage over Laertes that his
father is already dead and he can begin his role at once. In fact,
though his actual appearance will be deferred till the fourth act,
within a hundred lines of the play's opening he is reported already
in action, his menace enhanced by being associated with the
'portentous figure' of the Ghost. His attempt to regain by force
what his father fairly lost is as dubious in its nature as its occasion:

> Young Fortinbras,
> Of unimproved mettle, hot and full,
> Hath in the skirts of Norway here and there
> Sharked up a list of lawless resolutes
> For food and diet to some enterprise
> That hath a stomach in't.

But, for all this disorderliness of unrestrained passion, the very
rashness of ungoverned youth has in it something not
unadmirable. In the 'mettle hot and full' there is a fiery spirit,
and the readiness for an 'enterprise' of 'stomach' betrays an
adventurous daring. This is something we shall remember when
all but two acts ahead the other prince, the hero of the play,
confesses himself 'a dull and muddy-mettled rascal', asks if he is 'a
coward' and decides he must be 'pigeon-livered'. Evidently when
describing Fortinbras's 'mettle' Shakespeare already had in mind
another who would be said to lack it. 'Dull' is precisely what his
father's ghost would warn Hamlet not to be –

> Duller shouldst thou be than the fat weed
> That roots itself in ease on Lethe wharf,
> Wouldst thou not stir in this.

Hamlet's exclamation that he is 'dull and muddy-mettled' is
provoked by the passion of the Player, not of Fortinbras, but

when at length he encounters Fortinbras with his army the occasion is again one to show up his 'dull' revenge. The contrast between the two princes, prepared for in the opening scene, is explicitly confirmed in Act 4.

Yet Fortinbras's enterprise, we notice, is not now the same. It is still a somewhat dubious one, risking thousands of men's lives for a minute piece of land not big enough to hold them. But it is not land lost by his father, of whom we have ceased to hear. Fortinbras's story has turned out a strange one. For after Denmark has sent ambassadors to Norway in the first act and they have returned home in the second, his threat to Denmark is over and his forces are safely diverted against Poland. So all he requires of Denmark now, instead of the return of his father's lands, is 'quiet pass' across Danish territory en route to his new foe; and accordingly when he actually appears in Act 4 he is on his way to Poland and 'craves' of the Danish king the 'promised march' over his kingdom. All this is perfectly coherent and consistent with itself. What is not dramatically consistent is that the menace of Fortinbras's 'lawless resolutes' in the first scene should create an expectation that fails to be fulfilled. Why so much about the danger of invasion if so little was to come of it? Is it even consistent on the level of verisimilitude for there to be, day and night, seven days a week, a 'sweaty haste' of casting cannon and building ships if a formal embassy to Norway was enough to get the invasion called off? Surely more was purposed by those warlike preparations than the substantiation of Fortinbras's 'mettle'. Does it not look as though, even between the first scene which describes the preparations and the second in which the embassy is dispatched, Shakespeare had somewhat modified his plan? Can it be that the troops who ultimately do no more than march across Denmark were originally designed to do battle?

It seems also worth remarking that, when they were at their most threatening in the opening scene, nothing was heard of Fortinbras's uncle, the reigning King of Norway. He is first mentioned in the second scene when Claudius appeals to him to suppress his nephew's escapade (to name it by what it now seems to have shrunk to). Others besides Bradley have pointed to this uncle on the throne of Norway as completing the correspondence between Fortinbras's position and Hamlet's and have supposed him created for that end. But it might conceivably have been that Denmark's reigning uncle suggested a parallel for Norway not so much to balance the Norwegian prince with Hamlet as to provide a means of extricating him from an enterprise that had already gone too far for the drama's unfolding plan. This is not something to feel sure of, since the opening account of Fortinbras finding his desperadoes in the 'skirts' or outlying parts of Norway certainly does not regard *him* as a reigning monarch, so that it leaves the way for his uncle open. On the other hand, it is sometimes pointed out that if the dead Fortinbras forfeited literally 'all those his lands / Which he stood seized of ', there should be no king of Norway at all.[7] This too is not a point that I should wish to press; for Shakespeare, had he meant that, might have referred to the lost lands as the Norwegian kingdom, and he did not. 'All' may derive from Belleforest, who applies it, however, to the treasure (*toutes les richesses*) in the king's ship; the difficulty arises through transferring the forfeit to lands. It is not one that is likely to have occurred to Shakespeare, who could hardly have foreseen the arguments which might be based upon a single emphatic phrase, when what clearly matters to the play is not the specification of the lands but their sufficiency as a motive for Fortinbras's filial 'enterprise'.

There still remains, however, the discrepancy between the fear his enterprise occasions in the opening scene and the ease of its suppression. Something that begins by being important to the action of the play is subsequently not. And it is at least a little unexpected that the young prince 'of unimproved mettle hot and full' should turn out to be so docile. His bedridden uncle has only to learn what he is up to and 'he, in brief, obeys, / Receives rebuke from Norway', and promises never more to take up arms against Denmark. It is not the less surprising in that this meek and easily swayed youth is not only a fearless leader but a very capable army officer – as appears from his being able to transform his desperadoes, the 'lawless resolutes' he 'sharked up', into a perfectly disciplined force. When the time comes for them to pass across the stage and the kingdom of Denmark, nothing could better the decorum with which they respect the terms of their licence. Fortinbras has only to say 'Go softly on' to command their ordered and silent obedience, though Granville-Barker is the only critic I have found to remark on this.[8]

And yet the dangerously hot-mettled youth of the opening scene has not been allowed to vanish. The fourth act gives indeed a rather terrifying description of him in Shakespeare's favourite image for rebellion:

> The ocean, overpeering of his list,
> Eats not the flats with more impetuous haste
> Than young Laertes, in a riotous head,
> O'erbears your officers.

And his 'lawless resolutes' are still with him, 'the rabble' who call him lord. Heedless of all precedent and tradition upon which a stable society must be based – 'Antiquity forgot, custom not known' – they reject even their legal sovereign, crying, 'Choose we! Laertes shall be king.' And the doors of the palace 'are broke'.

What has happened, then, is that the 'lawless resolutes' originally sharked up by Fortinbras have been switched to Laertes. That Shakespeare, for whatever reason, has modified his initial plan I do not think it possible to dispute.

Fortinbras is still able to fulfil part of the role for which he was created. He still has his army and his enterprise, and the enterprise, although a new one, is still one which defies rational justification, as Hamlet does not forbear to remark. As the dauntless man of action he is still available for the designed contrast with the inactive self-questioning hero, in which he still exhibits the paradox of a man of a daring spirit in a dubious undertaking. The peculiar subtlety of the contrast lies in an ambivalence too often unperceived – as by critics who cannot allow Hamlet and Shakespeare to think that something not fine in itself may yet be finely pursued – and it may be thought to gain in subtlety now that Fortinbras, instead of an irregular adventurer heading a disorderly uprising, has become a 'delicate and tender prince' conducting a well-disciplined campaign. But now that he no longer fights for his father's lands, he has quite ceased to be an avenger and almost even a son; and the part of his role which made him the warring foe of Denmark has ended with its initial menace.

It may be that Shakespeare came to see that the play would not have room for such embroilments. But I suspect that the cause of the change was deeper. For it might well seem that the threat to peace would come more appropriately from within Denmark than without. At any rate, the role of revenger, for which Fortinbras was never perfectly suited, is more capably filled by Laertes, groomed for it from the outset, as soon as events are ready for him to take it over. And if he takes over with it the menace of insurrection, is it not because this comes to be seen as belonging to the revenger's role? At least we are given a glimpse, when the Danes rise in support of Laertes, of what they might have done for Hamlet and of what the dangers of action could be. It is true that the rebellion, for one that 'looks so giant-like', is very soon over; so that Granville-Barker found it 'not in itself very convincing' and decided that Shakespeare avoided 'enlarging the play's action' lest 'wider issues' should detract from the personal conflict.[9] Yet it is surely rather to be remarked that the rebellion, though short-lived, does happen and has a formidable appearance for the moment that it lasts. The persistence of this motif, even when it was shed by Fortinbras with whom it began, suggests that it was one Shakespeare was not willing to relinquish. We shall not be prying too curiously, I submit, if we perceive that at some level of his mind the idea of armed rebellion would not dissociate itself from the Hamlet story; and it cannot but be, I think, that, even while the play presents revenge as a bounden duty to which Hamlet's whole nature must commit him, Shakespeare also saw it as striking at the roots of civil order.

It may also be remarked that rebellion calls forth an assured reminder, though staggeringly ironic from Claudius, of the divinity that 'doth hedge a king'; and, more significantly, that at the very centre of the play, when 'The Mousetrap' has brought home to Claudius his danger and he is arranging to pack Hamlet off to England, there occurs that strangely resonant speech, from the unlikely lips of Rosencrantz, about 'the cease of majesty', describing how the death of a king, reverberating through innumerable lesser lives, brings them to 'boisterous ruin'.[10] These are sentiments more expected in the history plays, from which they may seem little more than a survival. Yet they have their relevance in a tragedy which holds one king under threat of death for the death he gave to another king, and they suggest what vibrations may be set up in the mind by the story of Hamlet's revenge for the murder of his father.

～

Fortinbras's role as we now have it links him inseparably with Poland; and this raises a further question. The political geography of the play embraces a good part of northern Europe, and, although Poland is kept well in the background, its connection with the action is precise. We recall that it was against 'the Polack' that Fortinbras's uncle supposed his nephew's forces were directed; that, once he discovered they were not, he took care that they should be, even to the securing for them of safe passage across Denmark; and that accordingly, when Fortinbras at length appears, he is marching against Poland, just as it is from Poland that he arrives back in Denmark at the end. The Polack as well as we seems to have been well warned of the attack, for he had already garrisoned the disputed 'patch of ground'; and he therefore shares the infection of the political disease upon which Hamlet comments. It is his dramatic function to be a party in Fortinbras's war. But was this the function the drama first envisaged for him, or, when the role of Fortinbras underwent a change, did that of Poland change with it?

The question is not an impertinent one, for, apart from the fact that it was not Fortinbras's first intention, nor surely Shakespeare's either, to take those 'lawless resolutes' to Poland, there is an initial reference to the Poles, very early in the play, which attaches them to quite a different action. It occurs of course in Horatio's account of Hamlet's father directly after the first appearance of the Ghost:

So frowned he once, when in an angry parle
He smote the sledded Polacks on the ice.

These lines have proved controversial; it is said that one does not deal blows in parley, and the Polacks themselves, through the spelling of the substantive texts (*pollax*) and a Fourth Folio emendation, have sometimes been turned into a poleaxe. But contemporary accounts show that in the marshy parts of Lithuania, which was then a part of Poland, the inhabitants regularly travelled in winter in horse-drawn sledges over the frozen pools. Clearly the smiting of the Polacks was a valiant exploit of King Hamlet's like that of his combat against 'Norway' with which the dialogue couples it. Almost at once the play goes on to a fuller narrative of the combat against Norway; and one might not unreasonably look for a similar elaboration later of its companion exploit. It is true that the Norwegian episode derives – with or without the intermediacy of the lost play – from Belleforest, who supplies no equivalent for the Polacks; yet, whether it came to Shakespeare from some undiscovered source or lay in his own invention, some incident of a battle on the ice had a vivid if momentary lodging in his imagination. This is as much as one can say for certain; more may be idle surmise. Yet if the incident did hold potentialities for development, the play itself, though it chose not to exploit them, may suggest what some of them were. If initial symmetry were kept, the threat of attack from Norway might have been matched by another from Poland – until the play by a neat device set them against one another instead; and young Fortinbras, seeking to recover the lands his father lost, might have had a counterpart in a Polack son attempting retaliation for the smiting on the ice. If any such possibility in fact occurred to Shakespeare, it must have been dismissed as early as the second scene, when the sending of ambassadors to Norway prepares for the switch of Fortinbras's campaign and when the introduction of the son of the counsellor who is destined to be killed by Hamlet shows the play's clear recognition of who its second revenger must be. Yet has anyone ever satisfactorily explained why Shakespeare chose for this counsellor a name which to any Elizabethan would inevitably connect him with Poland, or, as they used to call it, Polonia? Attempts to find an original for him in some Polonian figure outside the play have not been so obviously successful as to rule out the alternative, and perhaps more natural, possibility, that Polonius's name arose in Shakespeare's mind because something associated him there with the Poland of the play.

$\sim$

The counsellor and his son, as they appear in the play, even when Laertes has attracted Fortinbras's 'lawless resolutes' to him, are characters still in one piece, as Fortinbras is not. Once we have seen that his role changes from that of a hot-headed insurrectionary to that of a dignified soldier prince, it becomes almost absurd to discuss him as if he were a single coherent person. Yet even Granville-Barker, while observing his new courtesy, supposes that the expedition to Poland will prove his 'unimproved mettle'. L.C. Knights in condemning this Polish expedition makes a point of its being undertaken by 'the same Fortinbras who, earlier in the play, had "shark'd up a list of lawless resolutes" to regain the land lost by his father'; Harold Fisch sees him risking death in Poland with 'devil-may-care impetuosity'; and Kenneth Muir insists that Hamlet's 'delicate and tender prince', having 'secretly mustered a band of soldiers, who seem little better than brigands', is really a 'barbarous adventurer' all the time.[11] Eleanor Prosser goes still further in relating Fortinbras's character to a coherence of design: she maintains that by introducing him as 'a brash and inexperienced young hothead' Shakespeare has carefully prepared us to see him and his Polish campaign 'in their true light', which will show them as 'completely amoral'. Perhaps it is no wonder that she finds 'matter for alarm' when he returns to Denmark, and can 'see no hope' for the country when he succeeds to the throne.[12] But Miss Prosser is hardly accurate in contending that Fortinbras 'has no rights' in the kingdom; for, when the play's last scene allows him to say that he has, we cannot use its first scene to disprove this. The play has only neglected to explain what his rights are, apparently not having foreseen that he would need them. What we can, and surely must, say is that the reckless and lawless youth of the opening scene could not have had the dying Hamlet's vote, nor Shakespeare's, and was not meant to have it. But in Fortinbras's subsequent role as a commander not reckless nor lawless, but calm, well governed and well obeyed, efficient and victorious, Shakespeare has discovered for him the yet further role of a ruler to whom Denmark may safely be left.

It would be interesting to know precisely when the idea came to him for Fortinbras's final role. It must, I think, have been emerging when Hamlet was allowed to perceive, what his critics still do not, the paradoxical greatness of the prince who campaigned for a straw. That Shakespeare must have seen by that stage that there would be little competition – for it was hardly a role for Horatio – does not make his election of Fortinbras a less felicitous act of opportunism. The choice does involve, however, yet another shift for Fortinbras in the dramatic pattern. For even the designed contrast between his 'mettle' and the hero's, prepared for on his first introduction and confirmed in their fourth-act encounter, has all but disappeared in the mutual esteem whereby Fortinbras receives Hamlet's 'dying voice' and in return pronounces his funeral tribute.

Laertes, unlike Fortinbras, enacts in the play's last scene the role for which he was intended from the beginning. Coming into the play as Polonius's son, he was as revenger to be Hamlet's image but also and ineluctably his enemy. It is the coming together, in league against the hero, of the two opposite antagonists, the man his vengeance seeks and the man whose vengeance seeks him, that gives the catastrophe its subtlety, though this again is a subtlety, like that of Hamlet's dual role which causes it, too often overlooked. A typical comment is that of R.A. Law: 'The protagonist here meets and personally overcomes both of his villainous antagonists. One of these villains repents and is forgiven in dying; the chief villain dies unmourned.'[13] As Claudius's accomplice, matching his principal's stratagem of the unbated sword with a venom of his own procuring, Laertes no doubt deserves to be called a villain – how else could we tolerate a tragedy in which the hero, having already killed his father, now kills him? But what the critic fails to observe is the distinction the play makes between the villains, of which the repentance and forgiveness of one of them is the token. Moreover Hamlet not only overcomes; he is also overcome – by the villain he has called his 'brother'; and Laertes is not only forgiven; in dying he also forgives:

> Exchange forgiveness with me, noble Hamlet.
> Mine and my father's death come not upon thee.

The words in which Hamlet is forgiven remind one of the wrong he has done: his responsibility for a 'father's death' is recalled just as his own father's murderer is dying at his hands.

Laertes, as the son of his father, finally fulfils his role by helping Hamlet to fulfil his. But Fortinbras, who also began as the son of his father, has moved through a series of changes to a very different status. In one thing he is constant: for his various roles all present him in a martial character, which ultimately unites the fiery mettle of his beginning with the superb decorum of his final speech. Shakespeare is a deep and far-sighted planner; he is also a brilliant improviser. He appears in both roles in *Hamlet*, and both of them contribute to the fine artistry of its ending.

10

HAMLET AND THE FISHMONGER

POLONIUS
Do you know me, my lord?
HAMLET
Excellent well, you are a fishmonger.

(2.2.173–4)

Hamlet's famous retort to Polonius has confounded Shakespeare's commentators almost as much as it did Polonius. Some of the greatest of them, from Coleridge to Kittredge, have shown themselves baffled by it; and, in spite of numerous conjectures, its true significance in the play has never yet been explained.[1]

The most obvious function of this retort is to exhibit Hamlet's madness. Notwithstanding all that we have heard of this, we have not yet seen it for ourselves; so that, when the Queen announces that 'the poor wretch comes' and Polonius prepares to 'board' him, our mounting expectation will have to be fulfilled. For Hamlet to call the self-important counsellor of state a fishmonger is, as Kittredge put it in the notes to his edition, 'the very maddest thing that he could say'. And that is how it seems to strike Polonius:

He knew me not at first, a said I was a fishmonger, a is far gone.
(2.2.189–90)

For Kittredge this would seem to be enough. He disdains attempts to discover 'an occult sense', insisting that 'the remark is, in fact, merely a bit of Hamlet's pretended insanity'. Yet after a little more of Hamlet's talk Polonius comes to the opinion that, 'though this be madness, yet there is method in't'. Observing 'how pregnant sometimes his replies are', he acknowledges 'a happiness that often madness hits on which reason and sanity could not so prosperously be delivered of ' (2.2.208–14). The dramatist thus gives a hint, through Polonius's lips, of what he is about: he is using Hamlet's mad talk to glance at things which rational and connected discourse is unable to express. Instances of such 'happiness' need not be confined to those Polonius notices himself: once given the hint, we may naturally suspect in the word 'fishmonger' – Kittredge notwithstanding – a clue to some deeper meaning. I believe that, correctly understood, it connects with a fundamental motif of the play.

It is important not to let the fishmonger supply us with red herrings, and it may be as well to begin by reviewing some of the favourite interpretations hitherto. What Coleridge found in 'You are a fishmonger' was no more than an accusation of fishing: 'You are sent to *fish* out the secret', in his gloss. It is true that such fishing *is* Polonius's purpose; but there are two objections to accepting this as 'Hamlet's meaning'. Fishing, as has been pertinently remarked, is not what a fishmonger, a seller of fish, does; and, if it were, then to call Polonius a fishmonger would not exceed 'reason and sanity'. It would hardly suggest that the speaker was 'far gone'. It is necessary to insist on this, since in a recent number of *Notes and Queries* Coleridge's interpretation has been reasserted.[2] The writer there concedes that a fishmonger is not the same as a fisherman, but notes that the Wardens of the Fishmongers' Company denounced certain butchers to the Privy Council for selling meat in Lent and makes the astonishing inference that a fishmonger for Hamlet is 'someone who spies out secrets'. The observance of Lent was of course a matter in which fishmongers had direct concern: fasting days were not merely meatless days but fish-days, as indeed they were often called, and officers of the Fishmongers' Company who objected when fish-days were not kept were doing no more than their proper duty in protecting the interests of their trade. This can give no warrant for supposing that a fishmonger was, or was thought of as, a spy.

Nevertheless the context of the word in *Hamlet* suggests some equivocation. The dialogue continues:

> ... you are a fishmonger.

POLONIUS

> Not I, my lord.

HAMLET

> Then I would you were so honest a man.

(2.2.174–6)

And this second retort is as unexpected as the first; for what seemed to be a gibe is now turned to commendation, as a witty shift of meaning substitutes the literal sense of *fishmonger* for whatever else *fishmonger* might be taken to imply. A fishmonger, in the plain sense of the word, pursues an honest trade; but to make a point of this suggests that there is some doubt to dispel and hence implies that honest in another sense is what a fishmonger in another sense is not. There is an innuendo of sexual licence. Malone accordingly pointed out that *fishmonger* 'was a cant term for a *wencher*', citing in support *The Irish Hubbub* by Barnabe Riche (1617). There the author, satirizing whoremasters, wants to laugh 'especially at him that they call *Senex Fornicator*, an old Fishmonger, that many yeares since ingrost the French pox'.[3] This meaning, therefore, unlike that of one who spies or fishes, is established by a very clear example. It had a pretty good innings in nineteenth-century annotation; and assuredly if, when Hamlet says 'You are a fishmonger', we see Polonius as a wencher, this will enhance the joke at his expense.

What it will not do, however, is add point to the dialogue which follows. From honesty, in a double sense, Hamlet leads us to carrion, also in a double sense, and so to Polonius's daughter. And, while the sexual allusions intensify and thicken, it is not on Polonius's venery that they focus:

> ... I would you were so honest a man.

POLONIUS

> Honest, my lord?

HAMLET

Ay sir, to be honest as this world goes is to be one man
picked out of ten thousand.

POLONIUS

That's very true, my lord.

HAMLET

For if the sun breed maggots in a dead dog, being a good
kissing carrion – Have you a daughter?

POLONIUS

I have, my lord.

HAMLET

Let her not walk i'th' sun. Conception is a blessing; but as
your daughter may conceive – Friend, look to't.

(2.2.176–87)

The sexual proclivities that Hamlet's mind is running on are not
those of Polonius but of Polonius's daughter, and Polonius
appears to interest Hamlet through his power to help or hinder
these. Tieck thought Hamlet was taunting Polonius with making
opportunities for his daughter;[4] and, by analogy with the literal
sense of *fishmonger* as a supplier of fish for others' use, a
figurative sense has been postulated in which a fishmonger
supplies women. Though this goes beyond anything the context
can be said clearly to imply, that Hamlet, in calling Polonius a
fishmonger, is calling him a bawd or pander, is now the standard
explanation.

A brief but important article by M.A. Shaaber,[5] investigating
the evidence for this interpretation, attributes it to a note in Sir
Edmund Chambers's edition of the play for the Warwick
Shakespeare in 1894. This says, though without evidence,
'"Fishmonger" may be used in a sense which it appears
sometimes to bear, of a seller of women's chastity ... Hamlet
seems to suggest that Polonius would willingly make a market of
his daughter.' Tieck had already equated 'fishmonger' with
'fleshmonger', in its sense of 'pander' (German *Kuppler*), and one
might guess that it was the nineteenth-century German critics
who gave Chambers the idea. However that may be, his 'possible

explanation', becoming more positive, as these things will, in subsequent editors, was taken up and insisted on by Dover Wilson,[6] with the result that it is now regularly stated as a fact. Professor Shaaber cites three editions of the sixties – to which at least one more could be added[7] – which gloss *fishmonger* without question as a 'bawd' or 'procurer'. It may be as well to get clear that Shaaber has not, as the writer in *Notes and Queries* declares, 'conclusively refuted' this interpretation, nor sought to. What he has done is to show that the meaning has not been conclusively established, a somewhat different matter: the examples which have been used to demonstrate it in fact do not.

It is a respected method of lexicography to establish the meaning of a word through illustrations of its use. But the technique of Shakespearean annotation has too often been to use this method like a shotgun. A number of instances of a word's use are fired off indiscriminately in the hope that one or more will hit the mark. And if the report is loud enough one may easily persuade oneself, and others too, that this indeed has happened. Thus Dover Wilson, in the note which Shaaber has examined, brings together the passage from Riche's *Irish Hubbub* which shows *fishmonger* being used for whoremaster and a passage from the same author's *Herodotus* in which harlots are referred to as fish; adds two episodes allegedly about a fisherman's daughter, though one in fact is not while the other is about a fishmonger's daughter who apparently bore her husband's child; and on the strength of these allusions declares that a 'fishmonger's daughter' is therefore a prostitute and a 'fishmonger' a bawd. Professor Shaaber's demolition of this evidence is complete; the task need not be repeated, though a comment or two may be added.

In Middleton's *Anything for a Quiet Life*, which Dover Wilson misremembered, the fishmonger we hear of is not the French bawd's father but the father she invents for a young Englishman who needs to conceal his identity. That the fishmonger has to be a French one permits a joke about his selling poisons (*poissons*) (3.2.96–100); but it seems likely from the build-up of the dialogue that this linguistic mix-up merely adds a bonus to what would have been a joke in any case. It is sometimes easier to see that there was a joke about a fishmonger than to see what exactly the joke was, though with the knowledge that a fishmonger could mean a wencher we shall not always need to look further.

Of all the instances cited the one that comes nearest to suggesting that a fishmonger might mean a bawd is one that does not use the word *fishmonger* at all. Barnabe Riche in his translation of Herodotus (1584) speaks of 'such arrant honest women as are fishe for every man';[8] and the irony in *honest*, the context, and the original Greek (ἑταιραι) leave no doubt that Riche is talking about harlots. Yet what makes the women harlots in the English is that they are available 'for every man'; it does not inevitably follow that the word *fish* by itself could bear this meaning. It is possible, and perhaps probable, that *fish* could, then as in a later age, refer to that which a woman has and a man desires;[9] and, if that were once accepted, then a purveyor of such fish, as Shaaber concedes, could well be called a fishmonger. But to see how this might happen is not to say that it did. All *mongers* are not purveyors: a *whoremonger* is not. I believe this is the relevant analogy and that a *fishmonger*, in the sense of a dealer in women, was one who was concerned with his own use and not sale. We are thus brought back to the whoremaster of Riche's *Irish Hubbub* and Malone's 'wencher'. No evidence is forthcoming that the word *fishmonger* in itself had further sexual connotations. One is left with the suspicion that the equation of a fishmonger with a bawd is no more than a conjecture derived from the very passage in *Hamlet* which it purports to elucidate. Yet Dover Wilson makes this meaning the basis of his interpretation of the whole Hamlet-and-Ophelia plot. He asks himself 'why Hamlet should suddenly call Polonius a bawd and his daughter a prostitute – for that', he says, 'is what it all amounts to'; and he finds an explanation, where Tieck had found one before him, in Polonius's scheme to use his daughter to waylay Hamlet. Assuming therefore that Hamlet must have been aware of the scheme, he leaps to the conclusion that he must have overheard it and even invents a stage direction to enable him to do so.[10] I have argued elsewhere that such a supposition violates the Elizabethan dramatic convention by which characters who overhear make plain that they have done so;[11] and one may add that it mistakes the 'method' of Hamlet's madness and of the play's dramatic irony. We are all in Dover Wilson's debt for bringing to the surface some undercurrents of this dialogue: Hamlet's injunction 'Let her not walk i'th' sun' has a particular point when Polonius has just proposed to do precisely that by 'loosing' his daughter to the son (and sun) of Denmark. But this is Shakespeare's irony, not Hamlet's, and it is there for the audience, not Hamlet, to perceive. Perhaps the most fatal objection to Dover Wilson's explanation is that it makes Hamlet all too rational and sane. He would not have to be mad, or to seem mad, in order to call Polonius a bawd for tricking him into an assignation. The 'happiness' which madness 'hits on' will depend on a less logical thought process: we must be alert to more recondite connections.

One thing the dialogue has shown us is that Hamlet's interest in the conduct of Polonius is subordinate to his interest in Polonius's daughter. His calling Polonius 'a fishmonger' leads to some 'harping' on the daughter; and perhaps the question we should be asking is not so much how 'fishmonger' applies to Polonius as what it has to do with the daughter. It will be useful therefore to recall that among the passages cited in attempts to illumine this dialogue is one that refers specifically to 'a fishmonger's daughter'. It is a passage first cited by Walter Whiter and it is from Ben Jonson's *Christmas His Masque*, in which Venus says:

> I am *Cupids* Mother ... hee is a pretty Child, though I say it that perhaps should not ... I had him by my first Husband ... he came a moneth before his time, and that may make him somewhat imperfect: But I was a Fishhmongers daughter.[12]

As Shaaber remarks, this is very dubious evidence for supposing that a fishmonger's daughter meant a prostitute; indeed, having a child by one's husband has little enough to do with either whores or bawds. The characteristic of a fishmonger's daughter, it seems, is her readiness to give birth; and if commentators had not been looking so fixedly for bawds they might have seen the relevance of this to the daughter of a man who has just been called a fishmonger and is warned against letting her conceive. This Whiter at least observed, and it enabled him to infer 'that some opinion prevailed, which induced Hamlet, who is *still harping* on the *daughter* of Polonius, to mistake the father for a *Fishmonger*'. Happily ignoring the difference between Shakespeare's concern with conception and Jonson's with delivery, Whiter added the conjecture, 'Probably it was supposed that the daughters of these tradesmen, who dealt in so nourishing a species of food, were *blessed* with extraordinary powers of *conception*.' We may have our reservations about whether Hamlet did in fact 'mistake the father', and Whiter's guess about the cause of the daughter's fertility was astray; but he saw that her fertility was the crux of the matter, and thus presented his successors with the clue which, in their preoccupation with wenchers, bawds and prostitutes, they have strangely failed to follow up.

That this is indeed the clue is confirmed by another Elizabethan allusion which Dowden cites in an old Arden note, though apparently without recognition of its bearing and again without effect on later commentators. The necessarily condensed nature of Dowden's note may be responsible for its neglect, but, if we follow his direction to *The Jewel House of Art and Nature* (1594) by Sir Hugh Platt, we shall find there an account of the properties of salt, and in it this very remarkable passage:

> Salt doth greatlie further procreation, for it doth not onely stir vp lust, but it doth also minister fruitfulnesse. And therefore the Egyptians did vse to feed their bitches with salte meates, when they found them vnapt for generation. And Plutarch doth witnesse, that ships vpon the seas are pestred and poisoned oftetimes, with exceeding store of mice. And some hold opinion, that the females without any copulation with the males, doe conceiue only by licking of salt. And this maketh the Fishmongers Wiues so wanton, and so beautifull.[13]

The fishmongers' wives here seem to enter in a non sequitur. For, if copulation is superfluous, it cannot be necessary for them to stir desire by their beauty nor to gratify it by their wantonness. But 'this maketh' is ambiguous: the fundamental sequence of ideas is from the effect of salt, and hence of sea-water, upon fertility to the manifestation of this effect in mice on the one hand and fishmongers' wives on the other. That the effect in the one case is to dispense with and in the other to encourage copulation is no doubt inconsistent; but it will not disguise that the essential point about fishmongers' wives is their propensity to breed. No mention is made of fishmongers' daughters, and I am not clear whether *wives* is used in its limited modern sense or in the older sense of 'women'; but, since the effect is due to the salt sea-water and is found in women associated with the fish trade, there is obviously no reason why it should not extend to fishmongers' daughters; and the passage quoted from Jonson is evidence of a belief that it did. If we set the passages from Jonson and Platt side by side and discount their difference in particulars – the difference between wives and daughters, between readiness to mate and to give birth – we observe that common to both is the supposition that the womenfolk of fishmongers have a special aptitude for procreation.

The passages thus reinforce one another, and, though other illustrations would be welcome, these two are enough to demonstrate what Shakespeare must have had in mind when he made Hamlet say 'You are a fishmonger' and then 'Have you a daughter?' Though the point has been lost to centuries of comment, there can surely be no doubt that Platt and Jonson and the contemporaries for whom they wrote would have picked it up at once.

The crucial test of an interpretation is its fitness to the context. The significance we can now attach to the fishmonger's daughter makes sense of the relations between Hamlet and Ophelia as no other meaning does. To quote Dover Wilson's words about his different solution, it 'enables us for the first time to see these relations in proper perspective and as a connected whole'.[14]

In its immediate context the question Hamlet put to the 'fishmonger' – 'Have you a daughter?' – has the seeming abruptness of the mad. Yet the question is directly preceded by thoughts of kissing and breeding. These are things associated with 'carrion', whether a dead dog or a woman, and they are things to which a fishmonger's daughter, it appears, was believed to be unusually prone. The example of the sun and the dead dog gives the idea of mating and breeding an extremely disgusting form, which prompts a warning to the fishmonger of what his daughter should be protected from: 'As your daughter may conceive – Friend, look to't.' He must keep her away from the sun – her apparent source of danger, whether from its literal effect upon carrion or through its figurative allusion to the prince of the realm. That this advice is offered just when Polonius has proposed to 'loose' his daughter 'to him' is an irony that Hamlet can be in no position to appreciate; but, though he cannot be supposed to know what Polonius is planning, he does of course know perfectly well who Polonius is. In saying, 'He knew me not at first, a said I was a fishmonger', Polonius is ironically and characteristically mistaken. For Hamlet recognizes in him the father of the woman he might marry; and it is an imagination that dwells on her as a potential mate, all too liable to conceive and breed, that sees her father as a fishmonger. An association of ideas is clear; but it is not one that 'reason and sanity' determine. It has the character of obsession. Whether we think of Hamlet as mad, or only seeming or affecting to be mad, will ultimately make no difference.

In the larger context of the play this interpretation is equally illuminating. After Hamlet has seen Ophelia's father as a fishmonger, he hails him on their next encounter as 'Jephthah, judge of Israel' (2.2.422), and for a comparable reason. For Jephthah too was noted for having a 'fair daughter', as Hamlet reminds us by quoting a snatch of a popular ballad. ('Still on my daughter,' Polonius remarks.) And Jephthah's daughter is also one with a significant sexual legend. Yet, whereas the fishmonger had to be warned against letting his daughter go into the sun, what the Bible tells us about Jephthah is that in fulfilment of a vow he consigned his daughter to death.[15] And before she went to her death, instead of conceiving and breeding, she could only bewail her virginity. Through her Hamlet raises the same question as with the fishmonger's daughter while presenting a converse instance.

Which of these alternative figures is to be the emblem of Ophelia's lot is a matter which obsesses Hamlet's mind as revealed through his dialogues with her father. The approach to it by way of the fishmonger and Jephthah with their contrasting daughters has a pleasing symmetry as it prepares us for the encounter with Polonius's daughter herself. When Hamlet confronts Ophelia the crucial questions, already voiced obliquely, will be put to her directly:

Are you honest? ...
Are you fair? ...

(3.1.103–5)

We recall that fishmongers' wives did not conjoin these qualities. They combined beauty with wantonness, which is exactly what Hamlet would expect: 'The power of beauty will sooner transform honesty from what it is to a bawd than the force of honesty can translate beauty into his likeness' (3.1.111–13). At length he comes to the climactic question:

Wouldst thou be a breeder of sinners?

(3.1.122)

This question, introduced with an expostulatory 'Why', is in the nature of a protest. It comes straight upon Ophelia's confession that she has believed in Hamlet's love, and, with what it implies about the consequence of love, it indicates the character of Hamlet's recoil. What he is recoiling from is sexuality and generation, all that goes to the breeding of sinners. He sees Ophelia confronted with a choice between being the fishmonger's daughter or Jephthah's, and he makes the choice for her himself when he bids her get her to a nunnery and declares there shall be no more marriage.

This is the true significance of Ophelia's role in the play. It has often been misunderstood – as by those who suppose that Ophelia jilted or failed Hamlet or that he turned on her because she repelled his love-addresses and lent herself to her father's stratagem. It has often been found obscure: Bradley questioned 'whether from the mere text of the play a sure interpretation' could 'be drawn'.[16] And obscurity has even been held a virtue – by those who have praised Shakespeare for 'deliberately' leaving

Ophelia 'a problem'[17] and have found her 'vague and ambiguous' story a source of the play's attractiveness.[18] Yet I believe that, if we grasp the significance of what Hamlet says, his attitude to Ophelia, and the reasons for it, are quite plain.

One reason for Hamlet's antipathy to marriage the critics have regularly stressed. He has the example of his mother, who has made 'marriage vows / As false as dicers' oaths' (3.4.44–5). It is an example which Ophelia must not follow – although, since woman is identical with Frailty and beauty perverts chastity, he is more than fearful that she may. Yet his antipathy to marriage has another and still more essential aspect. Marriage sanctifies the instinct towards life and procreation, and this conflicts with Hamlet's yearning for release from the defilement of the flesh. His first soliloquy bemoans 'the uses of this world', entirely given over to 'things rank and gross in nature', and wishes God had not forbidden 'self-slaughter' (1.2.129–37); and in the soliloquy which comes near the mid-point of the play – and just before his encounter with Ophelia – he is still longing for an end to 'the heart-ache and the thousand natural shocks / That flesh is heir to' (3.1.61–4). The obverse of this death-wish is his revulsion from whatever would promote and perpetuate life. And this is expressed with some intensity in Hamlet's rejection of Ophelia's love, and of his own. Bradley held it 'essential to Shakespeare's purpose that too great an interest should not be aroused in the love-story' lest it should 'interfere with' more important interests.[19] Yet, far from interfering, the love-story is the brilliant means by which one aspect of the play's main theme is dramatized. Hamlet's inability to meet life's challenge, his reluctance to act out the part that life requires of him, is shown not least in his recoil from mating and procreation, his abhorrence of conception and breeding. This is an extremely important motif in the play and may be seen beginning when Hamlet calls Polonius a fishmonger.

11

HOW MANY GRAVEDIGGERS
HAS *HAMLET?*

The point about the children of Lady Macbeth is that they do not come into the play and are no concern of ours. The same is not true of those characters in *Hamlet* who, to quote A.W. Verity, 'are commonly described in criticisms of *Hamlet*' as 'Grave-diggers'.[1] These, minor figures though they are, have their indispensable moment when they are in possession of the stage, and every editor and every producer of the play needs to make up his mind about them.

How many gravediggers then are there? Every schoolboy knows the answer to be two, and on this point, if no other, most scholars would allow him to be right. It is the answer he will get if he consults such a work of reference as, say, F.G. Stokes, *A Dictionary of the Characters and Proper Names in the Works of Shakespeare* (1924): 'Grave-diggers (*Haml.*) See CLOWNS, TWO.' 'Clowns, Two ... *Haml.* (Grave-diggers.) v, 1.' And this answer is not only confirmed by long stage tradition but by a glance at the lists of dramatis personae in such standard editions as the Cambridge, Variorum (Furness), Arden (Dowden), Oxford (Craig), Yale, Kittredge and Alexander. That it is still accepted by the best modern textual scholarship appears from Sir Walter Greg, *The Shakespeare First Folio*, which, quoting the stage direction '*Enter two Clownes*', explains 'i.e. the Gravediggers'.[2] I believe it, however, to be wrong.

'*Enter two Clownes*' is a reading in which the good quarto and the Folio texts agree, and it is presumably what Shakespeare wrote. The editions I have just cited all retain it, but the description of the clowns as gravediggers, which these editions reserve to the dramatis personae, is in some others – less anxious to conserve tradition than to clarify the action – incorporated into the stage direction itself. Some recent editors go further: '*Enter* SEXTON *and* GRAVEDIGGER' (Sisson), or, still more specific, '*Two clowns* (*a sexton and his mate*) *enter*' (Dover Wilson). That one of the clowns is in fact a sexton is clear from the dialogue – here and elsewhere I quote the second quarto – 'I haue been Sexton heere man and boy thirty yeeres'; and it is equally plain that in the stage-action of the play he is busy 'graue-making'. The nature of the other clown is more obscure.

Yet the tradition which makes him also a gravedigger extends over more or less three centuries. The earliest extant text which presents him as such is not an edition of *Hamlet* itself but a playlet included in the collection of drolls published by Henry Marsh under the title of *The Wits, or, Sport upon Sport* in 1662. The ninth piece in this volume consists of what we know as Act 5 scene 1 of *Hamlet* as far as the entry of the funeral procession. It is called *The Grave-makers*, in the plural; its opening direction specifies the stage business, '*Enter two to dig the Grave*'; the prefixed short list of the 'Actors Names', anticipating Professor Dover Wilson, further defines the 'two' as '*Grave-maker, and his Man*'; and the speech headings use these 'names' throughout. *The Wits* purports to be a collection of drolls which have actually been, to quote Kirkman's title-page to the edition of 1673, 'Presented and Shewn ... in Publique'; but their modern editor, John James Elson, prefers to think that those of them which are excerpts from full-length plays were prepared by the publisher for reading and possible performance 'after the Restoration' rather than that they had already been 'acted in the turbulent days of the Rebellion and the Protectorate'.[3] I cannot say that I find very good reason for this scepticism; nor need it strengthen suspicion to observe that the text of *The Grave-makers*, notwithstanding some liberty of adaptation, evidently derives from the 1637 quarto of *Hamlet*. Instead of having been acquired via the actors of the drolls, the text was probably taken straight from a printed copy of the play. But that need not mean that publication was not inspired by stage performance. The playlet was called *The*

Grave-makers because it was as grave-makers that the *Hamlet* clowns were thought of; and it looks as though the tradition of the popular stage had established the second clown as a gravedigger by the middle of the seventeenth century, or even before.

He seems certainly to have been a gravedigger on the stage of the Restoration. Downes, the prompter, recording the cast of the first Restoration revival of *Hamlet* – by Davenant, who had seen *Hamlet* staged before the Civil War – referred to the two clowns as the first and second grave-makers.[4] Hazelton Spencer believes that it was the text prepared by Davenant and acted by Betterton from the early 1660s that eventually reached print in the quarto of 1676,[5] which claims to give the play 'as it is now Acted at his Highness the Duke of *York*'s Theatre'. This is the first edition of *Hamlet* to set out the dramatis personae, and its specification of 'Two Grave-makers' fixes the character of both clowns for all succeeding editions, though Capell's variant, 'Grave-diggers', has since his time been preferred. It was the 1676 quarto which also supplied the clowns of Shakespeare's text with their grave-digging equipment: '*Enter two Clowns with Spades and Mattocks.*' This stage direction, reprinted by the subsequent quartos, was taken over by Rowe and through him firmly planted in the editorial tradition. Capell, the only eighteenth-century editor after Rowe to rethink the stage directions completely, again provides a variant: oddly uncertain about grave-digging gear, he was content with '*Spades, &c.*' But, though some of the greatest editions, including the Cambridge and the Furness Variorum, have followed him, the 'mattocks' persist through most editors right down to Dover Wilson, though modernized by Neilson and Kittredge to 'pickaxes' and by Alexander to 'picks'.

Notwithstanding these editorial directions, the equipment bestowed on the clowns by Shakespeare has to be discovered from his dialogue, which calls for one spade and no more. 'Come my spade,' says the sexton, on settling to work – not 'our spades', I notice, though this is not conclusive. 'My spade' may be a vocative, an interpretation which the quarto punctuation slightly favours; but, if it is taken as a demand addressed by the sexton to his companion, then it may be this, along with the indubitable injunction to 'fetch mee a stoupe [Q2 soope] of liquer', which permits the editor of *The Grave-makers* and Professor Dover Wilson to regard the companion as the sexton's man or mate. Kittredge, reading even more into the text, describes him as the elderly sexton's 'young helper'. In point of fact, however, Shakespeare tells us nothing at all about him.

What seems clear from the dialogue, if we examine it closely, is that the sexton's companion takes no part in the grave-making. That is the obvious inference from his opening speech; when he says, 'Make her graue straight', he enjoins the action on another, but dissociates himself from it. In his third speech he underlines the effect of this by calling the sexton 'good man deluer' (in the Folio, Goodman Deluer), a name which Shakespeare would hardly have applied to *one* of the clowns if it had been appropriate to both. On the strength of this alone Walker observed, 'Hence it would appear that the Second Clown is not a grave-digger';[6] but he is the only scholar I find to have perceived it. Our impression that the two clowns are not of the same craft is deepened when Goodman Delver confounds his companion with the riddle about what man builds the strongest. The answer, 'a graue-maker', may make its joke if there is a slow-witted grave-maker who has failed to guess his own distinction. But the joke is a better one if Goodman Delver enjoys a double score: not only does he know the answer while the other does not, but as a grave-maker himself he is one of those who build the strongest while the other is not. The other, I take it, then, is not entitled to a spade, the insignium of 'auncient gentlemen' like 'Gardners, Ditchers, and Grauemakers'; and one spade is all the stage should show. He certainly does not dig; and, by the time the digging gets going, he has of course gone for the liquor.

If his being sent for the liquor has sometimes made him appear to be no more than Goodman Delver's mate, this is not quite one's first impression of him. At the beginning of the scene it is he who gives the instructions. When Delver objects, 'Is shee to be buried in Christian buriall ...?', the other puts him down firmly: 'I tell thee she is, therfore make her graue straight.' Here his superiority ends, though when the sexton is laying down the law he can still take the liberty of interrupting: 'Nay, but heare you good man deluer.' But then Delver brushes him aside with 'Giue mee leaue', and proceeds to talk him down, whereupon he subsides into the dull-witted fellow who asks innocent questions and cannot guess riddles, before being finally dispatched on a menial errand. *Vis-à-vis* Goodman Delver his status undergoes a rapid decline. There is indeed some inconsistency of characterization – or would be, if characterization were in question. In truth, the second clown's character is as indeterminate as his office. Or should one perhaps rather say that his character and office are exactly defined by the headings with which Shakespeare distinguished the two speakers, '*Clowne*' and '*Other*'? 'Other' is not the mate of the sexton in Elsinore, but he is the mate of 'Clowne' in the theatre, the stooge, as we may call him nowadays, who supplies the feed for the funny man's wit. In this role he is consistent, answering or asking questions, displaying knowledge or ignorance, as may be required of him to give scope for comic retort. And when he is no longer wanted he is ordered off the stage. For the liquor is obviously an expedient, and that it is never brought worries neither the clown who has sent for it nor us. The anonymous Other has no identity beyond his role, and when a named and identifiable character arrives to take it over is eliminated without trace. In what is to follow it will be Hamlet himself who plays the stooge; but his never ceasing to be Hamlet will now give to question and answer an altogether deeper significance.

If the second clown had really been a gravedigger, there might have been no great harm in his staying, since a digger can always dig. Yet as gravedigger no less than clown's mate he could only be an obstruction. I suspect that Shakespeare had seen graves being dug, and in this if in nothing else his experience may conceivably have been the same as mine. Graves are usually dug by one man, rarely except in performances of *Hamlet* by two. However blinded by stage tradition, many producers must surely have discovered what a recent production made plain, that, though two men may get into a grave together, both cannot easily dig. This, however, was one blunder that Shakespeare did not make.

12

'THUS DIEST THOU'

When the King receives from Hamlet, whom he thought he had sent to execution in England, a letter announcing his return, he is naturally astonished. His mystification is shared by Laertes, who, however, adds, in the version of the second quarto:

> but let him come,
> It warmes the very sicknes in my hart
> That I liue and tell him to his teeth
> Thus didst thou.

The last two lines are both imperfect, and the Folio text is superior in reading 'shall liue' and 'diddest', of which the former is presumably correct. 'Diddest' smooths the metre, and is the reading of all the editors, down to and including Dover Wilson, Kittredge, Alexander and Sisson. But can it be said to be satisfactory to sense? Why should Laertes get a warm glow of satisfaction from telling Hamlet, in whatever manner of insult, 'Thus diddest thou'? And why should so feeble a taunt give him that peace of mind that is envisaged as the dialogue continues?

KING
    ... Will you be rul'd by me?
LAERTES
    I my Lord, so you will not ore-rule me to a peace.
KING
    To thine owne peace ...

What is it that will bring Laertes 'peace'?

Laertes is of course in the dramatically celebrated situation of a son whose father has been murdered. Indeed that is the main reason for his being in the play; for, as the critics have repeatedly observed, it is his function to serve as a foil to the hero. In the last two acts he is, as Kittredge remarks, 'the typical avenger'. While Hamlet's passion for revenge grows dull and needs a spur, as he has told us in the last speech we have heard from him (4.4.33), the fury of Laertes needs rather to be reined in. Whereas Hamlet is made a coward by his conscience, Laertes consigns *his* conscience 'to the profoundest pit' (4.5.132). Hamlet understands 'the dread of something after death'; but Laertes dares damnation. Laertes is visited by no Ghost to call him to revenge; he needs none to tell him what his situation requires of him. As he comes tearing into the palace he shouts 'I'le be reueng'd / Most throughly for my father' (4.5.136–7); and in this second scene with the King, when he has been calmed down, his purpose is unchanged: 'And so haue I a noble father lost … but my reuenge will come' (4.7.25–9).

For one so perfectly at home in the revenge convention, revenge of course means killing his father's killer. The only thing that can bring him 'peace', then, is the death of Hamlet. About this the King at least has no illusions. The speech which begins by promising Laertes 'peace' proposes to give it him through 'an exployt' in which Hamlet 'shall not choose but fall'. And Laertes on his side, far from being taken aback by talk of Hamlet's 'death', consents to be ruled by the King so long as he himself can be the 'organ' in the 'exployt'. The two understand one another completely, and have evidently done so from the beginning. It was the prospect of Hamlet's death that Laertes was referring to when he said it warmed his heart. If there were any doubt about this, it would be dispelled by the bad quarto; for the memorial reconstruction clearly indicates the general sense, and in the crucial sentence comes close enough to the words, of the authentic text. The first quarto has:

LAERTES

> O he is welcome, by my soule he is:
> At it my iocund heart doth leape for ioy,
> That I shall liue to tell him, thus he dies.

Staunton quoted this last line in a note to his edition (1860) and thought its reading might 'by some ... be thought to be superior'. Prompted by it, Marshall, in *A Study of Hamlet* (1875),[1] tentatively proposed what is evidently the correct reading. What Laertes will exultantly cry in Hamlet's teeth, in a phrase which gains extra force from its antithesis with 'I shall liue' in the preceding line, is not 'Thus didst thou' but 'Thus diest thou.' Through the likeness of *d* and *e* in the secretary hand this is one of the easiest of all misreadings for a compositor to make.

It is very strange that Marshall's emendation has not been accepted, nor apparently much considered. One cannot tell whether Marshall himself would have adopted it in the text of his 'Henry Irving' edition if he had not died before the last volume, containing *Hamlet*, was finished. It is not mentioned in Dover Wilson's *Manuscript of Shakespeare's 'Hamlet'* nor in Sisson's *New Readings*. Perhaps its neglect has been due to the textual theory, only recently discredited, that the Folio and second quarto were independent of one another and that in a reading common to both they would therefore authenticate one another. But with a *d–e* confusion a common error must always be reckoned a possibility. And, now that the Folio is known to have made use of the second quarto, their common reading may be the more readily objected to. This may indeed be an instance in which the second quarto led the Folio astray. The first quarto makes it clear that 'diest' must have been at some stage in the promptbook and therefore that Shakespeare's manuscript was at least once correctly read.

Whatever the genesis of the error, its long life can only be deplored. For it mutes the dramatic effect just when the action begins its last turn towards catastrophe. Even before the villainous King outlines his final stratagem, the destined avenger is to exult in contemplation of the hero's death. When some future audience hears Laertes say at this point, 'Thus diest thou', will there not be a great gain in dramatic tension?[2]

13

LETTER TO A SIXTHFORMER

7 November 1984

22 North Crescent
Finchley
London N3 3LL

Dear Mr Jotischky[1]

Forgive me if I have not replied to your letter as promptly as you
may have hoped. It arrived while I was away from home and it
awaits attention, along with many others, now.

Of course I accept that *bias* can refer to the heavier weight of
one side of the bowl. But, as you know, the reference of the word
extends to, or is extended from, the curving course through
which the bowl in consequence moves. And this latter sense is the
one I find appropriate to Polonius's metaphorical usage. He is
instructing Reynaldo to use a method that is out of the straight,
i.e. devious, indirect.

I take your point about remarks that are 'prejudiced' (i.e.
biassed in the modern sense). One may regard Laertes as being
prejudged by a questioner who assumes the thing he seeks to find
out; wherefore the procedure, instead of putting an open
question, may be said to be one-sided. But one-sided seems to
me a much less natural meaning here than devious: a devious
course is surely a fairly exact description of how Reynaldo is told
to proceed. The context I think is decisive: the deviousness which
I take to be suggested by *bias* reiterates the idea of *windlasses* in
the same line and anticipates *indirections* in the next. The three

parallel expressions leave little doubt of what it is that Shakespeare has in mind. (Of course you may object to the same thing's being said three times; but that is a different matter from the present issue of the meaning. The reiteration may be part of the characterization of Polonius as fussily loquacious. But Shakespeare himself is not always above such repetition.)

Assays is a little more difficult. Being less concrete, its meaning is less easily pinned down. But the basic etymological meaning of *assay* appears to be a test, trial or experiment; and that seems to me to suit the context here. Polonius is recommending an experiment which hopes to achieve a result, a test of which one will at least see the outcome. From the sense of trial the word also of course means a try, an attempt or effort, especially one made with great exertion or determination, as in 'Make assay', 3.3.69. It is true that, as I have suggested in my note on that passage, it can sometimes refer to a military enterprise, as in the instance of 2.2.71, which you cite. But there the sense is governed by the context 'assay *of arms*', and it is *of arms* which supplies the connotation of battle. Without some such influence from the context I shouldn't care to gloss *assay* as 'attack, assault', which Onions's *Glossary* gives as one of its meanings (citing – NB though – this very line 2.2.71). In 2.2 Fortinbras is spoken of as attacking Denmark, or at least challenging its king to a trial of (military) strength; but in 2.1 Laertes is not, even metaphorically, in an analogous situation. He is not being directly challenged or confronted, indeed rather the reverse. But, if you preferred the paraphrase 'devious enterprises' instead of my proposed 'devious tests', I should have no objection.

I am afraid, however, I don't think it justifiable to conjecture that the 'original text', by which I suppose you mean Shakespeare's manuscript, may, instead of *windlasses*, have had *wanlass* (or *wanlasses*, since the metre requires the trisyllabic plural). Of course there is always the possibility of printers misreading their copy, but the reading here gives no cause for suspicion. The textual position is that Q2, generally taken by scholars to have been set from Shakespeare's autograph, has 'windlesses' (*sic*); and that cannot be a corruption from Q1, from which this line is absent; and it is exactly repeated in the Folio, which, although it sometimes copies from Q2, had access to independent authority. Where the textual authority is as strong as this, to reject a perfectly satisfactory reading in favour of a merely speculative alternative would not accord with sound textual principles. (In any case the meaning is unaffected, and since *wanlass* and *windlass* appear to be different forms of the same word – see *OED* under *windlass sb²* – a modernized edition might still prefer the modern spelling *windlass.*)

I hope I don't sound too dogmatic on this last (textual) point. On the other hand, perhaps I ought to. What else I ought to do, though, is to congratulate you on your interest in and perception of some of the difficulties of arriving at Shakespeare's meaning & your attempts to grapple with them. You have set me quite a task, you know, in which I hope I have acquitted myself adequately, though I don't know how much all this will help.

I am very glad that you & your set have in general found my edition helpful.

Yours sincerely,

Harold Jenkins

NOTES

INTRODUCTION

1 *Hamlet*, ed. Harold Jenkins (1982), 127.

2 Ibid., 135.

3 John W. Mahon and Thomas A. Pendleton (eds), '*Fanned and Winnowed Opinions*': *Shakespearean Essays presented to Harold Jenkins* (1987).

1 THE STRUCTURAL PROBLEM IN SHAKESPEARE'S *HENRY IV*

Of the numerous critical writings on *Henry IV*, I have read most and learnt from many. So, although my main thesis about its structure has not, as far as I am aware, been previously put forward, it necessarily incorporates some arguments which have. To my predecessors I gladly acknowledge my indebtedness. It is not least to some of those with whom I disagree – Professor Dover Wilson and Dr Tillyard; from their work on *Henry IV* I have derived much insight and stimulus. The most important discussions of the particular problem are, I think, the following:

The Plays of William Shakespeare, ed. S. Johnson (1765), 4.235, 355; *The Works of Shakespeare*, ed. C.H. Herford, Eversley edition (1899), 6.253–4; C.F. Tucker Brooke, *The Tudor Drama* (1912), 333–5; R.A. Law, 'Structural unity in the two parts of *Henry the Fourth*', *Studies in Philology*, 24 (1927), 223 ff.; J. Dover Wilson, *The Fortunes of Falstaff* (1943), 4 and *passim*; E.M.W. Tillyard, *Shakespeare's History Plays* (1944), 264 ff.; J. Dover Wilson,

1 Henry IV, New Cambridge Shakespeare (1946), vii–xiii; M.A. Shaaber, 'The unity of *Henry IV*', *Joseph Quincy Adams Memorial Studies* (1948), 217 ff.; H.E. Cain, 'Further light on the relation of *1* and *2 Henry IV*', *Shakespeare Quarterly*, 3 (1952), 21 ff.; Law, 'Links between Shakespeare's history plays', *Studies in Philology*, 50 (1953), 175–82; E.M.W. Tillyard, 'Shakespeare's historical cycle: organism or compilation?', and Law, 'Shakespeare's historical cycle: rejoinder', *Studies in Philology*, 51 (1954), 37–41; G.K. Hunter, '*Henry IV* and the Elizabethan two-part play', *Review of English Studies*, n.s. 5 (1954), 236 ff.

For further references, see *The Second Part of Henry the Fourth*, ed. M.A. Shaaber, New Variorum (1940), 558–63.

1 Westfield College was founded in 1882, with the specific object of preparing women for University of London degrees. It later became a constituent college of the University of London; men were first admitted as students in 1964. Constance Maynard (1849–1935) was Mistress of Westfield College from 1882 to 1913 (see page 4). [E.H.]

2 Quoted in *Henry IV Part 1*, ed. S.B. Hemingway, New Variorum (1936), 395.

3 For particulars of the most important, see the unnumbered note above, which will usually obviate the necessity of further reference in the footnotes to the works listed in it.

4 J. Upton, *Critical Observations on Shakespeare* (1746). See especially 11, 41–2, 70–1.

5 *The Plays of William Shakespeare*, Johnson–Steevens Variorum, 2nd edn (1778), 1.300; E. Capell, *Notes and Various Readings to Shakespeare* (1775), 164.

6 *1 Henry IV*, ed. G.L. Kittredge (1940), viii.

7 See R.W. Chambers, *Beowulf, an Introduction to the Study of the Poem*, 2nd edn (1932), 390.

8 'The intentional fallacy' is actually the title of an article by W.K. Wimsatt and M.C. Beardsley in the *Sewanee Review*, 54 (1946), 468 ff., repr. in Wimsatt, *The Verbal Icon* (1954).

9 L. Abercrombie, *A Plea for the Liberty of Interpreting*, British Academy Shakespeare Lecture (1930), 6.

10 Ibid., 22.

11 The connection here is reinforced by the Prince's use of his earlier image: 'all the budding honours on thy crest / I'll crop'.

12 A.C. Bradley, 'The rejection of Falstaff', *Oxford Lectures on Poetry* (1909), 262–3.

13   Ibid., 253.

14   Dover Wilson, *The Fortunes of Falstaff*, 120–1.

15   Cf. Luke 13.25–7.

16   This first-act soliloquy looks forward not only to the rejection of Falstaff but also to Vernon's vision of the Prince and his company before Shrewsbury, 'gorgeous as the sun at midsummer'.

17   See F.W. Moorman, 'Shakespeare's history plays and Daniel's "Civile Wars"', *Shakespeare Jahrbuch*, 40 (1904), 77–83.

18   S. Daniel, *The Civil Wars* (ed. L. Michel, 1958), IV.34, 48 [E.H.]

19   All this is very well exhibited by Cain, 'Further light on the relation of *1* and *2 Henry IV*'. But his conclusion that the two parts therefore have no continuity is invalidated because, like many others, he is content to isolate particular elements in the problem and does not examine it whole. Except when the views of others are being quoted or discussed, the word 'Falstaff' does not occur in his article.

20   This is a synthesis of several passages in Coleridge. The words in quotation marks are said of whatever can give permanent pleasure; but the context shows Coleridge to be thinking of literary composition. See S.T. Coleridge, *Biographia Literaria*, ed. J. Shawcross (1907), 2.9. Also relevant are 'On poesy or art', ibid., 2.262; and *Coleridge's Shakespearean Criticism*, ed. T.M. Raysor, 2 vols (1930), 1.223–4.

2 *KING LEAR*

1   *King Lear*, ed. K. Muir, Arden Shakespeare (1952), xxx. [E.H.]

2   Quoted ibid., 248. [E.H.]

3   See A.W. Schlegel, *Lectures on Dramatic Art and Literature*, tr. J. Black, 2nd edn (1889), 412. [E.H.]

4   See A.C. Bradley, *Shakespearean Tragedy* (1904), 247, 257–60. [E.H.]

5   See page xii. [E.H.]

6   See H. Granville-Barker, *Prefaces to Shakespeare*, 1st series (1927), 188–9. [E.H.]

7   A. Sewell, *Character and Society in Shakespeare* (1951), 112. [E.H.]

8   Bradley, *Shakespearean Tragedy*, 284 ff. [E.H.]

9   Ibid., 285. [E.H.]

10   Ibid., 291. [E.H.]

11   R.W. Chambers was head of the English department at University College, London, when Harold Jenkins was a student there (from 1927). See Chambers, *King Lear*, W.P. Ker Memorial Lecture 1939 (1940). [E.H.]

3 *MACBETH*

1 See *Johnson on Shakespeare*, ed. W. Raleigh (1908), 177. [E.H.]

2 Aristotle stressed the importance of pity and terror in tragedy in *Poetics*, 2.11. [E.H.]

3 See *King Lear*, 5.3.232. [E.H.]

4 See page 23. [E.H.]

5 See pages 24, 50. [E.H.]

6 A.J.A. Waldock, *Hamlet: A Study in Critical Method* (1931). [E.H.]

7 T.S. Eliot, 'Hamlet', *Selected Essays* (1932), 143. [E.H.]

8 A.C. Bradley, *Shakespearean Tragedy* (1904), 351. [E.H.]

9 See *Johnson on Shakespeare*, ed. Raleigh, 177. [E.H.]

4 THE CATASTROPHE IN SHAKESPEAREAN TRAGEDY

1 J. Fletcher, *The Faithful Shepherdess* [c. 1610], 'To the Reader'.

2 *Soliman and Perseda* (1599), 1.1.6–7.

3 F.R. Leavis, 'Diabolic intellect and the noble hero', in *The Common Pursuit* (1952), 152.

4 A.C. Bradley, *Shakespearean Tragedy* (1904), 60–1.

5 For example, *Macbeth*, ed. K. Muir, Arden Shakespeare (1951), li.

6 I. Ribner, *Patterns in Shakespearian Tragedy* (1960), 137 ff.

7 T.S. Eliot, 'Shakespeare and the Stoicism of Seneca', *Selected Essays* (1932), 130–1; Leavis, 'Diabolic intellect and the noble hero', 136 ff. For counter-arguments, see Dover Wilson, New Cambridge edition of *Othello* (1957), li–liv; J. Holloway, *The Story of the Night* (1961), 47, 55–6.

8 I suppose no modern production can recapture the suspense there must have been for the play's first audience, accustomed as they were to dramatic situations in which the seeming dead awakened. Even Desdemona had regained a moment's consciousness to speak three dying lines. It is not inconceivable that the ending of *Othello* gave suggestions for *King Lear*. Othello in his grief looks on Desdemona 'cold', and he reunites himself with her when he dies 'upon a kiss', as Romeo had done before him. But, if Lear's death gazing on Cordelia's lips has indeed its ultimate origin in the conventions of love tragedy, nothing can better illustrate the imagination's transforming power.

9 *The Plays of William Shakespeare*, ed. S. Johnson (1765), 6.159 (in *Johnson on Shakespeare*, ed. W. Raleigh (1908), 161–2); C. Lamb, 'On the tragedies of

Shakespeare', *The Works of Charles and Mary Lamb*, ed. E.V. Lucas (1903–5), 1.107; Bradley, *Shakespearean Tragedy*, 251–4.

5 *MUCH ADO ABOUT NOTHING*

This chapter was a lecture delivered at the University of Newcastle upon Tyne, 7 May 1982, slightly adapted.

1   G. Bullough (ed.), *Narrative and Dramatic Sources of Shakespeare* (1958), 2.78.

2   See H. Jenkins, 'The ball scene in *Much Ado about Nothing*', in B. Fabian and K. Tetzeli von Rosador (eds), *Shakespeare: Text, Language, Criticism: Essays in Honour of Marvin Spevack* (1987).

6 *AS YOU LIKE IT*

This was a lecture delivered to the Shakespeare Conference at Stratford-upon-Avon, 18 August 1953.

1   A. Quiller-Couch, *Shakespeare's Workmanship* (1918), 130. In spite of some radical disagreement, I have got a number of hints from 'Q''s essay.

2   This is not to imply that Shakespeare's 'golden world' is at all the same as the primitive life of the mythical golden age, in which, by contrast with the Forest of Arden, there was no winter wind, sheep went unshorn, and man, at peace with all creatures, neither killed the deer nor was threatened by the snake and lion. Virgil associated the simplicity of pastoral life with the golden age, and the two ideals were frequently combined, not to say confused, by later pastoralists (see R. Walker, *The Golden Feast* (1952), 133).

3   O.J. Campbell, *Huntington Library Bulletin*, 8 (1935), 85.

4   '*Enter Orlando*' says the Folio simply, but the dialogue justifies Theobald's '*with Sword drawn*'.

7 *TWELFTH NIGHT*

'Shakespeare's *Twelfth Night*', from *Rice Institute Pamphlet*, 45 (1959), reprinted by permission of the author and Rice University.

1   L. Hotson, *The First Night of 'Twelfth Night'* (1954), 97.

2   Ibid., 15.

3   C. Lennox, *Shakespear Illustrated* (1753), 1.237 ff.

4 For a survey and discussion of them, see K. Muir, *Shakespeare's Sources* (1957), 66 ff. The more important ones are now assembled in G. Bullough (ed.), *Narrative and Dramatic Sources of Shakespeare*, 2 (1958).

5 *Twelfth Night*, ed. H.H. Furness, New Variorum (1901), xvii.

6 I follow the emendation of Theobald, adopted by most editors, for the Folio *on't*.

7 The Folio omits *with*.

8 M. Crane, '*Twelfth Night* and Shakespearean comedy', *Shakespeare Quarterly*, 6 (1955). See also Mark Van Doren, *Shakespeare* (1939), 169: 'The center is Malvolio'.

9 In Charles Lamb's account of Bensley's Malvolio in the essay 'On some of the old actors'.

10 See especially M.P. Tilley, 'The organic unity of *Twelfth Night*', *Publications of the Modern Language Association of America*, 29 (1914).

11 See J. Russell Brown, *Shakespeare and his Comedies* (1957), 167.

12 On the style of Malvolio's speeches, see Van Doren, *Shakespeare*, 167.

8 HAMLET AND OPHELIA

This is a lecture originally delivered on 3 April 1963.

1 *The Plays of William Shakespeare*, ed. S. Johnson (1775), 8.311; J. Dover Wilson, *What Happens in Hamlet* (1935), 125 ff.; E.K. Chambers, *Shakespeare: A Survey* (1925), 187–8; R. West, *The Court and the Castle* (1958), 15; G.R. Elliott, *Scourge and Minister* (1951), xxx–xxxi; L. Kirschbaum, 'Hamlet and Ophelia', *Philological Quarterly*, 35 (1956), 388.

2 Dover Wilson, *What Happens in Hamlet*, 130.

3 Kirschbaum, 'Hamlet and Ophelia', 388.

4 S.T. Coleridge, *Shakespearean Criticism*, ed. T.M. Raysor, Everyman edn (1960), 1.27.

5 See *Hamlet*, ed. J.Q. Adams (1929), 258–60.

6 H. Gardner, 'Lawful espials', *Modern Language Review*, 33 (1938), 345 ff.

7 H. Jenkins, 'The tragedy of revenge in Shakespeare and Webster', *Shakespeare Survey* 14 (1961), 47–8.

8 Centring upon the nunnery scene, most interpretations of Ophelia ignore, and some wildly contradict, this very significant conclusion. A judgement on Hamlet's attitude to Ophelia is suggested by *Measure for Measure*, 2.2.166–8, which observes that the sun in which the carrion corrupts brings the violet to flower.

9   Laertes is usually thought of as some sort of villain. But Hamlet has more than his
     rank in mind when he calls him 'a very noble youth'. As the avenger of his father,
     he is comparable to Hamlet, as Hamlet indeed declares: 'By the image of my cause
     I see / The portraiture of his.' Yet, as the treacherous instrument of Claudius,
     Laertes no less than Hamlet dies through his own guilt at the moment of
     achieving his revenge.

9 FORTINBRAS AND LAERTES AND THE COMPOSITION OF *HAMLET*

1   H. Jenkins, 'The tragedy of revenge in Shakespeare and Webster', *Shakespeare
     Survey 14* (1961), 46–7. I ask indulgence if I repeat here one or two sentences
     from this earlier essay.

2   The outstanding exception is H.D. Gray, 'Reconstruction of a lost play',
     Philological Quarterly, 7 (1928), 260–3. See below, note 7.

3   R. Nevo, *Tragic Form in Shakespeare* (1972), 24–6.

4   A.C. Bradley, *Shakespearean Tragedy* (1904), 90.

5   See, on opposite sides, W.W. Lawrence, 'Hamlet and Fortinbras', *Publications of
     the Modern Language Association of America*, 61 (1946), 673 ff.; and R.A. Law,
     'Belleforest, Shakespeare, and Kyd', *Joseph Quincy Adams Memorial Studies* (1948),
     279 ff.

6   K. Muir, *Shakespeare's Tragic Sequence* (1972), 65.

7   This is stressed especially by H.D. Gray (see above, note 2). I do not think it
     answers his objection to suggest with E.A.J. Honigmann (*Stratford-upon-Avon
     Studies*, 5 (1963), 134) that 'lands / Which he stood seized of' could refer to
     'lands seized ... in war'; nor to say with Lawrence ('Hamlet and Fortinbras',
     683–4) that the uncle in Norway is only a tributary king – for this would make
     him, if only by permit, the holder of the forfeited lands and make nonsense of
     Fortinbras's campaign to get them back from Denmark.
        Gray supposes, partly on the strength of references to Fortinbras and Norway in
     Der Bestrafte Brudermord, that Fortinbras must have been in the *ur-Hamlet*, in
     which he envisages Hamlet seeking revenge for his father's death and Fortinbras
     campaigning for his father's lands joining forces together against Claudius. He
     conjectures that Shakespeare began with such a scheme in mind but then dropped
     the plot of revenge by force of arms for the more psychological drama that we
     know. Without wishing to extend speculation about the contents of an
     irrecoverable play, I find insuperable objections to this theory: Hamlet, if he is
     to remain an honourable revenger, cannot be in league with a foreign prince
     against the Danish king; Fortinbras, so long as he is his father's son, must stand
     against Hamlet, forced by the pattern of the story to be opponent and not ally;
     and, finally, a play with such a plot as Gray outlines, having moved further away
     from the traditional story than Shakespeare does, could not really be an *ur-Hamlet*.

8 H. Granville-Barker, *Prefaces to Shakespeare, III: Hamlet* (1937), 129: 'Incidentally the courtesy of his speech belies his and his army's earlier reputation.'

9 Ibid., 141–2.

10 On the significance of this passage and its placing, see K. Brown, 'Form and cause conjoined', *Shakespeare Survey 26* (1973), 18.

11 Granville-Barker, *Prefaces to Shakespeare, III* (1937), 129; L.C. Knights, *An Approach to Hamlet* (1960), 81–2; H. Fisch, *Hamlet and the Word* (1971), 47; Muir, *Shakespeare's Tragic Sequence* (1972), 61–3.

12 E. Prosser, *Hamlet and Revenge* (1967), 210, 236.

13 Law, 'Belleforest, Shakespeare, and Kyd', 292.

10 HAMLET AND THE FISHMONGER

1 As it was not in my British Academy Shakespeare Lecture, 'Hamlet and Ophelia' (1963); *Proceedings of the British Academy*, 49 (1963), 138–9. I hope and believe that nothing I said then is wrong; but I now know that the passage has a more precise significance than I then grasped. [Cf. pp. 140 ff., above. E.H.]

2 S.T. Coleridge, *Shakespearean Criticism*, ed. T.M. Raysor, Everyman edn (1960), 1.24; *Notes and Queries*, 217 (1972), 126–7.

3 B. Riche, *The Irish Hubbub* (1617), 25.

4 L. Tieck, *Dramaturgische Blätter* (1826), 2.83 (*Kritische Schriften*, 3 (1852), 262).

5 M.A. Shaaber, 'Polonius as fishmonger', *Shakespeare Quarterly*, 22 (1971), 179–81.

6 *Hamlet*, ed. J. Dover Wilson, New Cambridge edition (1934), lvi–lix, 170–1; J. Dover Wilson, *What Happens in Hamlet* (1935), 101–14.

7 The Pelican edition, by Willard Farnham. On Dover Wilson's authority this meaning is also incorporated into the latest editions of Partridge's *Dictionary of Slang* (1937).

8 Barnabe Riche, in *Tudor Translations*, ed. L. Whibley (1924), 216.

9 According to Farmer and Henley in their *Slang and its Analogues* (1890–4). (The obscene meanings are not included in their shorter *Dictionary of Slang* (1905), though taken over by Partridge into his.) The lack of examples of which Edward Dowden and Matthias Shaaber complain should not invalidate the authority of this work for its own age in a field where literary illustration is hardly to be expected.

10 Dover Wilson, *What Happens in Hamlet*, 105–8.

11 See 'Hamlet and Ophelia', pages 148–9 [E.H.].

12 *Ben Jonson*, ed. C.H. Herford and P. and E. Simpson (1925–52), 7.441; W. Whiter, *A Specimen of a Commentary on Shakespeare*, ed. A. Over and M. Bell (1967), 132–3.

13   H. Platt, *The Jewel House of Art and Nature* (1594), 2.8–9.

14   Dover Wilson, *What Happens in Hamlet*, 108.

15   Judges 11.30–40.

16   A.C. Bradley, *Shakespearean Tragedy* (1904), 153.

17   J.M. Patrick, 'The problem of Ophelia', *Studies in Shakespeare*, ed. A.D. Matthews and C.M. Emery (1953), 139–44.

18   L. Kirschbaum, 'Hamlet and Ophelia', *Philological Quarterly*, 35 (1956), 376–93.

19   Bradley, *Shakespearean Tragedy*, 160.

11 HOW MANY GRAVEDIGGERS HAS *HAMLET*?

1   *Hamlet*, ed. A.W. Verity (1904).

2   W.W. Greg, *The Shakespeare First Folio* (1955), 311.

3   *The Wits*, ed. J.J. Elson (1932), 33.

4   John Downes, *Roscius Anglicanus* (1708), 21.

5   H. Spencer, *Shakespeare Improved* (1927), 183 ff.

6   W.S. Walker, *A Critical Examination of the Text of Shakespeare* (1860), 3.270.

12 'THUS DIEST THOU'

1   F.A. Marshall, *A Study of Hamlet* (1875), 83.

2   Since this article was accepted for publication, the same emendation has also been proposed by a correspondent in *The Times Literary Supplement*, 21 June 1957.

13 LETTER TO A SIXTHFORMER

1   See Introduction, pages xii–xiii. The 'Letter' refers to *Hamlet* 2.1.65–6.

INDEX